REPRODUCING PERSONS

ALSO BY LAURA M. PURDY

In Their Best Interest? The Case against Equal Rights for Children

Feminist Perspectives in Medical Ethics (edited, with Helen B. Holmes)

REPRODUCING PERSONS

ISSUES IN FEMINIST BIOETHICS

—————————— LAURA M. PURDY

CORNELL UNIVERSITY PRESS | ITHACA AND LONDON

First published 1996 by Cornell University Press.

Printed in the United States of America

∞ The paper in this book meets the minimum requirements of the
American National Standard for Information Sciences—Permanence
of Paper for Printed Library Materials, ANSI Z39.48-1984.

Library of Congress Cataloging-in-Publication Data

Purdy, Laura M.
  Reproducing persons: issues in feminist bioethics/
Laura M. Purdy.
   p. cm.
  Includes bibliographical references and index.
  ISBN 0-8014-3243-X (cl. : alk. paper). —ISBN 0-8014-8322-0 (pbk. :
alk. paper)
  1. Human reproductive technology—Moral and ethical aspects.
2. Abortion—Moral and ethical aspects. 3. Feminist ethics. I. Title.
RG133.5.P87 1996
176—dc20   95-52019

Contents

Preface

In 1974, bioethics was not yet a recognized subdiscipline of ethics, although an increasing amount of work was appearing in the area, most of it focusing on a few hot topics such as abortion. Reproductive ethics did not really gel into a field until some ten years later. The essays in this volume span this twenty-year period of intense growth and specialization.

Reproduction has been the major point of intersection between the burgeoning fields of bioethics and feminist philosophy. I believe that there are at least two reasons for this. One is that reproduction is the most obvious place where sex makes a difference. Another is that the second wave of feminism was born (perhaps not coincidentally) at a time of accelerating social change and rapid development in reproductive biology.

I came at the issues with a feminism born in graduate school, an environment where women were scarcer than hen's teeth and the door marked "Faculty Women" had no takers, where the curriculum was heavy with courses such as Automata Theory and more traditional courses that did not notice gender. That my first published work was in reproductive ethics was mostly a matter of chance. *Roe v. Wade* had just come down from the Supreme Court, and I found myself attempting to articulate why I thought the opinion was right, even if not convincingly argued. Michael Tooley's groundbreaking article "Abortion and Infanticide" had just appeared, and when he was asked to write again on the subject, he, knowing that I was working on abortion, kindly asked whether I would like to collaborate with him. The result was "Is Abortion Murder?" in 1974. In the next ten years or so, I wrote several more pieces about reproduction, not particularly intending to establish it as an area of specialization (it did not yet exist), but drawn irresistibly to the issues. Most of my writing time in the next few years was taken up with a book on children's rights, but once that was finished the rest of the essays in this volume were written, several pulled out of me by calls for papers or invitations. The most recent, "What Can Progress in Reproductive Technology Mean for Women?" was finished in January 1995.

Only recently did I notice how many essays I had written and that they fit together like a jigsaw puzzle, with very little overlap, and with a couple of overarching themes. One is the aforementioned feminism, a feminism that seems sadly lacking in much mainstream work on reproduction. Another is parental responsibility toward children and future children, a theme that unites this bioethics work with my work on children's rights. This latter theme introduces what some might regard as an antifeminist note, given the inevitable tensions between women's welfare and that of fetuses, babies, and children. I believe that such tensions are an unavoidable feature of the moral landscape, however, and that no moral perspective can reasonably insulate itself from their existence via denial.

The Introduction sets the moral stage for the three groups of essays that follow, each containing both old and new work. The first group raises questions about the right to reproduce. It has seemed to me for a very long time that although there are good grounds for recognizing a legal right to reproduce, the automatic assumption that it entails a moral right to reproduce under any circumstances is questionable. Indeed, I believe that reproduction is morally wrong in some circumstances. This assertion tends to provoke strong emotions, and a demand for line-drawing principles, in a tone that suggests that none is conceivable. Yet humans have developed moral guidelines in many areas of life no less fraught with difficulty than this one, and much more careful thinking is clearly required here.

The second group of essays focuses on abortion. Disagreement about the morality of abortion has been a divisive theme in the United States since the 1970s, and so this emphasis needs no further justification. Each of the essays examines a different facet of the debate, ranging from the moral status of the fetus and potentiality arguments to a series of questions about women's rights.

The third group of essays takes up issues raised by new reproductive technologies and arrangements. Two of them examine arguments about surrogacy (or contract pregnancy), a topic that is proving to be nearly as controversial as abortion. Two others look at the general moral implications of the new developments, one defending them against objections that fail to take account of women's welfare, the other evaluating John Robertson's principle of procreative liberty within the context of that welfare.

It would be impossible to acknowledge all the people who have helped to shape the work in this volume over these many years by arguing with me, critiquing my work, or—once in a while—agreeing with me. Among them are the Wells and Hamilton students who have enrolled in my Reproductive Ethics seminars. I must also thank other feminist bioethicists, who, I fear, mostly sigh sadly at what they see as my wrong turns, but who have also, despite their distaste for some of my stands, provided me with some of the best criticism and strongest solidarity. Thanks also to John Ackerman, whose enthusiasm for this project made it exist, and the staff at Cornell University Press who helped make it esthetically pleasing. Last but not least, thanks to my husband, John Coleman, who both encouraged me to get things off my chest and onto paper and helped create the conditions that made the book possible.

LAURA M. PURDY

Ithaca, New York

REPRODUCING PERSONS

Introduction

> Magicians know to keep the audience's attention away from the action. But moral philosophers may be magicians who have tricked even themselves.
>
> —Virginia Warren, "Feminist Directions in Medical Ethics"

Several years ago a leading bioethics journal asked me to review a paper on how physicians should deal with severely hydrocephalic fetuses.[1] It carefully considered the fetus's interests, the role of the physician, and the impact of the decision on society as a whole. I kept waiting for the author to notice the fetus's location inside a woman and to recognize that she has interests and perhaps even rights. He never did.[2]

If this kind of experience were an anomaly, bioethics would already be feminist. Unfortunately, it is not an anomaly and bioethics is not feminist. Quite the contrary: women's interests are routinely discounted or ignored altogether. Recent feminist work documents and analyzes this phenomenon.[3] Sexism has been most apparent in reproductive matters, where, for

---

Parts of three earlier works are incorporated into the Introduction: "A Call to Heal Ethics," in *Feminist Perspectives in Medical Ethics*, edited by Helen B. Holmes and Laura M. Purdy (Bloomington: Indiana University Press, 1992), reprinted from *Hypatia* 4, no. 2 (Summer 1989) and 4, no. 3 (Fall 1989). Reprinted by permission of Indiana University Press. "Good Bioethics Must Be Feminist Bioethics," in *Philosophical Perspectives on Bioethics*, edited by Wayne L. Sumner and Joseph Boyle (Toronto: University of Toronto Press, 1996). *In Their Best Interest? The Case against Equal Rights for Children* (Ithaca: Cornell University Press, 1992). Reprinted by permission of the publisher.

[1] Thanks to Hilde Nelson for casting a critical eye over this manuscript and for several useful comments. This section of the Introduction was originally published in *Philosophical Perspectives in Bioethics*, ed. Wayne L. Sumner and Joseph Boyle (Toronto: University of Toronto Press, 1996).

[2] The happy ending here is that the author radically revised his paper to reflect my concerns, and it was ultimately published.

[3] See Susan Sherwin, *No Longer Patient: Feminist Ethics and Health Care* (Philadelphia: Temple University Press, 1992), and Helen B. Holmes and Laura M. Purdy, eds., *Feminist*

example, plenty of work on abortion still proceeds without any reference to women's concerns. And when the new reproductive technologies were beginning to burst on the scene in the early 1980s, their possible impact on women seemed to be the last thing on anybody's mind.[4] Now, despite the voluminous feminist literature on them, the mainstream debate seldom reflects issues raised by it.

As both feminism and bioethics mature, feminists are looking beyond reproduction, not only at other specific issues in bioethics, but also at the field as a whole. After all, bioethics is supposed to critique the health care system, so why does it fail to see so much that is wrong? For example, where was bioethics before it became common knowledge that medical research often fails to include women? Or that it concentrates on problems that plague men?[5] How could we have been so oblivious to the gender differences in physician–patient relationships, differences that lead doctors to suppose that women need tranquilizers when the same symptoms in a man suggest a heart workup?[6] And how come men's views about withdrawal of care are so much more likely to be taken seriously?[7] Why, too, has it taken so long for bioethics to notice when allocation decisions leave women providing the brunt of the care?[8] And so on.

As the magnitude and pervasiveness of such gender differentials come into focus, feminist philosophers have also started to analyze the overall structure of bioethics. Many of us are coming to suspect, as Susan Sherwin argues, that "the organization of bioethics reflects the power structures that are inherent in the health care field, which in turn reflects the power structures of the larger society."[9] It hardly needs saying that despite considerable progress for women in recent years, men—mostly white, middle-class, het-

---

Perspectives in Medical Ethics (Bloomington: Indiana University Press, 1992). There are also quite a few articles on specific topics written from a feminist point of view.

[4] See "The Morality of New Reproductive Technologies," in this volume, originally published in the *Journal of Social Philosophy* 18 (Winter 1987): 38–48. Written in the late 1970s and therefore somewhat dated, it discusses this question.

[5] See Sue V. Rosser, "Re-visioning Clinical Research: Gender and the Ethics of Experimental Design," in *Feminist Perspectives in Medical Ethics*, ed. Holmes and Purdy.

[6] For a recent eye-opening look at the medical establishment, especially gynecology and obstetrics, see John M. Smith, *Women and Doctors* (New York: Atlantic Monthly Press, 1992). Smith cites a 1990 American Medical Association report, "Gender Disparities in Clinical Decision-Making," which notes significant gender differences in such critical matters as kidney transplants, cardiac catheterization, and diagnosis of lung cancer (p. 18).

[7] See Steven H. Miles and Allison August, "Courts, Gender, and the Right to Die," *Law, Medicine, and Health Care* 18, nos. 1–2 (Spring–Summer, 1990): 85–95.

[8] See Virginia Warren, "Feminist Directions in Medical Ethics," in *Feminist Perspectives in Medical Ethics*, ed. Holmes and Purdy.

[9] Sherwin, *No Longer Patient*, p. 3.

erosexual men—are still in charge, both in society generally and in the medical profession, and, consciously or subconsciously, choose social arrangements that reflect their perceived interests. Worse still, individual practitioners may still be gripped by common sexist—even misogynist—attitudes for which medical education currently provides no antidote.[10]

The results for white women and members of other less powerful groups can be devastating. Sexist health care, for example, can rob women of physicians' respect, deprive us of safe and effective therapies, deny us the kind of birthing experiences we value, drug us into resignation at life's injustices, legitimize violence toward us, even undermine our last wishes about how to die. Consequently, we may be deprived of the kind of control over how we live that men take for granted. Although some writers question the value of such control, it is essential for the welfare of second-class citizens in societies where there is little support for positive rights.[11] An uncritical bioethics tolerates this outcome.

Bioethics is an offshoot of ethics. Academic ethics is not in the business of moral reform: it would be a waste of our beautifully trained minds for us, qua philosophers, to spend our time exhorting others to behave morally—although it may behoove us to do so, as citizens, in our spare time. However, it seems fully appropriate for us to attend to and publicize inconsistencies in society's professed values, as well as to devote ourselves to investigating moral problems connected with equality. Yet such work has constituted only a relatively small part of the discipline of ethics, which has for the most part been preoccupied either with arcane metaethical questions or with what it regards as broader practical matters.[12]

Although this emphasis might surprise a Martian, a sociological understanding of the liberal arts generally helps to explain how it might come about. It is, after all, the relatively well-to-do who are able to spend their lives in such speculation, and few are willing to risk undermining their own psychological comfort by focusing on the moral environment that makes it possible. Indeed, the history of ethics seems to confirm this insight, as it has generally either turned a blind eye to the kinds of inequalities that now seem so apparent, or has, worse still, actively propagated them.[13] Certainly,

[10] This is a point emphasized over and over by Smith, *Women and Doctors*.

[11] Doubts about the value of control are to be found in the literature on ecofeminism and in Daniel Callahan, *The Troubled Dream of Life: Living with Mortality* (New York: Simon & Schuster, 1993).

[12] In particular, traditional ethics has tended to define problems faced by men as more important than those faced by women. Thus, for example, there is a long history of just war theory, but relatively little on child-rearing.

[13] The dismal record with respect to women here is by now well known. See, for example, the writings of Aristotle, Kant, and others in Rosemary Agonito, *A History of Ideas on Women:*

contemporary ethics still usually leaves it up to feminists to bring concern for gender justice to discussions.[14]

Despite its birth in the radical 1960s, bioethics has for the most part followed its parent's example. Analyses sensitive to gender and other markers of disadvantage have often been rejected as uninteresting, bad scholarship, biased, ideological, or "political," and thus as having no place in a serious intellectual endeavor such as bioethics.

This rejection has been especially pointed where gender is at issue.[15] It has been difficult for feminist voices to be heard on particular issues. The question of the relationship between feminism and established bioethics theory is still relatively uncharted territory. Feminism is, after all, but one of a number of perspectives from which one might approach issues in bioethics. The existence of such diverse perspectives raises the question of whether there is a "right" one (or a group of "right" ones), or whether we are doomed to irreducible disagreement where they diverge.

My question here is whether there is anything so compelling about a feminist outlook that it must be included in bioethics. This question is meant neither to exclude concern with other socially debilitating markers nor to imply that gender injustice is always the most urgent concern. Gender is, *of course*, not the only subordinating marker in Western societies, and not necessarily the worst handicap in every situation. Furthermore, there is a hier-

---

A Source Book (New York: Putnam, 1977). It also seems to me that traditional ethics has been remarkably oblivious to class inequality as well as to matters of race. Of course, it may turn out that earlier writers in ethics were more sensitive to these issues than is now apparent from what we take to be the history of ethics.

[14] I suspect that Michael Levin's contempt for the issue is widely shared. In an unusually frank preface to his book *Feminism and Freedom* (New Brunswick, N.J.: Transaction Books, 1987), Levin writes: "The reader may be puzzled, as I myself have sometimes been, that a philosopher should devote several years of his finite existence to feminism, when he could be thinking about the problem of induction or a hundred other intrinsically more interesting topics. . . . I could mention that what made me a philosopher in the first place was impatience with ignorance and irrationality, salient traits of feminist writing" (p. x). No doubt he feels the same way about discussions of other kinds of inequality. For an excellent treatment of recent moral and political theory, see Susan Moller Okin, *Justice, Gender, and the Family* (New York: Basic Books, 1989).

[15] In some circles "feminism" has become such a dirty word that using it immediately ends serious discussion, even where framing the issue without using it hardly raises eyebrows. My suspicion is that feminism is more fundamentally threatening to the establishment than claims, say, of racial injustice. I do not know whether that is because threats to the gender status quo are more basic or whether they are just more immediate, given the relative numbers of white women and members of other racial groups in academe. In any case, a number of articles written from a feminist point of view have slipped past the gatekeepers since the early 1980s, although it was not until 1992 that the first book-length works were published. (See Sherwin, *No Longer Patient*, and Holmes and Purdy, eds., *Feminist Perspectives in Medical Ethics*.)

archy of values that hits individuals with more than one such marker particularly hard. So despite the existence of pervasive sexism, some women are still better off than some men, and some persons of either sex are better off than other members of their sex. For this reason rectifying gender injustice need not always be our first priority, even if *awareness* of gender and the difference it makes are always crucial.

To begin, we need to know precisely what "feminism" is, as all those to whom I have explained my project have immediately pointed out. Some seem still unsure of basic feminist theses; others, more abreast of recent controversies, wonder how one might fix on a single feminist viewpoint to work with.[16] I try to distinguish core theses of feminism from more debatable positions, which may be either theoretical views or positions on specific issues, such as contract pregnancy. Because they are still the subject of serious debate among feminists, it would be premature for bioethics to absorb them. However, I argue that what I call "core feminism" is essential for bioethics.

CORE FEMINISM

At the heart of all feminism—except perhaps the most aggressively deconstructionist theories—are two simple judgments. First, women are, as a group, worse off than men, because their interests routinely fail to be given equal consideration. Second, that state of affairs is unjust and should be remedied. As Valerie Bryson writes, "even in the most 'advanced' nations, it remains true that positions of public power are overwhelmingly held by men; meanwhile women as a group continue to work much longer hours than men (particularly in within the home) and to receive far less financial reward, while fear of sexual violence restricts their lives and they are denied full control over their own reproduction."[17] In poorer countries, woman's lot is often still worse than that of her male compatriots.

Some details of core feminism are themselves a matter of serious disagreement among feminists. Disagreement begins with how best to

---

[16] For example, a fundamental divide among feminists is between what Catharine Stimpson has called the "minimizers" and the "maximizers." The former want to minimize the meaning of sex differences, the later want to valorize what they see as basic differences between the sexes. See Ann Snitow, "A Gender Diary," in *Conflicts in Feminism*, ed. Marianne Hirsch and Evelyn Fox (New York: Routledge, 1990), p. 14. The consequences of these kinds of fundamental divisions are painfully evident in the more specific debates on such issues as pornography and reproductive technologies.

[17] Valerie Bryson, *Feminist Political Theory: An Introduction* (New York: Paragon House, 1992), pp. 261–62.

describe the ways women are worse off and how much worse off they are. Are women discriminated against? Oppressed? Enslaved? Is the problem that they are not viewed as Kantian persons? That they are not accorded equal treatment? That their interests don't count? And, how bad is the problem? Are most men simply thoughtless and unaware of the issues, as some liberals might assert, or are men so hostile that they'd like to see women eradicated from the earth, as some radicals seem to think? Also in dispute is women's basic nature, and hence the proper goals and strategies of feminism. Are women and men "really" different? If so, then it would seem that feminism's goal ought to be validating our differences and making sure that women are as well off as men. Or are we really quite alike by nature, so that the problem is to relieve women *and* men of the socialization that seems to leave us so different? Or is the truth somewhere in-between?

It is understandable that even well-meaning outsiders are put off by the sometimes bitter debates about such points—sometimes I am myself. However, it is crucial to keep in mind that they are often more academic than practical, and although their existence is sometimes taken as sufficient reason for rejecting feminism altogether, that hardly seems sensible. Disagreements about how best to liberate slaves hardly undermines the judgment that they ought to be liberated. Likewise, given the extent, pervasive nature—and consequences—of unwarranted gender assumptions, it would surely be foolish to suppose that it is evident in every case how to deal with them. Widespread feminist consciousness is but a newborn in the family of ethical debate, and there is every reason to expect a fruitful maturity to be preceded by tumultuous adolescence.

How would I lay out core feminism? Many people, both men and women, still conceive of women as incomplete persons, individuals who, in Kantian terms, do not share in human dignity, as they are supposedly not capable of autonomously chosen life plans. Like Aristotle and Rousseau, such individuals conceive of women primarily as servants whose role is to nurture others. Thus some find nothing immoral about systematically subordinating women's interests to the interests of others when they conflict. The consequences range from infanticide and starvation for little Indian girls, to more subtle forms of loss for Western women. As Valerie Bryson and others point out, women even in North America are disproportionately absent from positions of public power and prestige, work longer hours than

---

[18] Ibid. Also, as Robin Morgan points out, even Kurt Waldheim, former UN secretary general, wrote that "while women represent half the global population and one-third of the labor force, they receive only one-tenth of the world income and own less than one percent of world property. They are also responsible for two-thirds of all working hours" (cited on

men for less pay, are often denied sexual and reproductive freedom, and are subject to violence from men.[18]

I suspect that the most fruitful approach to developing a more extensive notion of core feminism would proceed by emphasizing the importance of equal consideration of interests. Equal consideration of interests would mean that women's interests would count as heavily as those of men and, where the two come into conflict, would be taken to outweigh those interests at least half the time. Such calculations would be made more complicated by the need to weight interests, with a more pressing interest sometimes trumping several less pressing ones.

This formal demand for equality constitutes the central notion of core feminism. It requires that any moral inquiry be alert to gender-related differences in treatment or outcome, that such differences be minimized or thoroughly justified, and that women's welfare be considered as important as men's where their interests are in conflict.

Fair-minded thinkers can hardly object to this approach. Nor could they reasonably object to certain attempts to flesh out this principle in particular situations. Thus, for example, how could it be moral to accept or promote social arrangements that put women, but not men, at risk of impoverishment if they choose to bear children?

However, what constitutes equal consideration of women's interests is much less clear in many other cases. Thus, for instance, it may as yet be unknowable whether permitting paid contract pregnancy so undermines women's status that it should be prohibited, as some radicals claim. We should, in any case, be pointing out the exploitive conditions to which women are currently subjected. Fleshing out and testing such judgments will have to be an interdisciplinary enterprise. It depends, after all, on empirical judgments about the lives of women and men and on the ethical analysis of those judgments. The former fall primarily within the realm of the social sciences, the latter within that of moral philosophy.

Despite such uncertainties, I would argue that there are even now many clear cases where, without justification, women's interests are accorded less weight than a man's interest in the same circumstance, to women's serious detriment.[19] We do not always need perfect understanding to clean up such cases; it is often surely possible to improve things even if settling them fully must await further insight.

---

p. 1, from Waldheim's "Report to the UN Commission on the Status of Women," in *Sisterhood Is Global*, ed. Robin Morgan (New York: Anchor Books, 1984).

[19] Again, for an excellent bibliography, see Sherwin, *No Longer Patient*; see also individual articles in Holmes and Purdy, eds., *Feminist Perspectives in Medical Ethics*.

Some theories about how society should be ordered are diametrically opposed to this approach, recommending hierarchical, rather than egalitarian, social and political arrangements. Aristotle, for example, thought he had reason to subject women and some men to the rule of other men. His arguments are pretty clearly inadequate, and I doubt that many contemporary thinkers would defend him on these issues. In any case, there are many different possible kinds of hierarchical theories, and presumably not all of these would justify subordinating women.

What is more interesting—and troubling—is the failure of more apparently egalitarian theorists, such as Locke, Rousseau, and Rawls, to notice the gender inequality implied by their views. In particular, these writers tend, in their more applied sections, to take families rather than individuals as basic, thus incorporating the public/private distinction and all the inequitable assumptions built into it. Excellent feminist work is being done on these theories, and there is no need for me to repeat it here.[20] Yet such work is often rejected in principle. Such a rejection shows that core feminism and the claim of injustice inherent in it must be evaluated at a very basic level.

OBJECTIONS TO CORE FEMINISM

What can be said against core feminism? Recall that core feminism says that women's interests are unjustly accorded less weight than those of men. So core feminism may be thought to go wrong in two basic ways. First, it may claim falsely that women's interests are not given equal consideration—that is, the first claim of core feminism is false. Second, although opponents may concede the point about women's interests, they may hold that this state of affairs is justifiable—a denial, that is, of the second claim of core feminism. Michael Levin takes the first path, sociobiologists often take the second.[21]

I take it that the evidence for the first claim of core feminism is overwhelming[22] and that any decent moral theorist would accept the second. Are

---

[20] See, for example, works such as Susan Moller Okin, *Women in Western Political Thought* (Princeton: Princeton University Press, 1979); Okin, *Justice, Gender, and the Family;* Lorenne M. G. Clark and Lynda Lange, eds., *The Sexism of Social and Political Theory* (Toronto: University of Toronto Press, 1979); Nancy J. Hirschmann, *Rethinking Obligation: A Feminist Method for Political Theory* (Ithaca: Cornell University Press, 1992); and Virginia Held, *Feminist Morality: Transforming Culture, Society, and Politics* (Chicago: University of Chicago Press, 1993).

[21] See Levin, *Feminism and Freedom,* and such sociobiologists as Edward O. Wilson, *On Human Nature* (Cambridge: Harvard University Press, 1978), and Richard Dawkins, *The Selfish Gene* (Oxford: Oxford University Press, 1976).

[22] For a brief overview of the claim that women are worse off, see Sherwin, *No Longer Patient,* chap. 1, esp. pp. 13–19.

there methodological reasons for rejecting these apparently unexceptionable claims? Let us start with the judgment that women's interests are systematically discounted. What kind of claim is that? It is a mixed claim, partly moral and partly empirical. The empirical data are appropriately gathered by social scientists and are relatively unproblematic. And, if one were skeptical about the validity of social science methods, then one would have to be equally skeptical of the denial of core feminism. More controversial is the choice of what data to gather, given differing opinions about what categories are relevant. Thus Michael Levin disagrees with Valerie Bryson, contending that "women in Western society are better off than men by every objective measure of well-being. Women live longer, enjoy better health, are less prone to insanity, alcoholism, drug abuse, and crime."[23] Evaluating such contradictory positions involves a decision about what factors are most important in a good life, as well as understanding the relevant causal relationships.[24] For example, if women lack full control over their fertility, how should we rank the consequences for their welfare, and how do they compare with the factors that lead more men to become criminals?

Are there any grounds on which this general enterprise might be rejected? The causal claims and the statistical measurements lean toward the empirical end of the spectrum. The investigations that lead to them may be relatively value free, as we have seen, although the decision about what questions to investigate is not. Doubts about specifics might appropriately be raised as questions about a researcher's standards of evidence, or even his or her honesty. However, if that is really what is at issue, it should be discussed in those terms, not dismissed as somehow "political."

To judge by some comments, political contamination is so fearsome that the only acceptable motivation for research is idle curiosity. But the disinterest in human affairs suggested by that motivation is as political in its way as research motivated by concern defined as political, because it suggests either that the status quo is fine (as there is no pressing need to do research necessary for evaluating it) or that any state of affairs would be fine (no matter how dreadful).

Such dismissal is especially unconvincing where the word "political" is left undefined—as is generally the case in these discussions. "Political" has become a derogatory term, but its use should not lead us to reject positions

---

[23] Levin, *Feminism and Freedom*, p. 7.

[24] For instance, we need to know why women live longer and why more men go insane, if those claims are true. These facts per se do not necessarily tell us that women or men are more unjustly treated. Thus women may live longer because of their stronger biological constitution, even though men get more effective medical care; men may go insane more frequently for genetic reasons or because their overblown expectations of their just deserts fail to be met, not because of unfair treatment.

without further justification. In any case, it is *issues* that are political, not positions on these issues. Whatever "political" is taken to mean, those who espouse one position on a particular issue have no case for rejecting a different position on the grounds that it is political. Yet this happens again and again as the unequal status quo is defined as neutral but criticisms of it are defined as "political."

So far we have been considering the epistemological status of the core feminist claim that women's interests are not accorded equal consideration. What now of the judgment that this state of affairs is unjust?

Surely this is a paradigmatic moral judgment: discussion of the merits of hierarchy is or should be, after all, a central issue in ethics. The philosophical lever that motivates and requires it is clear for any approach that takes universalizability for granted: unequal treatment must be justified by morally relevant reasons. So what grounds might there be for asserting some philosophical impropriety here, that the debate is, after all, merely "political"?

Perhaps questioning the assertion that women exist to nurture and serve is the sticking point—but isn't the discussion of human ends a properly moral question? Or perhaps the tender nerve is the sacred public/private distinction so closely tied to that conception of women's nature. Proponents of the traditional public/private distinction wouldn't want to have to concede that it is merely a political (as opposed to a moral) arrangement—one based on power rather than right. Nor can they have it both ways: either the so-called private world is a moral arrangement, in which case reasoned criticism of it must be moral talk, too, or it is a power-based arrangement, a fact that undermines their objection to allegedly political assaults on it. What feminists require here is, after all, moral consistency. Behavior that is regulated or prohibited in the public sphere among men may now often be visited on women in the so-called private sphere with impunity. If the public/private distinction is moral, then this discrepancy requires justification. Attempting to deflect moral attention from that fact by calling criticism "political" suggests reluctance to put at women's disposal the instruments men count on for fair adjudication of conflicts.

In short, I believe that the epithet "political" here is an attempt to preserve the domestic realm and gender matters in general from moral scrutiny. These issues are almost uniquely threatening to men's personal lives; in the worst cases, those lives are predicated on assumptions about women and justice that couldn't pass muster in a first-year course on critical thinking. Among them is the understanding that a wife will attend to children and household in order to free up the man for more socially valuable pursuits, that she will follow him wherever his career leads, and that because he provides most or all of the outside income his wishes and desires will prevail.

A clear view of this matter would explain the emotional reactions feminist work evokes. I can't help but think back here to what happened in the early 1980s when I proposed introducing a feminism course at the small women's college where I teach. My course description was anything but inflammatory: "An examination of the justifications proposed for different positions regarding women's role in society, including consideration of specific moral and political problems raised by such debate, such as reproductive rights, and equality in the workplace." With nothing more to go on than this rather drab description, and apparently no interest in hearing more, my colleagues asserted, among other things, that the students would be cheated by such a course and that it was inappropriate for a women's college. I was also asked to reassure the group that I wouldn't be indoctrinating my students. Perhaps these colleagues thought feminism means man hating or believed that gender issues for some reason can't be examined with the same rigor that characterizes good treatment of other issues in moral and political philosophy. Their hostility certainly prevented any discussion of their assumptions or mine.

Such events clearly communicate that, in the words of the classical dismissal, gender is "not a topic." Because it clearly is a topic in the empirical sense, what is really being conveyed here is that it's an *unworthy* topic. Why is it unworthy? Well, of course gender, like race, and so on, is, alas, merely a particular concern, whereas philosophy is confined to the universal. However, a glance at the history of philosophy shows us that philosophers have been preoccupied with both kinds of question.[25] Why should this issue engender such emotions unless it has a deeper meaning? Moreover, it would be inconsistent for bioethics to object to an approach it so clearly uses itself.

Core feminism focuses, in any case, on very broad issues. Remember that gender is not something that only women have, so noticing gender isn't just studying women.[26] And core feminism is interested in the *relationship* between women and men: What could be more universal than that? How is that different from studying relationships between men who fall into different categories, say, patients and physicians? Not only do these objections

---

[25] See also the work of Stephen Toulmin, "The Recovery of Practical Philosophy," *American Scholar* 57, no. 3 (Summer 1988): 337–52; and Albert R. Jonsen and Stephen Toulmin, *The Abuse of Casuistry: A History of Moral Reasoning* (Berkeley: University of California Press, 1988).

[26] Just as race is not something predicated only of people of color, class is not only what the poor have, and sexual orientation not just what homosexuals have. See Elizabeth V. Spelman, *Inessential Woman* (Boston: Beacon Press, 1988).

fail to make sense, but also their obvious inadequacy once again suggests some other agenda.

If what I have said so far is right, then there is nothing epistemologically suspect about core feminism: core feminism is the expression of an ordinary moral judgment. And, there is good reason for accepting it: both the statistics and the moral case for it are compelling.[27]

"Wait a minute!" some people will say: "I'm convinced by your argument that there is in principle nothing objectionably political about core feminism, but I still see no reason to accept its premises." Such people may hold that there is no evidence that women's interests are systematically subordinated. Or they might believe that the disparities in question are justifiable.

As I have said, there is no space here to construct these arguments. Doubting or denying the first premise seems to me to be possible only by shutting one's eyes to the ubiquitous evidence. In any case, this level of skepticism logically implies equal doubt about the contradiction to core feminism's first premise. But when you are in such an unsettled state with respect to a belief, intellectual honesty requires that you consider evidence that could help you make up your mind. That requires you to evaluate every case with an eye to possible unjust gender disparities. So even doubters, if they want to be considered careful thinkers, must add the lens of gender to their thinking. There is not much that can be said to those who are convinced that no gender disparities exist, except what Wittgenstein said in another context, "Don't think, but look!"[28]

What about those who doubt or deny core feminism's second premise? As before, doubters must be prepared to use gender analysis for testing arguments. Denyers generally hold untenable beliefs about human nature based on sociobiology or have an overly rigid conception of what it takes to keep human societies afloat.[29] They have a moral duty to reexamine their beliefs; otherwise they collude in an unfair system.

---

[27] For an excellent summary of facts and issues, see Sherwin, *No Longer Patient,* chap. 1.
[28] See Ludwig Wittgenstein, *Philosophical Investigations,* trans. G. E. M. Anscombe (Oxford: Basil Blackwell, 1963), sec. 66.
[29] For an excellent discussion of the pitfalls of sociobiology as applied to human behavior, see Philip Kitcher, *Vaulting Ambition* (Cambridge: MIT Press, 1985). For more socially oriented discussions, see Pauline Bart's response to Melford E. Spiro's *Gender and Culture* (New York: Schocken, 1980), "Biological Determinism and Sexism: Is It All in the Ovaries?," in *Biology as a Social Weapon,* ed. The Ann Arbor Science for the People Editorial Collective (Minneapolis: Burgess Publishing Company, 1977). There are many other discussions of possible social arrangements. For a start, see John Stuart Mill, *The Subjection of Women,* and *Feminist Scholarship: Kindling in the Groves of Academe,* ed. Ellen Carol DuBois, Gail Paradise Kelly, Elizabeth Labovsky Kennedy, Carolyn W. Korsmeyer, and Lillian R. Robinson (Urbana: University of Illinois Press, 1985).

If the specific claims of core feminism are so unproblematic, why is the feminist project so often rejected in principle? Why do people claim that the issue is uninteresting, that feminist scholarship is shoddy, and/or that it is biased, ideological, or "political"? In short, why is it thought to be intellectually disreputable, so that it need not be taken seriously by scholars?

What problems and issues one finds interesting or uninteresting is surely a somewhat subjective matter, one that depends considerably on one's upbringing and situation. The question of social equality might be expected to be of substantial interest to those who have good grounds for thinking that their interests count less than those of members of other groups. Conversely, it is plausible to believe that those whose interests prevail more often will find this topic less gripping. The cynical interpretation of the claim that feminism is uninteresting is that it is the easy way to avoid challenges to one's own status. I feel some attraction to that interpretation.

One might also contend that core feminism is uninteresting because it simply aims to bring practice into line with our professed ideals or because it raises no philosophically worthwhile questions.[30] The first version of this objection says that equal consideration for women's interests is uncontroversial: improving women's condition is just a matter of changing behavior, not moral revolution. Unfortunately, however, many people are still obviously unconvinced of the thesis that women should be treated as equals, and the resistance to specific proposals for improvements in women's welfare by those who allege their commitment to this ideal is often so fierce as to raise doubts about their sincerity. Such resistance may, of course, just be evidence of a psychological block; but it might also signal deeper philosophical problems: persistent sexism in the work of those who intend to be egalitarian lends some support to this possibility. The second version of this objection betrays an excessively generalized and abstract conception of what constitutes worthwhile philosophy. It seems to hold that only the highest level considerations are valuable and that lower level work simply plays out the implications already contained in the higher. The image here is reminiscent of Thomas Kuhn's distinction between revolutionary science and normal science. But that attitude underestimates the difficulties inherent in and the value of, a good deal of lower level work. Here, for example, taking new players into account both destabilizes old solutions and creates new quandaries.

What about the accusation of shoddy scholarship? That rejection of feminism seems no more solid. Of course there is shoddy feminist scholarship. Feminist scholarship may be shoddy because it is sloppy, ill thought-out, unimaginative, or poorly written, and so forth. Like all such scholarship, it should be ignored. But unless it can be shown that the core assumptions of

---

[30] Thanks to Dan Callahan for reminding me of this argument.

feminism are unsound, the existence of shoddy scholarship is hardly grounds for rejecting the whole enterprise. There's lots of appalling metaphysics around, but nobody any longer suggests that we can do without metaphysics: the answer is to do it better.

A special problem with some feminist scholarship is that it argues for different standards of scholarship, contending that existing ones are in some way biased. Such arguments not only threaten existing methods, but are also especially difficult to mount, because they require people to pull themselves up by their own methodological bootstraps. Promising work is rarely perfect to start with, and the appropriate response to it is constructive criticism, not derision.[31]

Rejecting core feminism on the grounds that it is biased or ideological is also unreasonable. When accused of bias, many feminists who are not philosophers tend to retort that bias is universal.[32] This response fails to distinguish between bias and tenable points of view; it also undermines core feminism by flirting with the kind of malignant relativism that pulls the rug out from under the assertions of injustice so central to feminism. In any case, unsubstantiated accusations of bias are suspect: intellectual honesty requires us to come to grips with positions and show how they go wrong.

To reject feminism on the grounds that it is ideological is equally untenable. It seems to me that the word is often used to describe philosophical systems one believes to be closed-minded and unfalsifiable. Because we disagree about what we think these are, it would be preferable to describe all systems as "philosophy" and do our evaluation of them via argumentation rather than value-laden terminology.

The last and most important objection to core feminism is that it is "political" and that good scholarship has no place for politics. The problem with this objection, as noted, is that words such as "politics" and "political" have come to be used in such a variety of ways that unless people stipulate how they are using them, it is hardly clear what they are objecting to. For example, *Webster's Ninth New Collegiate Dictionary* gives the following different meanings for "political": (1) "Of or relating to government, a government, or the conduct of government"; and (2) "Of, relating to, or involving politics, and especially party politics." The *Oxford English Dictionary* also sug-

---

[31] See, for example, some of the pieces in Claudia Card's recent anthology, *Feminist Ethics* (Lawrence: University Press of Kansas, 1991).

[32] For example, see a recent sympathetic review of *Issues in Reproductive Technology I: An Anthology* (New York: Garland, 1992), a feminist collection edited by Helen B. Holmes. The reviewer, Lois B. Moreland, writes: "Of what value is a feminist anthology? By definition, its perspective is biased. It is gender-centered. Its vision is limited" (*Politics and the Life Sciences* 12, no. 2 [August 1993]:301).

gests: (3) "Of, belonging, or pertaining to the state or body of citizens, its government and policy, especially in civil or secular affairs; public, civil, of or pertaining to science or art of politics"; and (4) "Belonging to or taking a side in politics or in connexion with the party system of government; in a bad sense, partisan, factions." Furthermore, *Webster's* adds under "politics," "the total complex of relations between people in society."

"Politics" and its cognates thus have radically different descriptive meanings. Worse yet, sometimes these terms are used in purely descriptive ways, but at others they are used in derogatory ways. We see something of these senses in definition (4). "Political" can mean partisan. To be partisan is not necessarily to be biased, although the word can be used to imply bias. Bias can take several forms: leaping to conclusions on the basis of too little evidence or evidence of the wrong kind; ignoring evidence that undermines one's conclusion, and so forth. It may also imply the kind of bad faith that leads people to be less alert to or even knowingly to commit these errors. Another common assumption is that whereas moral argument involves reasoned discourse, political discourse is instead rhetoric that aims at making the weaker argument appear to be the stronger, or that it is a mere epiphenomenon of power. Political discourse may also be rejected because it is motivated by anger, but of course even angry people may have good arguments.

Naturally, many words, such as "politics," have widely differing meanings, but the problem here is that it is the context that often leaves us in doubt about the subtleties of a given use. For example, consider Susan Sherwin's comment that "subordination of one group of persons by another is morally wrong, as well as politically unjust."[33] Precisely what distinction is she making here?

General rejections of the political in scholarship are still more puzzling.[34] Of course, we should be avoiding biased, partisan work. But that scholarship should not be messing with government, party politics, civil affairs, or political philosophy is a vastly different thesis. Surely it is reasonable to demand that discussions about these matters be, first and foremost, clear, with well-defined terms. This is such a fundamental point—and the solution so obvious—that one can hardly avoid the suspicion that the obfuscation is intentional. One interim solution is to refuse wherever possible to use "political."

---

[33] Sherwin, *No Longer Patient*, p. 56.
[34] See, for example, Karen Lehrman's recent "Off Course," attacking women's studies (*Mother Jones* [September–October 1993]: 45–51, 64, 66, 68). Lehrman accuses some women's studies classes of being political and praises what she takes to be nonpolitical mainstream treatments of the same issues; yet she never defines the word or asks what is central about the feminism that informs women's studies curricula.

ETHICS OR POLITICS?

One way to limit the use of "political" is to recognize how much it overlaps with "ethical" or "moral."[35] Some thinkers—including some pioneers in bioethics—seem to think that the scope of ethics is narrow and should be limited to immediate personal relationships, say, between doctor and patient, or nurse and doctor. But conceiving of ethics in this way cuts it off from broader structural issues. The model here is some versions of act utilitarianism that ignore universalizability as well as the subtler aspects of particular situations. Working in such a shrunken framework can be an interesting exercise and is often necessary for making decisions in an imperfect society. However, it is important always to return to the big picture, because only thus is it possible to see why some problems come up again and again.

Sticking to narrow contexts tends to support the status quo at the expense of human welfare. It fails to question why people find themselves in unfavorable circumstances and mindlessly applies what appear to be the relevant moral rules. Suppose, for example, that an individual physician, Sue, is trying to decide whether to do an abortion for Mary. If Sue accepts a narrow definition of health and believes that her job is to help Mary achieve health, she might conclude that it is inappropriate for her to do the abortion. However, Sue might also believe that social justice for women requires that women have access to abortion, and she knows that no other agency provides that service. Therefore, she does the abortion for Mary. Sue's decision is, I would argue, a moral one, not exclusively a social or political one, even though it may be seen as transcending the traditional boundaries of medical ethics. Bioethical decision making thus conceived ranges over all human activity, drawing on both values embedded in the context of health care and those exemplified by broader moral principles.

My perspective here closely reflects Ezekiel Emanuel's conception of the logical structure of bioethics. As he argues in *The Ends of Human Life*, the apparently "endless irresolution" of specific problems in bioethics occurs because the values intrinsic to health care cannot resolve the conflicts that arise within it. Instead, they demand recourse to broader principles of political philosophy, defined as that which "is primarily concerned with the proper ends of human activities and what people should and should not do to realize those ends."[36] Emanuel goes on to say: "How we confront and resolve them will both reflect and affect our understanding of ourselves as human beings, of the good life, of social justice, of the proper way to care

---

[35] I use the two interchangeably.
[36] Ezekiel Emanuel, *The Ends of Human Life: Medical Ethics in a Liberal Polity* (Cambridge: Harvard University Press, 1991), p. 13.

for the disabled, debilitated, and dying. Medical ethics is a measure of our own moral vision; these questions force us to articulate our ideals and values, our ethical self-understanding, and to assess their worthiness."[37] According to him, the liberal political philosophy widely accepted in the United States discourages law and public policy from advancing particular notions of the good. Hence, health care ethics reflects the splintered values of the political concepts underlying it.[38]

Emanuel's general diagnosis makes sense; however, it is not clear why these higher principles are principles of political philosophy rather than principles of plain old ethics. What is ethics, if not a discipline "concerned with the proper ends of human activities and what people should and should not do to realize those ends"? Perhaps Emanuel sees judgments in political philosophy as those about which reasonable people may disagree, whereas moral judgments are those we are compelled by reason to accept. However, in my opinion that approach would overestimate both the compelling nature of ethical judgments and the freedom from constraint inherent in political philosophy. So, although I believe that Emanuel has the general picture right, I think that we are unable to reach a consensus about many issues in bioethics because of the pluralism of our *moral* beliefs.

Getting clear about the boundaries and areas of overlap between the moral and political realms seems, in any case, long overdue. It would make sense to label as "political" theory that which deals directly with government, but much of political theory does not. Most of the material in the political theory courses I took, for instance, could just as well have been labeled "moral theory." The lines seem even more blurred today when leading political theorists, such as Susan Moller Okin, Michael Walzer, and

---

[37] Ibid., p. 4.

[38] Emanuel (ibid., p. 7) distinguishes three other possible positions on this issue of the source of values used in health care ethics and argues, convincingly, I believe, that his own political conception is superior. First, there is the teleological view that holds that all the relevant values are intrinsic to the health care enterprise. Second, there is the applied ethics view that derives the values in health care ethics from more general moral principles. And third, there is a view that recognizes two moral worlds competing for center stage in health care ethics, a professional role morality and what Emanuel calls "common" morality (pp. 26–29). He comments:

Each of these three approaches should be rejected. Professional ethics is not separated from, derived from, or to be balanced against political philosophy. Instead, it is best to see that the intrinsic ends of a profession are incomplete; they need specification and balancing through political philosophy. A complete account of the purposes of the profession—a specification of its ends, a balancing of its internal ends, a balancing of its internal ends with nonprofessional ends—requires political philosophy. Professional ethics can be fully articulated only by references to political values. Professional ethics and political philosophy are not in conflict or at cross-purposes, but professional ethics is insufficient without the values articulated in political philosophy. (p. 29)

Ezechiel Emanuel himself, are so active in what it seems reasonable to call *ethical* theory.

Clear thinking necessitates the conceptual housekeeping that inquires into such distinctions. In its absence, dust and cobwebs infiltrate the scene, and we find it hard to see what is wrong with rejecting some works as "political." Once the metaphysical Pledge has been applied, however, the primarily moral nature of the enterprise emerges. Positions seen by some as threatening can no longer be deprived of standing on allegedly epistemological grounds. That in turn forces the would-be moral gatekeepers to recognize and come to terms with radical challenges.

Thus we see clearly that ethics that turns a blind eye to particular forms of unfairness is broken and in need of repair. The tendency to discount women's interests is, as I have suggested, pervasive in bioethics: it requires constant vigilance to penetrate the apparently seamless discussions that leave no moral space for women, as did the paper on hydrocephalic fetuses. What is distinctive about bioethics is that women are especially at risk in the medical establishment: erroneous or self-interested assumptions about our bodies and minds are close to the surface here, and the delivery of care is so value laden that it cannot help but reflect them. Bioethics that fails to be alert to women's vanishing interests is, whether intentionally or not, biased: it condones the promotion of all other interests at the expense of women's. In short, there is no "safe" neutral territory here between biased bioethics and feminist bioethics.

Rethinking gender assumptions from scratch is a major undertaking. But because the issues are so much clearer in bioethics, it may be possible for those who think there is no gender injustice to confine their inquiries to that field. What, after all, do women want from the health care system? Like men, we want help in staying healthy. We want safe, effective, respectful therapies when we are ill or injured. And, because reproduction happens in our bodies, we also want help in carrying out our reproductive goals. Other legitimate life goals may also require medical support. We generally want to keep on living as long as we are content with the quality of our lives. In dying, we want our wishes about that process respected, and we want no unnecessary pain or suffering. Practices that repeatedly leave women worse off in these respects should be evidence enough of my contentions—and targets for change.

WHITHER FEMINIST BIOETHICS?

I have been arguing that what distinguishes feminist from biased ethics is the premise that a woman's welfare is as important as anybody else's. Biased ethics turns a blind eye to women's needs even as it attends to the needs of others. Biased ethics fails to scrutinize denials of core feminism (and the equivalent cores for other disadvantaged groups), and is all too ready to accept attempts to justify discrimination and discrepancies in welfare.

Feminist ethics documents how existing practices harm women unfairly and unjustifiably and focuses on how to avoid such outcomes. Feminism, writes Alison Jaggar, "seeks to identify and challenge all those ways, overt but more often and more perniciously covert, in which western ethics has excluded women or rationalized their subordination. Its goal is to offer both practical guides to action and theoretical understandings of the nature of morality that do not, overtly or covertly, subordinate the interests of any woman or group of women to the interests of any other individual or group."[39] I have argued that the moral minimum for those who wish to escape biased ethics is to recognize that because women and men are now so dissimilarly situated, even apparently gender-neutral principles may well affect them very differently.

Contrary to popular belief, this approach does not imply that one sees gender bias everywhere. It does imply the resolve to root it out where it exists. Considering how oblivious people—including feminists—have been to even blatant instances of bias, our alertness to its more subtle manifestations is necessary, even if it strikes unsympathetic souls as a paranoid conviction that bias is everywhere.[40]

How to proceed? Enough good feminist bioethics exists to light the way for those of good will who are unsure quite how to begin. The path is rocky, given the disputes among feminists alluded to, but openness to the idea that traditional approaches are inadequate is a good start. Awareness of possible gender inequity is compatible with a variety of positions on the kinds of disparities that exist between women and men. Of course, it matters whether we are liberals who emphasize equality of opportunity or radicals more interested in welfare, whether we are reasonably optimistic about the potential for harmonious relations among humans or members of FINRRAGE.[41] Those who start with such different assumptions often reach different conclusions about particular issues, but active awareness of possible gender inequity will help to set the framework for fruitful dialogue. The basic point is that checking for gender problems should become as

[39] Alison Jaggar, "Feminist Ethics: Some Issues for the Nineties," *Journal of Social Philosophy* 20, nos. 1–2 (Spring–Fall 1989): 91.
[40] The problem here is that developing a feminist consciousness seems to be akin to having not one, but a series of scales drop from one's eyes. The quantum nature of the experience is reminiscent of Plato's view of how we are to come to know the forms. Fortunately, the recipe is somewhat clearer!
[41] FINRRAGE stands for Feminist International Network of Resistance to Reproductive and Genetic Engineering.

integral to bioethics as is checking for spelling errors: just as we no longer let a study "go public" before passing it through a spellcheck program, it shouldn't go out without a gender check. If we do this, then to the extent that the health care establishment take bioethics seriously, the most obvious discrepancies in care will diminish.[42]

As I have suggested, we need to keep a weather eye out for possible gender injustice. But is that all there is to it? What about the more sophisticated and demanding recommendations coming from new feminist work in bioethics? Both Susan Sherwin and Virginia Warren emphasize how sexist ostensibly neutral theories can be. From there they go off in different directions, although their suggestions intersect at some points. Warren distinguishes between substance and process, arguing that in both we need to become more sensitive to male perspectives that we now take as the whole story.[43] For example, she believes that such a perspective concentrates on situations where competition is a central element or focuses on their competitive aspects; inquiries are often transformed into a power struggle. Sherwin argues that feminist bioethics requires of us a new attention to context, reconsiders the nature and importance of basic moral concepts, such as relationships and character, and always keeps the political dimension in mind.

Eradicating unjust gender discrepancies in bioethics will certainly entail some fundamental rethinking. We have to pay close attention both to what problems we take up and the ways we deal with them; we certainly have to reanalyze basic concepts and principles, even if some emerge more or less intact. Fortunately, the more general work in feminist ethics is a fruitful source of inspiration here. Where this will lead is anybody's guess, although it seems safe to say that bioethics will look very different when we are done.

FEMINIST ETHICS

If feminist bioethics needs to look toward feminist ethics, where to start?[44] The obvious place is a critique of traditional ethical theory. Many of us who've been in the trenches trying to teach and apply ethical theories have long had doubts about the usefulness of anything like currently accepted approaches. As we are all acutely aware, there are several ethical theories. Their conclusions about a given case are often incompatible; even when

[42] I take it for granted that women should be treated at least as well as men; men should, of course, not drop to women's current level. We will then have something like equal consideration in care.

[43] See Warren, "Feminist Directions," in *Feminist Perspectives in Medical Ethics*, ed. Holmes and Purdy.

[44] This section of the Introduction was originally published in *Hypatia* 4, no. 2 (Summer 1989): 9–14. Somewhat revised versions were subsequently published in Holmes and Purdy, eds., *Feminist Perspectives in Medical Ethics*; and in the Appendix of Purdy, *In Their Best Interest? The Case against Equal Rights for Children* (Ithaca: Cornell University Press, 1992).

conclusions coincide, justifications tend to diverge. We are therefore compelled to pick a single theory if we wish to ensure consistent answers. But which to choose—and why? Although a few seem to me to be downright untenable, there are serious problems with all: whichever we choose opens us up to reproach on theoretical grounds even before we attempt to apply it. Complicating the picture further is the obscurity, and even inconsistency of some moral theorists (take Kant or Rousseau, for example), so that radically different interpretations of any given theory may be possible. Once we have chosen an interpretation, we may discover that there is, even then, no guarantee of help with the particular problem we wish to address. So although we may still march students through the traditional theories and make token bows in their direction in research on practical problems, their link with moral problem solving seems ever more tenuous.[45]

Some have reacted by espousing relativism[46] or retreating to the theoretical—ethics as a free-for-all or as an intellectual game. But who then will address the social problems now threatening us? Journalists? Politicians? Diplomats? Generals? And, equally serious, notice that there is no salvation from the slippery slide that pulls not only applied ethics but also ethical theory itself from our grasp. The latter, after all, requires debatable assumptions in fields such as philosophy of mind and language, not to mention empirical beliefs about how humans function and about the world at large. Of course, these assumptions depend in turn on further debatable assumptions in logic, epistemology, and metaphysics. So to be consistent, we might have to withdraw from all but the most basic areas of philosophy.

One way to proceed is to choose the least problematic moral theory—the one whose costs we are least reluctant to pay. In so doing, we adopt a set of principles, arranged neatly in our preferred pecking order. But it's often hard to have much confidence in that particular ranking. I myself, for example, am drawn to utilitarianism. Many of the problems attributed to it arise from implausible, straw-person interpretations that bear little resemblance to the spirit in which it was developed. Some problems are real, but have solutions no more distasteful than those necessary to patch together other moral theories. Some problems can be resolved at the cost of importing into the theory conflicts that otherwise arise only at its margins by positing utility for values such as freedom and justice. Other people are drawn to liberal theories, say, contractarianism, or Kantian imperatives; I

---

[45] I have sometimes thought that one way to recognize the canon in a field is to think about what we are afraid not to teach.

[46] Susan Sherwin seems to take this path in *No Longer Patient,* but despite her explicit embrace of moral relativism, it seems clear from her subsequent comments that she rejects the notion that there are no intellectual constraints on moral reasoning. See chapter 3.

think they often find themselves smuggling in assumptions about utility. So our practical reasoning about specific issues often is less divergent than one might have expected.

Blurring boundaries makes it easier to achieve some kind of consensus, although it is difficult to escape the suspicion that it is a result not of the accurate application of particular moral theories but of ideas that were already floating in the air. The same problem affects a more principle-oriented approach to ethical problem solving such as the one espoused by Tom Beauchamp and James Childress. In their excellent text *Principles of Biomedical Ethics* they lay out a number of general moral principles, declining to align them in any hierarchical order that would clarify what to do when they conflict.[47] The resulting flexibility is appealing, but it seems to import into the core of decision making a disturbing degree of relativism. Thus, despite its promise of practical guidance, moral theory seems to leave us in the lurch just when we need it most. Whether this state of affairs is the "temporary" result of the inability to develop an adequate universal theory or a perhaps irremediable reflection of reality, as Tristram Engelhardt seems to assert, remains to be seen.[48]

The fact that traditional theories often fail to provide much guidance for practice is both a problem and a possible exit from this apparent impasse. Attempting to resolve concrete problems brings us nose to nose with problems for which the standard theories have little wisdom. What kind of situation are we dealing with? How is it most appropriately described, and what criteria can we use to tell? Who is to count in the moral deliberations and why? What are the most relevant facts and what are the grounds for deciding? As we grapple with such matters, the questions of which moral principle should ultimately prevail may recede almost to the vanishing point, while texture and context are in the forefront.

Feminist writers have been especially active in exploring such ideas, stimulated in part by Carol Gilligan's *In a Different Voice* and Nel Noddings's *Caring*.[49] One emerging consensus is that it is important to concentrate on the context and details of problematic situations, instead of trying to deduce what ought to be done from highly abstract and general principles. This approach seems to be to be a possible way out of the aforementioned difficulties, and given the block we have come to, one well worth investigating.

[47] Tom L. Beauchamp and James F. Childress, *Principles of Biomedical Ethics*, 4th ed. (Oxford: Oxford University Press, 1994).

[48] H. Tristram Engelhardt, Jr., "Applied Philosophy in the Post-Modern Age: An Augury," *Journal of Social Philosophy* 20 (Spring–Fall 1989): 42–48.

[49] Carol Gilligan, *In a Different Voice* (Cambridge: Harvard University Press, 1982), and Nel Noddings, *Caring* (Berkeley: University of California Press, 1984).

Some have taken this precept as a thoroughgoing rejection of traditional moral theory, assuming that an intuitive approach to specific situations will carry us through. But concentrating on particular situations without the benefit of underlying principles leaves us forever unable to resolve many conflicts or to generalize from one case to another. Yet without such generalization we lose our way in the ever-multiplying thickets, unable to use anything we have learned in the past, ever in danger of incoherent action.

Take, for example, the promising emphasis on notions of caring and preserving relationships. It helps keep our feet on the ground as we deliberate about how to live. Often enough, if we care about others, it will be obvious what ought to be done. Many, perhaps most, situations calling for moral decision making involve choosing between our own selfish desires and others' welfare. Should a doctor lie to cover up negligence? Should a parent squelch a kid's natural curiosity because answering questions gets tiresome? Everybody knows the answers, the question is whether people care enough to do the right thing.

But not every problem can be resolved in this appealing way. "Caring" cannot show us when we may legitimately say "no" to preserve our own well-being or how to resolve a genuine conflict of interests. Moreover, not every relationship is worth preserving. Caring *will* compel us to consider the kinds of communication, compromise, and concern about long-term effects now sorely lacking in much moral decision making. It should help us rule out practices that belittle or ignore suffering. But if it is focused too narrowly on particular others with whom we have relationships, it might also have some tendency to narrow our vision to exclude awareness of the broader kinds of social and political context crucial to good moral reasoning.

Concern for particulars is an admirable antidote to the lifeless, overly broad, strokes to which we have been so often subjected by moral philosophers. But unless we can formulate principles that help us apply our insights about caring to more general contexts and get beyond preoccupation with particular cases, we are no better off than proponents of situation ethics. Also, as some have been pointing out, if this approach is not adopted by all, we simply perpetuate the status quo, in which women are expected to do and in fact do most of the caring.[50]

Without principles, we cannot consistently press the most basic claims motivating moral theories. Thus, values such as caring are defensible against possible alternatives only if we conceive of ethics as a social institution whose chief function should be justly to promote the well-being of all. Furthermore, only this kind of basic moral assumption safeguards us

---

[50] E.g., Claudia Card, "Women's Voices and Ethical Ideals: Must We Mean What We Say?," *Ethics* 99, no. 1 (October 1988): 125–35.

from the naturalistic fallacy and equips us to wend our way with some art through the moral labyrinth.

Universalizability—the principle that only a morally relevant difference between two cases justifies different treatment of them—provides a minimal, yet demanding, constraint on moral reasoning. Insensitively applied, it can be used as a bludgeon to lump superficially similar cases together, obscuring morally relevant distinctions, or vice versa. The principle by itself does not determine how narrowly to draw distinctions or what their content should be. The kind of close attention to detail, circumstance, and interests feminist ethics demands is fully compatible with universalizability so conceived. Rejecting the principle altogether because it is wrongly applied would leave moral decision making rudderless.

One might want to argue that caring people will make good decisions, so there is no need for even such a minimal structure. But, as I have argued, good decision making implies principle. And one of our chief aims as feminist moral philosophers should be to create justifiable formal and material principles that can be understood and used by all. Without such a structure we are in danger of creating yet another ghetto. When the dust settles, there is no telling what feminist ethics will look like. But what we do not want is a "special interest" ethics that can be ignored or relegated to the already large collection of theories among which people can arbitrarily pick and choose. What I hope for in the long run is that feminism will permeate all ethics, leaving "feminist ethics" to wither away. Only this outcome safeguards us from "respectable" theories that ignore women's interests.

What characteristics might we want to predicate of feminist ethics? I would argue for embracing the very broadest conception of feminism: "recognition that women are in a subordinate position in society, that oppression is an intolerable form of injustice . . . that it is possible to change society in ways that could eliminate oppression, and that is a goal of feminism to pursue the changes necessary to accomplish this."[51]

Feminist ethics might then be taken to include discussions that:

(1) *Emphasize the importance of women and their interests.* Stressing justice for women seems to me to be the minimum condition for describing any work as "feminist." But I think we want, during this time of experimentation and ferment, to avoid any semblance of rigid orthodoxy about the form that this emphasis should take. We shouldn't be branding some work as "not really feminist" so long as it is premised on the aforementioned feminist assumptions. This does not mean, of course, that we should not feel free to criticize other views or argue for our own. Feminist scholars have been

[51] Susan Sherwin, "Feminist and Medical Ethics: Two Different Approaches to Contextual Ethics," *Hypatia* 4, no. 2 (Summer 1989): 70 n. 7.

documenting in damning detail the invisibility (or worse) of women and their interests in most traditional work. Insisting on gender as a required category of analysis is a step in the right direction. Studies of mainstream medical ethics theory that include women are good examples of another.

(2) *Focus on issues specially concerning or affecting women.* We need to be broad-minded, in part to avoid the kind of sectarian warfare that could undermine this still-fragile enterprise. However, subject matter alone is not enough to render a work feminist: it should not be classified as such unless it also meets the test suggested under category (1). There is room here for a broad array of narrowly directed case studies. There is also room for "unsexy," "housekeeping" issues that might be ignored as too trivial to merit philosophical treatment by nonfeminists. Last, but not least, much of the recent work in reproductive ethics seems to fall most appropriately in this category.

(3) *Rethink fundamental assumptions.* Feminists need to reconsider both substantive principles and philosophical methods. Excellent instances of the former are the criticisms of atomism,[52] proposals for new models of human relationships,[53] and discussion of the moral relevance of gender,[54] as well as the aforementioned principles about detail and context. Valuable examples of the latter are Virginia Warren's criticism of the gladiator theory of truth,[55] and the concern about abstraction raised by Sheila Ruth.[56]

(4) *Incorporate feminist insights and conclusions from other fields and disciplines.* Interdisciplinary work like ethics (and medical ethics, in particular) requires substantial general knowledge. It must include awareness of how feminist work is transforming other disciplines; otherwise, we will not be able to fit our own contributions into an organic growing whole. These categories are neither exhaustive nor mutually exclusive: surely, the future will reveal a fascinating variety of approaches, strategies, arguments, and values. Let us hope that the rich stream of work we are witnessing, work that is now beginning to include long-overdue sensitivity to related oppressions, will steadily broaden its reach to every corner of the moral landscape.

---

[52] See Alison Jaggar, *Feminist Politics and Human Nature* (Totowa, N.J.: Rowman and Allanheld, 1983).
[53] Virginia Held, "Non-Contractual Society," in *Science, Morality, and Feminist Theory,* ed. Marsha Hanen and Kai Nielsen, *Canadian Journal of Philosophy* (suppl. vol. 13, 1987).
[54] Okin, *Justice, Gender, and the Family.*
[55] Warren, "Feminist Directions in Medical Ethics," in *Feminist Perspectives in Medical Ethics,* ed. Holmes and Purdy, p. 44 n. 5.
[56] Sheila Ruth, "Methodocracy, Misogyny, and Bad Faith: The Response of Philosophy," in *Men's Studies Modified: The Impact of Feminism on the Academic Disciplines,* ed. Dale Spender (Oxford: Pergamon, 1981).

A PROPOSAL

I have argued elsewhere that feminist work as just defined has a great deal in common with an intelligent utilitarianism.[57] Why might one elect to use a utilitarian basis for a new feminist theory? First of all, it is consequentialist: judgments about the moral worth of an action are based on its consequences.[58] Only such a consequentialist theory can hope to break free of precepts based on old prejudices. Second, utilitarianism demands that the interests of every party affected by an action be taken into equal account. Only this approach promises that the interests of women and other members of other disadvantaged groups not be, once more, ignored or discounted. Third, utilitarianism requires that alternatives to a given action be thoroughly explored. This requirement builds in consideration of longer-term possible consequences of the chosen action and its alternatives; such consideration is essential in safeguarding the interests of women and members of other disadvantaged groups. Last, but not least, utilitarianism realistically links morality to people's real values: finding happiness and avoiding unnecessary misery. This approach keeps morality grounded in the real world, paying attention to individual needs, needs that have so often been ignored when they belong to women and other members of disadvantaged groups.

Feminist thinkers often call for just these kinds of features in a new moral theory. Carol Gilligan speaks of "a moral universe in which men, more often than women, conceive of morality as substantively constituted by obligations and rights and as procedurally constituted by the demands of fairness and impartiality, while women, more often than men, see moral requirements as emerging from the particular needs of others in the context of particular relationships."[59] Some philosophers, mostly women, have built on these findings by enthusiastically arguing for a new morality based on these values.

For example, in a pioneering paper, "A Feminist Approach to Ethics," Susan Sherwin urges upon us an ethic that "rejects the predatory conception of human interaction inherent in any theory that is essentially concerned with preserving the separateness of persons."[60] A good theory will, on the

---

[57] Laura M. Purdy, "Do Feminists Need a New Moral Theory?," paper presented at the conference Explorations in Feminist Ethics, Duluth, Minn., October 1988; printed in abbreviated form in Purdy, *In Their Best Interest?*

[58] For a critical discussion of consequentialism, see *Consequentialism and Its Critics,* ed. Samuel Scheffler (Oxford: Oxford University Press, 1988).

[59] Gilligan's position here is described by Owen Flanagan and Kathryn Jackson, in "Justice, Care, and Gender: The Kohlberg-Gilligan Debate Revisited," *Ethics* 97, no. 3 (April 1987): 623.

[60] Susan Sherwin, "A Feminist Approach to Ethics," *Dalhousie Review* 64, no. 4 (Winter 1984–1985): 711.

contrary, assume empathy and promote emotional and political bonds.[61] In a similar vein, Caroline Whitbeck has argued for what she calls a "responsibilities view," a morality that exhorts us to contribute to others' welfare. This approach entrusts individuals with certain tasks, together with the discretion required for carrying them out.[62] We may, Virginia Held emphasizes, even be responsible for individuals with whom our relationship is not voluntary.[63] In the words of Eva Kittay and Diana Meyers, our "central preoccupation is a responsiveness to others that dictates providing care, preventing harm, and maintaining relationships."[64] One assumption common to all these comments is that if we care about others, what needs to be done will often be obvious. The same assumption, it seems to me, underlies the practice of utilitarianism: the urgent needs of others are often clear, and it is our duty to try to meet them. Furthermore, a feminist ethic implies equal attention to the welfare of all affected parties, and, as I have suggested, utilitarianism seems to be the only theory that demands such attention to be taken for granted.

When I read *In a Different Voice* several years ago, I did not imagine how influential it would become. It did strike me that Carol Gilligan's work might have some bearing on the (it seems to me) peculiar distaste for utilitarianism that for the most part pervades academic philosophy. For what she says about the concerns of girls and women about caring, responsibility, and relationships is reminiscent of what I have always understood as desirable utilitarian assumptions. Misapplication could bias the theory against women, but it is not—contrary to what some others who drum us out of any meaningful moral arena from the start might say—rotten at the core. As Lea Campos Boralevi suggests, "this concern was not only different from Ancient Greek and Roman thinkers, in whose societies autonomous legal personality was given to the *pater familias*, a man with his family, including children, women, slaves and servants. It was also different from modern philosophers, such as Locke and Rousseau, who tried to give an autonomous personality to single *individuals* excluding women, or better, including women's interests in those of the men to whom they were closely related—fathers, brothers, or husbands."[65]

[61] Ibid.
[62] Caroline Whitbeck, "A Different Reality: Feminist Ontology," in *Beyond Domination*, ed. Carol C. Gould (Totowa, N.J.: Rowman and Allenheld, 1983), p. 79.
[63] Held, "Non-Contractual Society."
[64] Eva Feder Kittay and Diana T. Meyers, "Introduction," in *Women and Moral Theory* (Totowa, N.J.: Rowman and Allenheld, 1987), p. 3.
[65] Lea Campos Boralevi, "Utilitarianism and Feminism," in *Women in Western Political Philosophy*, ed. Ellen Kennedy and Susan Mendus (New York: St. Martin's Press, 1987), p. 164.

History underlines the affinity between feminism and utilitarianism. Boralevi asserts that "the way in which women's happiness was thought to be obtained differed slightly from one utilitarian thinker to the other, but utilitarians were all fundamentally and positively concerned with the happiness of women."[66] Utilitarianism equally took into account the happiness of each individual creature, and some of its proponents pressed women's case both theoretically and in practice.[67]

Given the methodological postulates favorable to women's interests, the historical concern of utilitarians, and my dimly perceived intuition that utilitarianism's humane approach to morality might have some bearing on the contempt heaped upon it, it has been all the more surprising to see it ignored or discounted in recent work on feminist ethics.

Utilitarianism ignores justice, is too demanding, and involves dubious comparisons of interpersonal preferences: such are the by-now traditional objections to the theory. It is not, by and large, these issues, however, that trouble prominent feminist theorists. For example, Susan Sherwin dismisses utilitarianism thus: "the most widely accepted theories of our time are inadequate for addressing many of the moral issues we encounter in our lives, since they focus entirely on such abstract qualities of moral agents as autonomy or quantities of happiness."[68] Caroline Whitbeck, too, characterizes all contemporary ethics as "rights views."[69]

This classification of utilitarianism with traditional individualistic theories seems to me far wide of the mark, whereas suggestions for a new feminist ethic are often astonishingly like any reasonably sympathetic interpretation of utilitarianism.[70] For example, diminishing suffering is one of utilitarianism's most urgent charges. We are to achieve this end by choosing actions and social policies that entail the least possible suffering.[71] Such

---

[66] Ibid., p. 164. However, Terence Ball in his article "Utilitarianism, Feminism, and the Franchise: James Mill and his Critics," *History of Political Thought* 1 (Spring 1980): 91–115, suggests that this claim ought to be tempered somewhat. Ball argues that James Mill's views are ambivalent at best and that it would be difficult to view Bentham as a feminist. But both Mill and Bentham agreed in principle that women's happiness counts equally in moral decision making; it is their views about the conditions that must be satisfied to bring about that end that are hardly tenable. Again, however, the problem involves application, not basic principle.

[67] For example, philosophic radicals founded University College, the first institution of higher learning that did not discriminate on the basis of class, religion, or sex (Boralevi, *Utilitarianism and Feminism*, p. 170).

[68] Susan Sherwin, "Feminist Ethics and in Vitro Fertilization," in *Science, Morality, and Feminist Theory*, ed. Hanen and Nielsen, p. 265.

[69] Whitbeck, "A Different Reality," p. 79.

[70] For an elaboration of this interpretation, see Wendy Donner, *The Liberal Self* (Ithaca: Cornell University Press, 1991).

[71] See Jeremy Bentham, *Principles of Morals and Legislation*, ed. J. H. Burns and H. L. A. Hart (London: Methuen, 1982), and John Stuart Mill, *Utilitarianism*, esp. chap. 2, where he writes: "the happiness which forms the utilitarian standard of what is right in conduct, is not the

a program corresponds, so far as I can tell, in all important respects exactly with Sheila Mullett's proposals for moral sensitivity and ontological shock and praxis.[72] The first is "painful awareness of suffering"; the second is commitment to awareness and action; the third involves a shift from individualistic perspectives to collective ones.[73]

Feminist ethics adamantly opposes all forms of egoism and selfish individualism. So does utilitarianism. Its motto, "the greatest happiness of the greatest number,"[74] is intended to convey its concern with everyone's welfare. Such a charge involves responsibilities toward all, based on need rather than contract. But this concern is no theoretical, duty-driven affair. John Stuart Mill argues that

> education and opinion . . . should so use that power [over human character] as to establish in the mind of every individual an indissoluble association between his own happiness and the good of the whole—especially between his own happiness and the practice of such modes of conduct, negative and positive, as regard for the universal happiness prescribes; so that not only he may be unable to conceive the possibility of happiness to himself, consistently with conduct opposed to the general good, but also that a direct impulse to promote the general good may be in every individual one of the habitual motives of action, and the sentiments connected therewith may fill a large and prominent place in every human being's sentient existence.[75]

This emotional linking of interests is by far the best guarantee against the individualism feminist theory rightly condemns.

Sandra Harding excoriates contemporary moral theory for its fascination with justice at the expense of human welfare: "to the observer armed with gender theory, egoism, utilitarianism, and formalism all appear to address characteristically masculine problems of how to elaborate rules for adjudicating competing rights and duties between generalized autonomous individuals. None takes as an equally important problem how to elaborate ways of resolving conflicting responsibilities to dependent particular

---

agent's own happiness, but that of all concerned. . . . As the means of making the nearest approach to this ideal, utility would enjoin, first, that laws and social arrangements should place the happiness, or . . . the interest, of every individual, as nearly as possible in harmony with the interest of the whole." John Stuart Mill, *Utilitarianism*, in *The Utilitarians* (New York: Dolphin Books, 1961), p. 418.

[72] Sheila Mullett, "Shifting Perspective: A New Approach to Ethics," in *Feminist Perspectives: Philosophical Essays on Method and Morals*, ed. Lorraine Code, Sheila Mullett, and Christine Overall (Toronto: University of Toronto Press, 1988), pp. 110–17.

[73] Ibid., pp. 115–16.

[74] Despite its logical incoherence. . . .

[75] Mill, *Utilitarianism*, pp. 418–19.

others."[76] She goes on to ask: "Should moral theory take the development of a concept of justice and political theory and the project of constructing the just state as central when those goals, even if achieved, would not by themselves bring about greater social welfare? Is justice sufficient to maximize social welfare?"[77]

It is ironic that Harding should castigate utilitarianism for insisting on a narrow conception of justice at the expense of social welfare, as that is precisely what it refuses to do.[78] The price for utilitarianism, as it may be for feminist ethics, is rejection by many members of the philosophical establishment.[79] In both cases, the charge is unwarranted, and, I think, for similar reasons.

Formal justice, in the guise of a carefully drawn account of universalizability, must be espoused by both. Although, as I have suggested earlier, the appropriateness of universalizability for feminist ethics has been the subject of hot debate, I believe that it is a minimum criterion for any ethic. The crucial point, as I see it, is that feminist theory will expect finer distinctions and perhaps untraditional morally relevant differences. The kind of close attention to detail, circumstance, and interest feminist ethics demands is fully compatible with universalizability so conceived. If we can make the case for how we apply universalizability, that should compel every moral thinker to heed us.

Nor are the demands of material justice overlooked. Mill's comments about material justice are often thought inconsistent with his adherence to the principle of utility, but careful reading of chapter 5 of *Utilitarianism* suggests that this idea is mistaken. There, he argues that justice is simply a set of the most general and important dictates of utility.[80] Proponents of other theories of justice appear to be unable to recognize this concept as justice.

"Care" reasoning, however, seems to me to follow a similar logic. Take the notorious Heinz case: a man's wife will die unless he steals medicine from a druggist. The boy Jake's analysis is that he should of course steal, as life is more important than property. His decision that life has priority over property is deemed to demonstrate a sophisticated understanding of jus-

[76] Sandra Harding, "Is Gender a Variable in Conceptions of Rationality? A Survey of Issues," in *Beyond Domination*, ed. Gould, p. 56.
[77] Ibid.
[78] Ibid.
[79] See contemporary critiques of utilitarianism, as well as comments about women's moral capacities by "great" philosophers, such as Kant or Rousseau; see also Kohlberg's work.
[80] For example, he mentions our need for security. This view assumes certain facts about human nature, which might be different. If they were different, then the dictates of justice would be different, too.

tice. But is it anything more than recognition that property is meaningless without life—a clearly utility-maximizing judgment?

The girl Amy is unwilling to declare so unambiguously that Heinz should steal the drug: What are the likely consequences of that course of action, she asks? Her analysis seems to me frankly utilitarian, as she appears to be concerned mainly with averting suffering, although Gilligan describes what she proposes as "maintaining relationships." But I don't think this distinction makes a big difference: if, as recent feminist work has rightly emphasized, relationships are essential for survival (let alone happiness), then the practice of having relationships has utility. Averting suffering tends to nourish relationships and therefore has utility.

The difference between Amy's and Jake's analyses seems to me to be mainly in Amy's unwillingness to put up with the terms of the puzzle, because she sees that bad consequences will follow no matter which course is chosen. The boy's willingness to accept the lesser evil is taken as a sign of his intellectual and moral maturity, even though its results in unnecessary suffering avoided by her less theoretical, more down-to-earth approach.

It is exactly this kind of vision and flexibility that is desirable in feminist ethics. Susan Sherwin urges us to consider not just the immediate features of a given case. At least as important are the assumptions underlying particular solutions, as well as their long-term consequences, especially political consequences.[81] Thus decisions must take into account not only the interplay of principles immediately involved (say, autonomy and nonmaleficence), but also the ultimate consequences of choosing one or the other in our society.

Sherwin is fearful of theories, such as utilitarianism, that compel us to separate the intrinsic morality of technologies from questions about their particular applications.[82] But this objection is, I think, inconsistent with her desire for context-sensitive judgments. She is rightly concerned to ensure that what we might call "deep" context gets taken into account. Doing so for a given situation or society, however, tells us nothing about other ones.

Furthermore, only consequentialist theories require such distinctions of us, as they demand the fullest and most sensitive understanding of social conditions. Most important, perhaps, they must take power asymmetries into account; otherwise the intent to rectify imbalances is impotent and suffering caused by them continues.

---

[81] Sherwin, "Feminist Ethics and in Vitro Fertilization," in *Science, Morality, and Feminist Theory,* ed. Hanen and Nielsen, pp. 281–83.

[82] I am using "intrinsic" here in a slightly odd way. By it I mean an evaluation of the consequences that necessarily follow from the fixed features of an act. This is compatible with an act's having no intrinsic morality.

Consider, for example, the question of surrogate motherhood. I think that in some worlds the practice would lead to more happiness than suffering. Practiced in our own sexist, racist, capitalist world, the possibility of harm is so great that we must stringently regulate it or perhaps even ban it altogether.[83] Only distinguishing necessary from contingent features of the practice (the latter arising from the context within which practice occurs) allows us to make this bifurcated judgment. Failing to differentiate these features deprives us of the use of beneficial technologies where circumstances preclude the envisioned harm. It is the rights- and justice-based theories Sherwin objects to that ignore the realities of deep context by attempting to focus on isolated actions.

Similar kinds of comment are appropriate in response to objections that utilitarianism allows for neither special relationships nor concern with specific individuals. The theory could hardly ignore the psychological facts of human existence. One of these is that we form attachments to particular individuals, whose welfare is specially important to us. No judgment could therefore possibly maximize utility unless it takes seriously this fact about our relationships with others. So long as there are clear rules about the boundaries of such special relationships, utilitarianism can incorporate them without violating universalizability.[84]

Attention to context is thus mandatory for any decent analysis; context dictates where special provisions, such as affirmative action, are appropriate. The same point justifies devoting ourselves to particular causes, such

---

[83] Purdy, "Surrogate Mothering: Exploitation or Empowerment?" and "A Response to Dodds and Jones," *Bioethics* 3, no. 1 (January 1989): 18–34, 40–44.

[84] As Kai Nielsen rightly points out in "Afterword: Feminist Theory—Some Twistings and Turnings," in *Science, Morality, and Feminist Theory,* ed. Hanen and Nielsen. He says:

> To recognize that *my* friends have a special claim on me that others do not is to recognize, for someone who understands what morality is, that *your* friends also have a similar claim on you . . . unless there is some morally relevant and in turn universalizable difference between you, your friends or your situation and me. It also involves believing that the moral point of view at crucial junctures requires impartiality. But again such a commitment to impartiality and universalizability does not require and should not require, moral agents to seek to be, what they cannot be anyway, to wit, detached, identityless atomic individuals. (p. 390)

Mill, too, addresses this and related points quite fully. He argues that

> those among them who entertain anything like a just idea of its [utilitarianism's] disinterested character sometimes find fault with its standard as being too high for humanity. They say it is exacting too much to require that people shall always act from the inducement of promoting the general interests of society. But this is to mistake the very meaning of a standard of morals, and confound the rule of action with the motive of it. It is the business of ethics to tell us what are our duties, or by what test we may know them; but no system of ethics requires that the sole motive of all we do shall be a feeling of duty. . . . It is the more unjust to utilitarianism that this particular misapprehension should be made a ground of objection to it, inasmuch as utilitarian moral-

as the feminist movement.[85] There are many injustices in the world, and it probably makes sense to allocate effort where we feel the most emotional pull, so long as all serious problems get addressed by somebody. Fighting women's oppression may sometimes seem to have less immediate utility than benefiting oppressors, but this can hardly be true in the long run. However, urgent threats not in our particular bailiwick may require us temporarily to scale back or drop our commitments altogether. Examples might be widespread homelessness, a life-threatening epidemic, an invasion from outer space.[86]

Feminist thinkers are correct, I think, in their insistence that we need to pay attention to the needs and desires of others not insofar as they are exemplars of the human condition, but as idiosyncratic selves. We cannot rely on assumptions about what we would want if we were in others' shoes or on judgments about what people ought to want: it is necessary to study particular others to see what they want. But utilitarianism, unlike any other moral theory, again requires precisely the same thing. The only way to increase happiness is to get people what they really need and want.

This need sometimes conflicts with the requirements of justice. In a utilitarian world, however, the conflict conforms with concerns advanced by feminist ethics. What people want now may interfere with what will make them happy in the long run. This can be the outcome either when current desires are satisfied at the expense of future ones or when development is deflected from the most ultimately satisfying deployment of our talents. Furthermore, we can sometimes justifiably be asked to forego our own satisfaction on behalf of others. Therefore, one of the most pressing tasks of

---

ists have gone beyond almost all others in affirming that the motive has nothing to do with the morality of the action, though much with the worth of the agent. . . . The great majority of good actions are intended not for the benefit of the world, but for that of individuals, of which the good of the world is made up; and the thoughts of the most virtuous man need not on these occasions travel beyond the particular persons concerned, except so far as is necessary to assure himself that in benefiting them he is not violating the rights, that is, the legitimate and authorized expectations, of anyone else. ("Utilitarianism," pp. 419–20)

[85] Rosemarie Tong rejects my utilitarian approach, arguing that "there is an enormous difference between seeking to diminish everyone's suffering *in general*, all the while neglecting to ask *who* it is that suffers, and seeking to diminish women's suffering *in particular*. Once again, feminists favor the concrete approach of binding the wounds of a specific oppressed group over the abstract idea of fighting suffering qua suffering. A feminist approach to ethics, unlike other practical approaches to ethics, mobilizes women to take charge of their moral destinies." But, because the harm to women caused by sexism is so great, I do not see any incompatibility in these positions except when some overwhelming catastrophe threatens humanity. See Rosemarie Tong, *Feminine and Feminist Ethics* (Belmont, Calif.: Wadsworth, 1993), p. 225.

[86] These points address some of Susan Sherwin's comments in "A Feminist Approach to Ethics."

any decent moral theory is to find the right mix of preference satisfaction and concern for long-term personal and social interests. Mill's psychology, by encouraging some desires at the expense of others, is designed to make the job easier.

Where feminist thinkers seem to diverge from utilitarianism most strongly is on the question of the nature of the self. Many feminists conceive of the self as socially constituted, not merely as strongly influenced by social factors. Because Mill's psychology is a variation on the latter theme, these feminists reject it. It seems to me, however, that this relational notion of the self remains to be elucidated in a fully clear and persuasive manner, and I am as yet unconvinced that it would dissolve or otherwise lessen the importance of most of the interpersonal conflicts that now constitute many of the critical moral questions facing us.

It has become a commonplace among feminists that we cannot just "add women and stir," as theoretical frameworks based on sexist assumptions disintegrate in their absence. We are committed to analyze the whole intellectual structure of Western civilization: our task is overwhelming. It is therefore sensible to salvage what we can and not feel compelled to reinvent *every* wheel.

Ethics is no exception. In our eagerness to start anew, let us not ignore gifts from the past: we may be dissatisfied with some of the implications of rights-based theories, for example, but it would be ungrateful to forget how rights talk has improved our lot. Furthermore, recognizing the close links between our fledgling feminist ethics and earlier theories may well help us to formulate our ideas and face whatever difficulties they may have in common.

Utilitarianism has had a checkered career. It is true that the theory may be characterized in different ways, depending on which writers, works, or comments ones takes as primary. A more or less sympathetic eye can construct more or less appealing versions of the theory. And, as with any moral theory, the intelligence and sensitivity of those apply it make a huge difference.[87] Utilitarianism, at its best, has much to offer feminists, and I believe that feminists should reassess their negativism about it.

---

[87] Conversely, as Mill pointed out, "there is no difficulty in proving any ethical standard whatever to work ill, if we suppose universal idiocy to be conjoined with it" (*Utilitarianism*, chap. 2, p. 425).

PART I

THE RIGHT TO REPRODUCE:

LIMITS AND CAVEATS

Human societies place tremendous emphasis on reproduction, and pronatalism is still a powerful force in many cultures. It is generally expected that individuals will have children. Many people—and some governments—seem to feel that having children is a duty. In the United States, although there are those who believe that only the selfish fail to have children, concern about producing the next generation takes the form of a right to reproduce that says that you may have children if you are able and so desire.

Even though the Constitution is silent on this matter of reproduction, various Supreme Court decisions have spied reproductive rights in the penumbra of other fundamental rights. International documents on rights, such as the United Nations Declaration of Human Rights, assert the right to found a family.

The strongest element in the right to reproduce, both legal and moral, is thought to be negative: individuals cannot usually be prevented from having children if they are able to. Exceptions include persons, such as prisoners, who are regarded as having forfeited their normal rights, and those such as soldiers, who have been impressed into allegedly urgent state business. Consistent with the general emphasis on negative rights, there are few positive rights available to help those who are experiencing difficulty exercising their right to reproduce.

Many people see the moral right to reproduce as an absolute right that should not be qualified in any way. That position is, in part, a laudable reaction to past attempts to limit births among individuals and groups considered inferior. So the justification for placing the right to reproduce beyond argument is that people have gone so far wrong on this issue in the past that one can no longer entertain the possibility of limits without risking racist or sexist disaster. Seeing the right to reproduce as an absolute right thus entails a moral pessimism that considers even initially enlightened moral discussion as the first step toward a slippery slope to oppression. This refusal to discuss the morality of reproduction is also considered the most potentially successful way of combating prejudiced disapproval of reproduction on the part of poor women, especially poor women of color, and of single, disabled, menopausal, or lesbian women.

Yet having children necessarily falls in the realm of morality. It affects the children themselves, other intimates, and society at large. It may be true that many calls for limits are morally untenable, but there may be justifiable limits on reproduction that need to be considered. In the end, the political dangers of asserting limits on reproduction might be great enough to outweigh the harm that could come of unlimited reproduction. Finally, scientific advances and social conditions make it imperative to consider possible expansion of the right to reproduce. On the one hand, fans of the rapidly developing new reproductive technologies are pressing for enabling legislation (see for instance Chapter 13, "*Children of Choice:* Whose Children? At What Cost?"); on the other, deteriorating social conditions threaten to empty the right to reproduce of meaning for ever larger numbers of people.

Careful examination of the ramifications of the right to reproduce would fill several volumes. Only a few can be sketched out here, and these essays represent a narrow, but important, part of the topic. Both Chapter 1, "Genetics and Reproductive Risk: Can Having Children Be Immoral?," and Chapter 2, "Loving Future People," take up the question of whether one should refrain from having children when they are at risk of serious harm from genetic or broader biological factors. The first is a recently revised version of an old paper that found its way into several anthologies. The second, written in 1992, considers a variety of responses that have appeared since the first paper was originally published in 1976. Chapter 3, "What Can Progress in Reproductive Technology Mean for Women?," written in 1995, argues that feminist treatments of genetic and reproductive risk fail adequately to consider women's interests. Chapter 4, "Are Pregnant Women Fetal Containers?," considers the question of what women owe their existing fetuses, a question that has become ever more pressing in recent years as the discipline of fetal medicine has developed new awareness of how women influence their fetuses' well-being. All four papers try to reconcile women's autonomy and well-being with concern for children. This problem would be much more tractable if one could simply assert either the primacy of women's autonomy or that of the offspring; however, neither approach would do justice to the moral complexity of the situation. Unfortunately, attempting to find tenable compromises entails contradiction, incoherence, and the charge of ad hoc accommodation. Furthermore, although I still think these reproductive problems are pressing issues, I have come to believe that they should play a relatively small role in overall health policy and that work on them must continue to emphasize that fact.

What about other problems? One of the most urgent is to cope with the ever-growing human population. Newer wrinkles involve single or lesbian women having children independently of men and, most recently of all, technologically created pregnancy in postmenopausal women. Calls for limits on reproduction have appeared in connection with each of these issues. Some, like the population question, have led to voluminous scholarly debates; all have broader political overtones that quite often interfere with reasoned discussion.

For example, the population debate now appears to be mired in disagreement about whether redistribution of resources would satisfy everybody's fundamental needs or whether the issue of population needs to be addressed independently of such redistribution. Espousing the latter position automatically brands one as a racist and a political conservative, no matter what considerations lead one to that conclusion. Likewise, few progressives are willing to raise the issue of when, if ever, it might be irresponsible to bring a child into the world, for fear of being thought sexist, racist, or "ableist."

I find these questions about responsible parenting among the most fascinating dishes on the applied ethics menu, for they raise fundamental questions about gender, gender roles, technology, and the good society. I look forward to exploring more of them in the future.

What, for instance, should we think about single women choosing to have children on their own? Although it is clearly preferable, other things being equal, to have a second adult deeply involved in child raising, there appears to be no evidence that children are necessarily harmed by living in a single-parent household. Likewise, despite widespread negativism about lesbian households, there seems to be no evidence that children are harmed by living in them, and some reason for thinking that they could be superior to the average heterosexual home. So society's attempts to prevent lesbians from having children (as in their exclusion from in vitro fertilization programs) are unjustifiable, products, no doubt, of fear and hatred of homosexuality. Postmenopausal pregnancy also seems relatively unproblematic. On the one hand, the outcry against it most probably relies on the position that natural is good and that women have no business fulfilling their desires in such an unnatural way. If it were based on concern about the offspring of such pregnancies, the outcry would have to include men who father children at the same late age. On the other hand, however, it seems morally dubious to have children who will most likely be orphaned at a young age. Even if they are provided for financially, what about their emotional well-being? These are some of the issues that will need to be explored in the future.

CHAPTER 1

Genetics and Reproductive Risk:

Can Having Children Be Immoral?

Is it morally permissible for me to have children? A decision to procreate is surely one of the most significant decisions a person can make. So it would seem that it ought not be made without some moral soul searching.

There are many reasons why one might hesitate to bring children into this world if one is concerned about their welfare. Some are rather general, such as the deteriorating environment or the prospect of poverty. Others have a narrower focus, such as continuing civil war in one's country or the lack of essential social support for childrearing in the United States. Still others may be relevant only to individuals at risk of passing harmful diseases to their offspring.

There are many causes of misery in this world, and most of them are unrelated to genetic disease. In the general scheme of things, human misery is most efficiently reduced by concentrating on noxious social and political arrangements. Nonetheless, we should not ignore preventable harm just because it is confined to a relatively small corner of life. So the question arises, Can it be wrong to have a child because of genetic risk factors?[1]

This essay is loosely based on "Genetic Diseases: Can Having Children Be Immoral?" originally published in *Genetics Now,* ed. John L. Buckley (Washington, D.C.: University Press of America, 1978), and subsequently anthologized in a number of medical ethics texts. Thanks to Thomas Mappes and David DeGrazia for their helpful suggestions about updating the article.

[1] I focus on genetic considerations, although with the advent of AIDS the scope of the general question here could be expanded. There are two reasons for sticking to this relatively narrow formulation. One is that dealing with a smaller chunk of the problem may help us to think more clearly, while realizing that some conclusions may nonetheless be relevant to

Unsurprisingly, most of the debate about this issue has focused on pre-natal screening and abortion: much useful information about a given fetus can be made available by recourse to prenatal testing. This fact has meant that moral questions about reproduction have become entwined with abor-tion politics, to the detriment of both. The abortion connection has made it especially difficult to think about whether it is wrong to prevent a child from coming into being, because doing so might involve what many people see as wrongful killing; yet there is no necessary link between the two. Clearly, the existence of genetically compromised children can be pre-vented not only by aborting already existing fetuses but also by preventing conception in the first place.

Worse yet, many discussions simply assume a particular view of abortion without recognizing other possible positions and the difference they make in how people understand the issues. For example, those who object to aborting fetuses with genetic problems often argue that doing so would un-dermine our conviction that all humans are in some important sense equal.[2] However, this position rests on the assumption that conception marks the point at which humans are endowed with a right to life. So aborting fetuses with genetic problems looks morally the same as killing "imperfect" people without their consent.

This position raises two separate issues. One pertains to the legitimacy of different views on abortion. Despite the conviction of many abortion ac-tivists to the contrary, I believe that ethically respectable views can be found on different sides of the debate, including one that sees fetuses as develop-ing humans without any serious moral claim on continued life. There is no space here to address the details, and doing so would be once again to fall into the trap of letting the abortion question swallow up all others. How-ever, opponents of abortion need to face the fact that many thoughtful in-dividuals do *not* see fetuses as moral persons. It follows that their reasoning process, and hence the implications of their decisions, are radically differ-ent from those envisioned by opponents of prenatal screening and abortion. So where the latter see genetic abortion as murdering people who just don't measure up, the former see it as a way to prevent the development of per-sons who are more likely to live miserable lives, a position consistent with a worldview that values persons equally and holds that each deserves a high-quality life. Some of those who object to genetic abortion appear to be

the larger problem. The other is the peculiar capacity of some genetic problems to affect ever more individuals in the future.

[2] For example, see Leon Kass, "Implications of Prenatal Diagnosis for the Human Right to Life," in *Ethical Issues in Human Genetics,* ed. Bruce Hilton et al. (New York: Plenum, 1973).

oblivious to these psychological and logical facts. It follows that the nightmare scenarios they paint for us are beside the point: many people simply do not share the assumptions that make them plausible.

How are these points relevant to my discussion? My primary concern here is to argue that conception can sometimes be morally wrong on grounds of genetic risk, although this judgment will not apply to those who accept the moral legitimacy of abortion and are willing to employ prenatal screening and selective abortion. If my case is solid, then those who oppose abortion must be especially careful not to conceive in certain cases, as they are, of course, free to follow their conscience about abortion. Those like myself who do not see abortion as murder have more ways to prevent birth.

HUNTINGTON'S DISEASE

There is always some possibility that reproduction will result in a child with a serious disease or handicap. Genetic counselors can help individuals determine whether they are at unusual risk and, as the Human Genome Project rolls on, their knowledge will increase by quantum leaps. As this knowledge becomes available, I believe we ought to use it to determine whether possible children are at risk *before* they are conceived.

In this chapter I want to defend the thesis that it is morally wrong to reproduce when we know there is a high risk of transmitting a serious disease or defect. This thesis holds that some reproductive acts are wrong, and my argument puts the burden of proof on those who disagree with it to show why its conclusions can be overridden. Hence it denies that people should be free to reproduce mindless of the consequences.[3] However, as moral argument, it should be taken as a proposal for further debate and discussion. It is not, by itself, an argument in favor of legal prohibitions of reproduction.[4]

There is a huge range of genetic diseases. Some are quickly lethal; others kill more slowly, if at all. Some are mainly physical, some mainly mental; others impair both kinds of function. Some interfere tremendously with normal functioning, others less. Some are painful, some are not. There seems to be considerable agreement that rapidly lethal diseases, especially

---

[3] This is, of course, a very broad thesis. I defend an even broader version in Chapter 2, "Loving Future People."

[4] Why would we want to resist legal enforcement of every moral conclusion? First, legal action has many costs, costs not necessarily worth paying in particular cases. Second, legal enforcement tends to take the matter out of the realm of debate and treat it as settled. But in many cases, especially where mores or technology are rapidly evolving, we don't want that to happen. Third, legal enforcement would undermine individual freedom and decision-making capacity. In some cases, the ends envisioned are important enough to warrant putting up with these disadvantages.

those, such as Tay-Sachs, accompanied by painful deterioration, should be prevented even at the cost of abortion. Conversely, there seems to be substantial agreement that relatively trivial problems, especially cosmetic ones, would not be legitimate grounds for abortion.[5] In short, there are cases ranging from low risk of mild disease or disability to high risk of serious disease or disability. Although it is difficult to decide where the duty to refrain from procreation becomes compelling, I believe that there are some clear cases. I have chosen to focus on Huntington's disease to illustrate the kinds of concrete issues such decisions entail. However, the arguments are also relevant to many other genetic diseases.[6]

The symptoms of Huntington's disease usually begin between the ages of thirty and fifty:

> Onset is insidious. Personality changes (obstinacy, moodiness, lack of initiative) frequently antedate or accompany the involuntary choreic movements. These usually appear first in the face, neck, and arms, and are jerky, irregular, and stretching in character. Contradictions of the facial muscles result in grimaces; those of the respiratory muscles, lips, and tongue lead to hesitating, explosive speech. Irregular movements of the trunk are present; the gait is shuffling and dancing. Tendon reflexes are increased. . . . Some patients display a fatuous euphoria; others are spiteful, irascible, destructive, and violent. Paranoid reactions are common. Poverty of thought and impairment of attention, memory, and judgment occur. As the disease progresses, walking becomes impossible, swallowing difficult, and dementia profound. Suicide is not uncommon.[7]

The illness lasts about fifteen years, terminating in death.

[5] Those who do not see fetuses as moral persons with a right to life may nonetheless hold that abortion is justifiable in these cases. I argue at some length elsewhere that lesser defects can cause great suffering. Once we are clear that there is nothing discriminatory about failing to conceive particular possible individuals, it makes sense, other things being equal, to avoid the prospect of such pain if we can. Naturally, other things rarely are equal. In the first place, many problems go undiscovered until a baby is born. Second, there are often substantial costs associated with screening programs. Third, although women should be encouraged to consider the moral dimensions of routine pregnancy, we do not want it to be so fraught with tension that it becomes a miserable experience. (See Chapter 2, "Loving Future People.")

[6] It should be noted that failing to conceive a single individual can affect many lives: in 1916, 962 cases could be traced from six seventeenth-century arrivals in America. See Gordon Rattray Taylor, *The Biological Time Bomb* (New York: Penguin, 1968), p. 176.

[7] *The Merck Manual* (Rahway, N.J.: Merck, 1972), pp. 1363, 1346. We now know that the age of onset and severity of the disease are related to the number of abnormal replications of the glutamine code on the abnormal gene. See Andrew Revkin, "Hunting Down Huntington's," *Discover* (December 1993): 108.

Huntington's disease is an autosomal dominant disease, meaning it is caused by a single defective gene located on a non-sex chromosome. It is passed from one generation to the next via affected individuals. Each child of such an affected person has a 50 percent risk of inheriting the gene and thus of eventually developing the disease, even if he or she was born before the parent's disease was evident.[8]

Until recently, Huntington's disease was especially problematic because most affected individuals did not know whether they had the gene for the disease until well into their childbearing years. So they had to decide about childbearing before knowing whether they could transmit the disease or not. If, in time, they did not develop symptoms of the disease, then their children could know they were not at risk for the disease. If unfortunately they did develop symptoms, then each of their children could know there was a 50 percent chance that they, too, had inherited the gene. In both cases, the children faced a period of prolonged anxiety as to whether they would develop the disease. Then, in the 1980s, thanks in part to an energetic campaign by Nancy Wexler, a genetic marker was found that, in certain circumstances, could tell people with a relatively high degree of probability whether or not they had the gene for the disease.[9] Finally, in March 1993, the defective gene itself was discovered.[10] Now individuals can find out whether they carry the gene for the disease, and prenatal screening can tell us whether a given fetus has inherited it. These technological developments change the moral scene substantially.

How serious are the risks involved in Huntington's disease? Geneticists often think a 10 percent risk is high.[11] But risk assessment also depends on what is at stake: the worse the possible outcome, the more undesirable an otherwise small risk seems. In medicine, as elsewhere, people may regard the same result quite differently. But for devastating diseases such as Huntington's this part of the judgment should be unproblematic: no one wants a loved one to suffer in this way.[12]

There may still be considerable disagreement about the acceptability of a given risk. So it would be difficult in many circumstances to say how we should respond to a particular risk. Nevertheless, there are good grounds for a conservative approach, for it is reasonable to take special precautions

---

[8] Hymie Gordon, "Genetic Counseling," *JAMA* 217, no. 9 (August 30, 1971): 1346.

[9] See Revkin, "Hunting Down Huntington's," 99–108.

[10] "Gene for Huntington's Disease Discovered," *Human Genome News* 5, no. 1 (May 1993): 5.

[11] Charles Smith, Susan Holloway, and Alan E. H. Emery, "Individuals at Risk in Families— Genetic Disease," *Journal of Medical Genetics* 8 (1971): 453.

[12] To try to separate the issue of the gravity of the disease from the existence of a given individual, compare this situation with how we would assess a parent who neglected to vaccinate an existing child against a hypothetical viral version of Huntington's.

to avoid very bad consequences, even if the risk is small. But the possible consequences here *are* very bad: a child who may inherit Huntington's disease has a much greater than average chance of being subjected to severe and prolonged suffering. And it is one thing to risk one's own welfare, but quite another to do so for others and without their consent.

Is this judgment about Huntington's disease really defensible? People appear to have quite different opinions. Optimists argue that a child born into a family afflicted with Huntington's disease has a reasonable chance of living a satisfactory life. After all, even children born of an afflicted parent still have a 50 percent chance of escaping the disease. And even if afflicted themselves, such people will probably enjoy some thirty years of healthy life before symptoms appear. It is also possible, although not at all likely, that some might not mind the symptoms caused by the disease. Optimists can point to diseased persons who have lived fruitful lives, as well as those who seem genuinely glad to be alive. One is Rick Donohue, a sufferer from the Joseph family disease: "You know, if my mom hadn't had me, I wouldn't be here for the life I have had. So there is a good possibility I will have children."[13] Optimists therefore conclude that it would be a shame if these persons had not lived.

Pessimists concede some of these facts but take a less sanguine view of them. They think a 50 percent risk of serious disease such as Huntington's is appallingly high. They suspect that many children born into afflicted families are liable to spend their youth in dreadful anticipation and fear of the disease. They expect that the disease, if it appears, will be perceived as a tragic and painful end to a blighted life. They point out that Rick Donohue is still young and has not experienced the full horror of his sickness. It is also well-known that some young persons have such a dilated sense of time that they can hardly envision themselves at thirty or forty, so the prospect of pain at that age is unreal to them.[14]

More empirical research on the psychology and life history of suffers and potential sufferers is clearly needed to decide whether optimists or pessimists have a more accurate picture of the experiences of individuals at risk. But given that some will surely realize pessimists' worst fears, it seems unfair to conclude that the pleasures of those who deal best with the situation simply cancel out the suffering of those others when that suffering

---

[13] *The New York Times*, September 30, 1975, p. 1. The Joseph family disease is similar to Huntington's disease except that symptoms start appearing in the twenties. Rick Donohue was in his early twenties at the time he made this statement.

[14] I have talked to college students who believe that they will have lived fully and be ready to die at those ages. It is astonishing how one's perspective changes over time and how ages that one once associated with senility and physical collapse come to seem the prime of human life.

could be avoided altogether.

I think that these points indicate that the morality of procreation in such situations demands further investigation. I propose to do this by looking first at the position of the possible child, then at that of the potential parent.

POSSIBLE CHILDREN AND POTENTIAL PARENTS

The first task in treating the problem from the child's point of view is to find a way of referring to possible future offspring without seeming to confer some sort of morally significant existence on them. I follow the convention of calling children who might be born in the future but who are not now conceived "possible" children, offspring, individuals, or persons.

Now, what claims about children or possible children are relevant to the morality of childbearing in the circumstances being considered? Of primary importance is the judgment that we ought to try to provide every child with something like a minimally satisfying life. I am not altogether sure how best to formulate this standard, but I want clearly to reject the view that it is morally permissible to conceive individuals so long as we do not expect them to be so miserable that they wish they were dead.[15] I believe that this kind of moral minimalism is thoroughly unsatisfactory and that not many people would really want to live in a world where it was the prevailing standard. Its lure is that it puts few demands on us, but its price is the scant attention it pays to human well-being.

How might the judgment that we have a duty to try to provide a minimally satisfying life for our children be justified? It could, I think, be derived fairly straightforwardly from either utilitarian or contractarian theories of justice, although there is no space here for discussion of the details. The net result of such analysis would be to conclude that neglecting this duty would create unnecessary unhappiness or unfair disadvantage for some persons.

Of course, this line of reasoning confronts us with the need to spell out what is meant by "minimally satisfying" and what a standard based on this concept would require of us. Conceptions of a minimally satisfying life vary tremendously among societies and also within them. *De rigeur* in some circles are private music lessons and trips to Europe, whereas in others providing eight years of schooling is a major accomplishment. But there is no need to consider this complication at length here because we are concerned only with health as a prerequisite for a minimally satisfying life. Thus, as we draw out what such a standard might require of us, it

---

[15] The view I am rejecting has been forcefully articulated by Derek Parfit, *Reasons and Persons* (Oxford: Clarendon, 1984). For more discussion, see Chapter 2, "Loving Future People."

seems reasonable to retreat to the more limited claim that parents should try to ensure something like normal health for their children. It might be thought that even this moderate claim is unsatisfactory as in some places debilitating conditions are the norm, but one could circumvent this objection by saying that parents ought to try to provide for their children health normal for that culture, even though it may be inadequate if measured by some outside standard.[16] This conservative position would still justify efforts to avoid the birth of children at risk for Huntington's disease and other serious genetic diseases in virtually all societies.[17]

This view is reinforced by the following considerations. Given that possible children do not presently exist as actual individuals, they do not have a right to be brought into existence, and hence no one is maltreated by measures to avoid the conception of a possible person. Therefore, the conservative course that avoids the conception of those who would not be expected to enjoy a minimally satisfying life is at present the only fair course of action. The alternative is a laissez-faire approach that brings into existence the lucky, but only at the expense of the unlucky. Notice that attempting to avoid the creation of the unlucky does not necessarily lead to *fewer* people being brought into being; the question boils down to taking steps to bring those with better prospects into existence, instead of those with worse ones.

I have so far argued that if people with Huntington's disease are unlikely to live minimally satisfying lives, then those who might pass it on should not have genetically related children. This is consonant with the principle that the greater the danger of serious problems, the stronger the duty to avoid them. But this principle is in conflict with what people think of as the right to reproduce. How might one decide which should take precedence?

Expecting people to forego having genetically related children might seem to demand too great a sacrifice of them. But before reaching that conclusion we need to ask what is really at stake. One reason for wanting children is to experience family life, including love, companionship, watching kids grow, sharing their pains and triumphs, and helping to form members of the next generation. Other reasons emphasize the validation of parents as individuals within a continuous family line, children as a source of immortality, or perhaps even the gratification of producing partial replicas of

[16]I have some qualms about this response, because I fear that some human groups are so badly off that it might still be wrong for them to procreate, even if that would mean great changes in their cultures. But this is a complicated issue that needs to be investigated on its own.

[17]Again, a troubling exception might be the isolated Venezuelan group Nancy Wexler found, where, because of inbreeding, a large proportion of the population is affected by Huntington's. See Revkin, "Hunting Down Huntington's."

oneself. Children may also be desired in an effort to prove that one is an adult, to try to cement a marriage, or to benefit parents economically.

Are there alternative ways of satisfying these desires? Adoption or new reproductive technologies can fulfill many of them without passing on known genetic defects. Sperm replacement has been available for many years via artificial insemination by donor. More recently, egg donation, sometimes in combination with contract pregnancy,[18] has been used to provide eggs for women who prefer not to use their own. Eventually it may be possible to clone individual humans, although that now seems a long way off. All of these approaches to avoiding the use of particular genetic material are controversial and have generated much debate. I believe that tenable moral versions of each do exist.[19]

None of these methods permits people to extend both genetic lines or realize the desire for immortality or for children who resemble both parents; nor is it clear that such alternatives will necessarily succeed in proving that one is an adult, cementing a marriage, or providing economic benefits. Yet, many people feel these desires strongly. Now, I am sympathetic to William James's dictum regarding desires: "Take any demand, however slight, which any creature, however weak, may make. Ought it not, for its own sole sake be satisfied? If not, prove why not."[20] Thus a world where more desires are satisfied is generally better than one where fewer are. However, not all desires can be legitimately satisfied, because as James suggests, there may be good reasons, such as the conflict of duty and desire, why some should be overruled.

Fortunately, further scrutiny of the situation reveals that there are good reasons why people should attempt with appropriate social support to talk themselves out of the desires in question or to consider novel ways of fulfilling them. Wanting to see the genetic line continued is not particularly rational when it brings a sinister legacy of illness and death. The desire for immortality cannot really be satisfied anyway, and people need to face the fact that what really matters is how they behave in their own lifetimes. And

[18]Or surrogacy, as it has been popularly known. I think that "contract pregnancy" is more accurate and more respectful of women. Eggs can be provided either by a woman who also gestates the fetus or by a third party.

[19]The most powerful objections to new reproductive technologies and arrangements concern possible bad consequences for women. However, I do not think that the arguments against them on these grounds have yet shown the dangers to be as great as some believe. So although it is perhaps true that new reproductive technologies and arrangements should not be used lightly, avoiding the conceptions discussed here is well worth the risk. For a series of viewpoints on this issue, including my own "Another Look at Contract Pregnancy" (Chapter 12), see Helen B. Holmes, *Issues in Reproductive Technology I: An Anthology* (New York: Garland, 1992).

[20]William James, *Essays in Pragmatism*, ed. A. Castell (New York: Hafner, 1948), p. 73.

finally, the desire for children who physically resemble one is understandable, but basically narcissistic, and its fulfillment cannot be guaranteed even by normal reproduction. There are other ways of proving one is an adult, and other ways of cementing marriages—and children don't necessarily do either. Children, especially prematurely ill children, may not provide the expected economic benefits anyway. Nongenetically related children may also provide benefits similar to those that would have been provided by genetically related ones, and expected economic benefit is, in many cases, a morally questionable reason for having children.

Before the advent of reliable genetic testing, the options of people in Huntington's families were cruelly limited. On the one hand, they could have children, but at the risk of eventual crippling illness and death for them. On the other, they could refrain from childbearing, sparing their possible children from significant risk of inheriting this disease, perhaps frustrating intense desires to procreate—only to discover, in some cases, that their sacrifice was unnecessary because they did not develop the disease. Or they could attempt to adopt or try new reproductive approaches.

Reliable genetic testing has opened up new possibilities. Those at risk who wish to have children can get tested. If they test positive, they know their possible children are at risk. Those who are opposed to abortion must be especially careful to avoid conception if they are to behave responsibly. Those not opposed to abortion can responsibly conceive children, but only if they are willing to test each fetus and abort those who carry the gene. If individuals at risk test negative, they are home free.

What about those who cannot face the test for themselves? They can do prenatal testing and abort fetuses who carry the defective gene. A clearly positive test also implies that the parent is affected, although negative tests do not rule out that possibility. Prenatal testing can thus bring knowledge that enables one to avoid passing the disease to others, but only, in some cases, at the cost of coming to know with certainty that one will indeed develop the disease. This situation raises with peculiar force the question of whether parental responsibility requires people to get tested.

Some people think that we should recognize a right "not to know." It seems to me that such a right could be defended only where ignorance does not put others at serious risk. So if people are prepared to forego genetically related children, they need not get tested. But if they want genetically related children, then they must do whatever is necessary to ensure that affected babies are not the result. There is, after all, something inconsistent about the claim that one has a right to be shielded from the truth, even if the price is to risk inflicting on one's children the same dread disease one cannot even face in oneself.

In sum, until we can be assured that Huntington's disease does not prevent people from living a minimally satisfying life, individuals at risk for the disease have a moral duty to try not to bring affected babies into this world. There are now enough options available so that this duty needn't frustrate their reasonable desires. Society has a corresponding duty to facilitate moral behavior on the part of individuals. Such support ranges from the narrow and concrete (such as making sure that medical testing and counseling is available to all) to the more general social environment that guarantees that all pregnancies are voluntary, that pronatalism is eradicated, and that women are treated with respect regardless of the reproductive options they choose.

CHAPTER 2

Loving Future People

Moral philosophers often wonder what a better world would look like.[1] It seems clear that eradicating war and poverty and building ecologically sustainable economies, among other things, would improve life immensely for many people. Only achieving such goals will enable us to provide the clean water, nutritious food, safe shelter, education, and medical care essential for human welfare; by themselves, these goods would go far toward helping people to fashion satisfying lives. We will not have a morally bearable world until everybody enjoys them.

In the United States and elsewhere, individuals in increasing numbers lack these basic prerequisites for a decent life, and our first priority should be to create a floor of well-being below which no one would be allowed to fall.

Prominent among such policies would be promoting justice for women. Most, if not all societies, define women in such a way that it seems right to subordinate us to men; the resultant inequality of burdens and benefits is still being documented. A just society would get rid of this inequality. To recommend such a state of affairs is not to embrace a libertarian moral theory but rather to assert the importance of women's equal autonomy within a more caring and egalitarian society.

Although many details of this just society remain to be worked out, feminists are sketching out its main lines. They include truly equal education

From *Reproduction, Ethics, and the Law,* edited by Joan Callahan (Bloomington: Indiana University Press, 1995). Reprinted by permission of Indiana University Press.
[1] Thanks to Joan Callahan and Dorothy Wertz for their helpful comments on this essay.

that equips us to take up whatever work suits our talents and interests, sufficient compensation for all occupations to enable us to live independently of men if we wish, and the right to determine whether and when we will have children. They assume social support for those decisions, including the resources necessary for bearing and rearing healthy children. The gap between the conditions in which most women now live and this feminist utopia is huge. At present, many women lack the equal educational and work opportunities that would help to guarantee decent living conditions, including a safe environment and appropriate medical care, for themselves and their children. Justice requires that we get closer to this ideal.

Having reached this conclusion, the main work of the moral philosopher, qua philosopher, is done: moral or political exhortation is not part of the job description.[2] However, there remain a few problems to mop up. Among them is the question of possible moral limits on women's reproductive rights.[3]

REPRODUCTION

Although there is no explicit constitutional right to procreate, it is generally assumed that such a right is implied by other fundamental constitutional rights. It is also assumed that it is, in any case, morally justifiable to assert such a right and that this right should be protected by law. Certainly, the assumption that individuals have a right to control their own bodies is deeply embedded in the Anglo-American intellectual tradition, and that right, because of reproductive biology, might reasonably be taken to imply for women, if not for men, a moral right to reproduce that should be protected by law. At present there are significant legal limits on women's reproductive rights, and, given the contemporary political climate, more are likely to be forthcoming. I believe that such legal limitations are unjustifiable.[4] It does not follow, though, that there are no *moral* limits on reproduction.

The right to reproduce is one of those moral rights that has been more assumed than argued for; it could, no doubt, be traced back to earlier days when human existence was more threatened by underpopulation than

[2] Working for change is the job of political activists. Of course, moral philosophers can be activists, too; in fact, given our positions of moral authority, we may well have a moral duty in this regard.

[3] This introduction is intended to emphasize the priority of fighting for human welfare, especially for women's basic welfare, a priority that may well seem to disappear in any treatment of a limited and problematic area. (I am not excluding in the scope of my concern here the welfare of other sentient creatures; however, I will be concentrating on human welfare.)

[4] Even if there is no clear constitutional right to procreate, the consequences of failing to act as if there is one would be at present very harmful to women. See Chapter 4, "Are Pregnant Women Fetal Containers?"

overpopulation.[5] The whole network of expectations and assumptions about reproduction is usually taken for granted and viewed as obvious, natural, and legitimate. However, cultural changes and technological developments have begun to inspire more serious scrutiny of these issues, even if a good deal of it still seems to me to be tied to fairly parochial "popular wisdom."[6]

The most plausible case for recognizing a moral right to reproduce comes, it seems to me, from a utilitarian moral theory coupled with the desire for children.[7] As I have suggested elsewhere, it is good, other things being equal, for desires to be satisfied.[8] Unfortunately, the potential for harm via reproduction means that very often things are not equal. Seeking to satisfy the urge to reproduce may increase the suffering created by overpopulation, contribute to the failure to meet the needs of existing children, channel women into rigid and narrow social roles, promote technologies that harm women, and bring to existence children who are more likely than average to lead miserable lives.[9]

If we are consistent in our concern about human happiness, it seems clear that we must attend to the welfare of future people. For the most part, it is possible to envision social policies that will further both the good of existing persons and the interests of future ones;[10] but here, sharp conflicts may emerge between the desires of the former and the interests of the latter. Most people want children, and they want their own children—that is, children who carry their own genetic material.

In the late 1970s, I began wondering whether it is ever wrong to have children and wrote a paper arguing that if you are at risk for a serious illness,

[5] My position that it is sometimes wrong to reproduce in the usual way does not require me to show that there is such a right. For if there is, it doesn't follow that it can always be morally exercised; if there isn't, it is still necessary to lay out the conditions for morally acceptable reproduction.

[6] Consider, for example, the recent debate about the nature and justification of the desire for children that is emerging in the feminist debate about artificial reproductive technologies. For further readings, see Michelle Stanworth ed., *Reproductive Technologies; Gender, Motherhood, and Medicine* (Minneapolis: University of Minnesota Press, 1987), and Helen B. Holmes and Laura M. Purdy, eds., *Feminist Perspectives in Medical Ethics* (Bloomington: Indiana University Press, 1992).

[7] For an examination of other possibilities, see Ruth F. Chadwick, "Having Children: An Introduction," in *Ethics, Reproduction, and Genetic Control*, ed. Ruth F. Chadwick (London: Croom Helm, 1987), pp. 3–10. The status of the desire for children, in particular its sources and consequences, needs much more thorough scrutiny.

[8] See Chapter 1, "Genetic and Reproductive Risk: Can Having Children Be Immoral?"

[9] Bringing to existence children who are more likely than average to lead miserable lives is not entirely unconnected with suffering created by overpopulation, etc.

[10] It may not be possible to reconcile the two if either the population grows too large or the definition of basic welfare is too inclusive, so that acute conflicts arise between present needs and future ones.

such as Huntington's disease, a good case can be made against your pro-creating; that paper still provokes animated—and highly emotional—dis-cussion. (See Chapter 1 for a more recent version of it.) And, despite the proliferation of fascinating new questions in biomedical ethics, this core is-sue still haunts us. Its most recent incarnations involve "fetal abuse," neonatal AIDS, and genetic therapy.[11]

I originally claimed that although there is good reason to reject legal in-terference in individual decisions about reproduction, we need much more open discussion of the ethical dimensions of such decisions, for exercising our legal rights can sometimes be morally wrong. Because we ought to try to provide every child with at least a normal opportunity for a good life, and because we do not harm possible people if we prevent them from ex-isting, we ought to try to prevent the birth of those with a significant risk of living worse than normal lives.[12] I then went on to argue that Huntington's disease presents such a risk.

My argument has been attacked on various grounds connected with the particularities of Huntington's disease.[13] A second objection could be based on women's privacy rights: women have only just been achieving some measure of control over their bodies, and this control is by no means either secure or universal; we should therefore encourage society to keep its nose out of these matters, even to the point of withholding moral evalua-tion of the reproductive decisions women make. This concern is extremely

---

[11] See, for example, Chapter 4, "Are Pregnant Women Fetal Containers?"; John D. Arras, "AIDS and Reproductive Decisions: Having Children in Fear and Trembling," *The Milbank Quarterly* 68, no. 3 (1990):353–82; and Noam Zohar, "Prospects for 'Genetic Therapy'—Can a Person Benefit from Being Altered?," and Jeffrey P. Kahn, "Genetic Harm: Bitten by the Body That Keeps You?," both in *Bioethics* 5, no. 4 (October 1991): 275–308.

[12] Robert Simon has pointed out to me that there are good reasons for thinking in terms of a more objective criterion than "opportunity for a normal life." These reasons center on the otherwise difficult-to-manage relativistic element in judgments about what is "normal."

[13] The main objection has been that Huntington's disease doesn't require such moral re-straint. It is argued that potential parents are usually going ahead without knowing for sure whether they have the disease. If they don't, then their children are not really at risk. Even if they do, there is only a 50 percent risk that each child will be afflicted with the disease. And, even if a child turns out to have the disease, he or she will have between twenty and fifty years of good life. My evaluation of these factors has not changed in the time since I wrote the article; they seem to me, if anything, to increase the horror of the disease. In par-ticular, the prospect of a short life seems to me especially tragic, because not only of the de-pression quite likely to be caused by knowledge of it, but also of the loss to all those (like women) whose early lives are often taken up with the demands of others. It takes many women well into middle age to overcome the sexist upbringing that deprives them of the self-confidence to make more choices based on their own interests. Deaths of people in their prime also deprives society of some of its best and wisest members. In case such consider-ations don't move you, it is always possible to find still more dreadful diseases, like Tay-Sachs, where they don't apply.

important, but we should nonetheless be wary of asserting the necessity for such an extreme suspension of judgment where there is potential for serious harm to others.[14]

Two other objections have emerged against the position that procreation is sometimes irresponsible. One comes from philosophers who hold that it is morally permissible to create children unless there is reason to think that they would prefer death to the life they live. The other comes from disability-rights activists who hold that it is, among other things, bias against disabled people, and not well-grounded moral argument, that motivates such recommendations. I concentrate here on the second case, except where the two intersect.[15]

ARGUMENTS FROM DISABILITY

Marsha Saxton and Adrienne Asch argue against abortion for disability.[16] Both also distinguish between abortion for disability and the attempt to avoid conception on those grounds. Asch writes: "Although I have serious moral qualms about selective abortion for sex or disability, I do not have moral objections—albeit social and psychological ones—to deciding not to conceive if one knows that one's offspring will be of one sex or will have a certain disability. I consider women who refrain from childbearing and rearing for these reasons to be misguided, possibly depriving themselves of the joys of parenthood by their unthinking acceptance of the values of a society still deeply sexist and ambivalent about people with disabilities."[17] Neither Asch nor Saxton rejection abortion in general, but they clearly think that aborting an existing fetus is morally worse than failing to conceive

---

[14] I argue in Chapter 4, "Are Pregnant Women Fetal Containers?," that although it would not be reasonable at this point to make prenatal harm a crime, it is still wrong for women to act in ways that are likely to harm their fetuses. Among other things, most of such harm arises because of factors beyond women's control such as lack of access to good prenatal care and that could be remedied if society made avoiding it a priority. So unless society does what it can, it is hypocritical and unjust to blame women for causing prenatal harm.

[15] Two points about my focus here. First, I am uneasy about contributing to the balkanization of progressive political movements that arises from criticizing our allies rather than those with whom we have far more basic disagreements. However, it also seems important to try to develop the strongest positions possible in order to facilitate social change. Second, because I am considering primarily the arguments of disability-rights writers, the following discussion seems narrowly centered on the question of disability. It should be understood that concern for painful or limiting disease is not thereby excluded.

[16] Marsha Saxton, "Born and Unborn: The Implications of Reproductive Technologies for People with Disabilities," in *Test-Tube Women: What Future for Motherhood?*, ed. Rita Arditti, Renate Duelli Klein, and Shelley Minden (London: Pandora, 1984); Adrienne Asch, "Can Aborting 'Imperfect' Children Be Immoral?," in *Ethical Issues in Modern Medicine*, ed. John Arras and Nancy Rhoden (Mountain View, Calif.: Mayfield Press, 1989).

[17] Asch, "Can Aborting 'Imperfect' Children Be Immoral?," p. 321.

one.[18] Yet it seems to me that their arguments, if sound, are as telling against failing to conceive as aborting. For this reason, and because more general questions about abortion would quickly obscure the specific question I want to consider here, my argument focuses simply on the question of what we want for future people.[19]

One of the clearest and most powerful messages to come from both Asch and Saxton is that much suffering of disabled persons arises not from their disabilities but from the social response to their disabilities. The United States is, in many ways, an uncaring society that, despite its relative wealth, tolerates a great deal of preventable misery on the part of those who must depend more than others on community resources. Support for individuals with disabilities is often both miserly and, because of the influence of special interests and erroneous preconceptions about their needs, not offered in the form that would be most useful to them.[20]

Asch and Saxton are certainly right here: it is clear that the plight of disabled persons would be much improved if each had all the help possible. And such help should be available: we waste billions on the military and other boondoggles, whereas a fraction of that amount would enable us to create a society that would meet people's needs far better.

Quite apart from our evaluation of disabilities themselves, however, this nasty state of affairs raises the question of the extent to which we ought to take into account socially imposed obstacles to satisfying lives when we try to judge whether it is morally right to bring a particular child into the world. As a dyed-in-the-wool consequentialist, I cannot ignore the probable difficulties that await children with special problems. It seems to me that only the truly rich can secure the well-being of those with the most serious problems. Given the costs and other difficulties of guaranteeing good care, even very well-to-do individuals might well wonder whether their offspring will get the care they need after their own deaths. This question is still more acute for those who aren't so well off—the vast majority of the U.S. population. Furthermore, it would be unwise to forget that women are always at risk for divorce and its financial

[18] Asch writes in support of abortion because of women's right to control their bodies; she also asserts that because legally newborns are persons, it is wrong to deprive them of medical care unless they are dying. She does not discuss the philosophical assumptions underlying these positions. Adrienne Asch, "Real Moral Dilemmas," *Christianity and Crisis* 46, no. 10 (July 14, 1986): 237–40.

[19] My arguments also hold for those who regard the relevant kinds of abortions no more morally significant than failing to conceive.

[20] See for a recent, moving discussion a series of articles in *The Progressive*, August 1991. (Mary Johnson, "Disabled Americans Push for Access," Laura Hershey, "Exit the Nursing Home," and Joseph P. Shapiro, "I Can Do Things for Myself Now," pp. 21–29.) These articles highlight both the ignorance and bad faith involved in much of current practice.

aftermath.[21] Although the solution is obvious—more social responsibility for individual needs—it is beginning to look as though none of us will see that come about in our lifetime. It seems to me that this consideration should be, in the case of some decisions about future children, decisive.

Other facets of the inadequacy of the social response to disabled people involve common habits, attitudes, and values. Ignorance leads even basically nice people to behave in hurtful ways; less good-hearted ones may be thoughtless or cruelly unsympathetic. In addition, apparently innocent values we hold make life difficult: "we, especially in the United States, live in a culture obsessed with health and well-being. We value rugged self-reliance, athletic prowess, and rigid standards of beauty. We incessantly pursue eternal youth," writes Marsha Saxton.[22] Certainly, excessive admiration for independence, athleticism, and narrow conceptions of beauty make life more painful than it need be for many; they are especially problematic for some disabled people. They constrict the range of prized achievement and characteristics in unjustifiable and harmful ways and could often be traced, I suspect, to unexamined gender-, race-, or class-based prejudice. It would therefore be desirable to see much of the energy now directed toward promoting these values channeled toward others, such as intellectual or artistic achievement, creating warm and supportive emotional networks, and opening our eyes to the beauty of a wide variety of body types. Unfortunately, our culture doesn't seem to be moving in that direction. It's all very well to believe that such social values shouldn't count, but that doesn't do much to lessen their impact on our children.[23]

Furthermore, there are serious objections to lumping health and well-being together with these other suspect values. Good health and the feeling of well-being it helps to engender are significant factors in a happy life. They enable people to engage in a wide variety of satisfying activities and to feel good while they are doing them. When they are absent, our suffering is

---

[21] The recent series of recessions (from 1991 to 1995) which have created widespread unemployment, cuts in federal and state welfare programs, and the increasingly serious health insurance crisis, should give pause to those of modest means who assume that they will be able to make sure their children's needs will be met. Furthermore, it is by now generally known that women usually fare poorly after divorce, especially if they have stayed at home to take care of children. Alimony is now rare, and divorced mothers must now earn a living (with nonexistent or rusty job skills). Because they are usually granted custody of the children, and, given the inadequate child support offered by most fathers, they must somehow cover child care expenses, too. With a divorce rate of 50 percent, no woman can be sure that she will not find herself trapped in such difficult circumstances.

[22] Saxton, "Born and Unborn," p. 303.

[23] Anybody who has tried to raise thoughtful and caring children knows how difficult it is to teach them these values, as well as the hostility they face if they accept them. It does not follow that we should give up on such projects, but we need to be realistic about their toll. Therefore, we should think twice about imposing some burdens on children.

caused not by our consciousness of having failed to live up to some artificial social value but by the intrinsic pain or limitation caused by that absence.

Denigrating these values is doubly mistaken. First, denying the worth of goals that can be achieved only partially (if at all) by some people would seem to require us to exclude from the arena of desirable traits many otherwise plausible candidates.[24] Perhaps more important, it also denies the value of less-than-maximal achievement of such values and hence undermines the primary argument in favor of allocating social resources to help people cope with special problems. If health and well-being are not valuable, what moral case is there for eradicating the social obstacles Asch and Saxton complain of so bitterly? Surely, it is just their importance that obliges us to provide the opportunity to help people reach the highest levels of which they are capable. If health and well-being are of no special value, what is wrong with letting a person languish in pain or sit in the street with a tin cup when a prosthetic leg or seeing-eye dog could make them independent?

Second, it is important to resist the temptation to identify with our every characteristic. Members of oppressed groups quite rightly want to change society's perception of the features that oppressors latch onto as the mark of their alleged inferiority.[25] Such is the source of such slogans as "Black is beautiful!," of the emphasis on gay pride, and of the valorizing of women's nurturing capacity. However fitting this approach may be in some cases, its appropriateness for every characteristic does not follow. Moral failings are one obvious example.

More generally, we need to think through more carefully any leap from qualities to persons. First, qualities must be evaluated on independent grounds, not on their connection with us. Then, it is important to keep in mind that to value some characteristic is not necessarily to look with contempt on those who lack it. That would suggest, among other things, that teachers always (ought to) have contempt for their pupils. On the one hand, we may admire diametrically opposed characteristics that could not, by their very nature, be found in a single individual. Consider your widely read couch potato friend: Do you really have contempt for her because she isn't Mikhail Baryshnikov? Or the converse? On the other, our assessment of and liking for individuals is not determined in any obvious way by whether they exemplify our favorite traits. Don't we all know people who, given their characteristics, ought to be our dearest friends—yet we just don't click? And don't we all have friends who don't meet our "standards" at all?

---

[24] This approach to grading values might lead to a reductio ad absurdum rejection of any value, even that of life itself as, after all, not everybody can live.
[25] Thanks to Dianne Romain for helping me to think more clearly about this issue.

None of this is to deny that it might be appropriate in some contexts for disability-rights activists to downplay the effects of certain impairments. It might be helpful, for example, to remind able-bodied individuals forcefully that people with physical problems are people first and foremost. That would help reinforce the point that their needs, like those of other citizens with special difficulties, should be secured as unobtrusively and respectfully as possible and that they ought not to be viewed as mere objects of pity.

THE DEMANDS OF LOVE

Perhaps the worry here is that because some disabled people cannot become healthy or fully able no matter what we do, society will—in a fit of pique—declare that it is not worth doing anything at all. But that would be true only if the help were motivated by a quasi-esthetic perfectionism.

Doubts and questions about the motivation of those who argue for preventing certain births lurk continuously in the wings here. There are indeed those who seek "perfection" in others. Their desire for it, their narrow and rigid standards, and their utter lack of human empathy with those who fail to "measure up" justify wariness: it would be inexcusable to ignore the lessons of history or to allow ourselves to be taken in by those who seek to camouflage their bigotry with lofty rationalizations. However, it would be equally inexcusable to dismiss the possibility that a caring and coherent position can lead, by an altogether different route, to the same conclusion that it is wrong knowingly to bring some children into the world.[26]

When I look into my heart to see what it says about this matter I see, I admit, emotions I would rather not feel—reluctance to face the burdens society must bear, unease in the presence of some disabled persons. But most of all, what I see are the demands of love: to love someone is to care desperately about his or her welfare and to want only good things for him or her. The thought that I might bring to life a child with serious physical or mental problems when I could, by doing something different, bring forth one without them, is utterly incomprehensible to me. Isn't that what love means?

Appeals in love in ethics generally are unhelpful. The exhortation to love or care for another does not usually tell you what to do: for example, it may be that the best way to help an alcoholic mate is to leave the relationship, even if that causes a lot of suffering. Nor does an appeal to love tell us how

---

[26] For a paper on a closely related example, see Janice G. Raymond, "Fetalists and Feminists: They Are Not the Same," in *Made to Order: The Myth of Reproductive and Genetic Progress*, ed. Patricia Spallone and Deborah Lynn Steinberg (Oxford: Pergamon, 1987).

to resolve conflicts of interest: it suggests that even legitimate interests of our own must always be subordinated to those of others. Until everybody takes it, this approach leads to rather lopsided relationships.

Where the appeal to love and care does have enormous power, however, is in the quite common conflict between our own desires and the welfare of others, where those desires either fail to constitute a legitimate interest, or where the disparity between the two is clear. Thus, if your life could be saved by someone's pulling a hair from my head, love would dictate allowing the pulling, despite my legitimate interest in protecting my body from attack.

So, to say that love is relevant here is to say that there is sometimes a disparity between a future person's interest in a healthy body and the interest in procreation. Defending that viewpoint requires showing that the moral right to reproduce is relatively weak and that the moral right to a healthy body is relatively strong.[27] Given the potential for harm to another that reproduction can involve, it seems to me that the presumed right to reproduce one's genetically related offspring is indeed the weakest element in the right to control your body. I concentrate here on the argument for healthy bodies—the claim that people are better off without disease or special limitation, and that this interest is sufficiently compelling in some cases to justify the judgment that reproducing would be wrong.

Disagreement about my claim could be about ends or means. That is, it could be about the value of health pure and simple, or it could be about its value in comparison to the means necessary to procure it. Surely, it is hard to disagree about the former: if you could ensure good health for everyone at no cost, say, by pushing an easily accessible button, then failing to push it would be indefensible. But that doesn't, of course, determine the lengths to which we should be prepared to go if ensuring or trying to ensure good health takes more than that. It seems that Asch and Saxton are in the odd position of holding that it is generally questionable to try to avoid health problems by altering reproductive behavior, but that we should go to great lengths to repair or compensate for health problems once children with them are born.[28]

This position appropriately emphasizes how much suffering from disability and disease is unnecessary, arising as it does from our failure as individuals and as a society to take away their sting. Clearly, greater social

---

[27] If ought implies can, we don't, strictly speaking, have a right to a healthy body. But that is not to say that we ought not to be trying to do the best we can.

[28] Asch does make some distinction between problems for which changes in reproductive behavior are appropriate and lesser ones for which they are not. She asks whether "we wish to abort for disability that will not cause great physical pain or death in early childhood."

responsibility would cause some health problems simply to dissolve, just as early surgery can repair a heart valve, leaving no trace of disease, or wheelchair ramps can open up new worlds; other once life-threatening diseases, such as diabetes, could, if well controlled, become relatively minor irritations. Frustration at the blindness, inertia, and selfishness that now stand between those with certain disabilities and a satisfying life is understandable, and activism to remove barriers and get needed support is justifiable and urgent.

However, it seems to me that some of the arguments intended to further that goal can be, as I suggested earlier, inadequate and counterproductive. Downplaying in every context the suffering that can be caused by the disability itself as Saxton and Asch do, is, I think, an example. Thus Saxton, at one point, seems to claim that *all* suffering is social: "the 'suffering' we may experience is a result of not enough human caring, acceptance, and respect."[29]

SUFFERING

I do not doubt that a great deal of the suffering caused by disease and disability does arise from a lack of caring. Perhaps all the suffering felt by some people is of this sort—people with minimal or cosmetic problems or those who have been able to tailor their desires to their circumstances. But in other cases, even were every conceivable aid available, the disease or disability itself would remain and be itself the cause of limit or pain. Neither immense human caring nor the most sophisticated gadgetry will restore freedom of movement to the paraplegic, for example. And it is not only major disability that can cause misery: I have both observed and felt it in connections that might well be dismissed as minor by those who are not experiencing them. In my own case, for example, my inability to see adequately at a crucial period in my development as a dancer was in part responsible for the failure to progress enough to make a career worthwhile. Yet that was a goal toward which I had worked since I was a small child and for which both I and my parents had made major sacrifices.[30] Although I

Adrienne Asch, "Reproductive Technology and Disability," in *Reproductive Laws for the 1990s*, ed. Sherrill Cohen and Nadine Taub (Clifton, N.J.: Humana Press, 1988), pp. 88–89. I would include chronic pain, serious physical or mental limitation, and mental suffering (including the prospect of an early but not imminent death) to the list of conditions to which people shouldn't be subjected.

[29] Saxton, "Born and Unborn," p. 308.

[30] The ease with which some dismiss the pains of others is unnerving; some of this arises no doubt from mere thoughtlessness, lack of experience, or the attempt to "cheer up." It hurts nonetheless. I was struck by a letter to Ann Landers that reads in part:

was able to make another satisfying life for myself, not everybody who has this kind of experience is so lucky.

That the degree of suffering may not be directly correlated with the apparent severity of disability may be taken as a reason for giving up on the idea of avoiding the birth of children at risk for serious health problems. After all, discussions of this issue always focus on the most severe diseases and disabilities, assume that these are the ones that cause the most suffering, and usually end with the trump question: Where do we draw the line? But my guess is that it is true that the most severe disabilities do often cause great suffering; it is just that more minor ones can also do so more often than most of us suppose—and not just because the environment is so harsh. That seems to me to be good reason for being concerned about both kinds rather than grounds for throwing up our hands.

Of course, it is necessary to draw some lines, because everybody carries deleterious genes, and hardly any of us are free of at least minor inadequacies in health functioning. Common sense would suggest some preliminary guidelines, however. Being a carrier, for example, is not an issue unless the relevant gene is dominant and carries with it the threat of serious problems or is recessive but your mate also carries it. Likewise, decisions about what constitutes a major threat depend to a considerable extent on the environment a child can reasonably be expected to live in. Demanding certainty in these judgments would be irrational, but that does not mean that we should ignore the probabilities. Different people obviously have different intuitions about such matters, but that does not mean that we should give up on attempting to achieve some consensus through discussion and debate.

Concern about the broader context of reproduction raises important questions about the morality of creating children who will face other kinds of hardships. What, for instance, of those who by their very existence as females, or African Americans, can be expected to live especially difficult lives? It would be tempting to say that there is nothing intrinsically undesirable about such characteristics: whatever special difficulties such persons face are purely a social matter, and hence my thesis about refraining

---

I, too, have suffered because some people have no idea what living with a handicap is like.

I am 33 years old and have multiple sclerosis. I have been told countless times how lucky I am to be able to park in a special place, work only half days, etc. I try to explain calmly that I'd gladly park anywhere and work all day in exchange for the privilege of good health. Surprisingly, that doesn't make an impression. I've been told, "I could handle that," and "It's no big deal," or "They'll find a cure soon." . . .

I pray a cure will be found soon, but in the meantime it is a VERY big deal to those of us who have it. Anyone who doubts that can speak to my children. We used to live in Montana and climb mountains. Now my life is completely different. We can't even walk around the zoo because Mom has MS. (*The Ithaca Journal*, December 6, 1991).

from reproduction would not hold here. Unfortunately, however, that answer will not do. For my argument ultimately depends more on the degree and inevitability of the suffering than its source. So, where we can be certain about the degree of possible harm, there is at least a prima facie case against reproduction in these cases, too.[31] If we want to reproduce in a situation of this sort, we need to ask ourselves whether we truly have the welfare of our possible offspring at heart or whether we are merely gratifying a desire of our own. Dealing with such situations in the detail they deserve is impossible here, but it does seem reasonable to point out one consequence of the purely social nature of the problem, namely, that we might in general be both less certain of the drawbacks and that there is more possibility of unexpected social progress.

Before going any further here, it is important to note two points. First, discussion about what we owe others tends to stick with the minimum; second, what might be an appropriate moral framework for thinking about the present might not be adequate for thinking about the future.

Thinking in terms of the moral minimum seems both to keep us on the firmest moral ground and is consistent with the moral atmosphere we are most used to. It also closely resembles the legal definitions and principles that parallel our moral thinking, structures intended to facilitate legal decision making. Such legal premises are in part, too, a legacy of the narrow classical liberalism that still colors our perceptions of what a good society should look like. Thus, we tend quite naturally to fall into talking in terms of "minimally bearable lives," rather than satisfying—or even downright happy—ones. And, although we may feel quite sure that it is wrong to bring into existence those whose lives will be truly miserable, there is a great deal more uneasiness about the judgment that we ought on moral grounds to refrain from bringing to existence those, who, despite much legitimate dissatisfaction, can be expected to prefer life to the alternative.

This intellectual groove is a serious problem, I believe, even for the garden-variety moral decisions that face us every day; however, it clearly fails to guide us in an intelligent and compassionate way when decisions

---

[31] Consider Joel Feinberg's comments on this question: "If before the child has been born, we *know* that the conditions for the fulfillment of his most basic interests have already been destroyed, and we permit him nevertheless to be born, we become a party to the violation of his rights. It bears repeating that not all interests of the newborn child should or can qualify for prenatal legal protection, but only those very basic ones whose satisfaction is known to be indispensable to a decent life. The state cannot insure all or even many of its citizens against bad luck in the lottery of life. . . . On the other hand, to be dealt severe mental retardation, congenital syphilis, blindness, deafness, advanced heroin addiction, permanent paralysis or incontinence, guaranteed malnutrition, and economic deprivation so far below a reasonable minimum as to be inescapably degrading and sordid, is not merely to have 'bad luck.'" *Harm to Others* (Oxford: Oxford University Press, 1984), p. 99.

affecting future people are at stake. If individuals can harm each other only by worsening their condition, then by definition, we cannot harm future people if avoiding the harm also means that a particular person will not be brought to existence.[32] According to your moral perspective, avoiding such harm becomes either supererogatory or morally suspect.[33] In either case this perspective undermines not only the kind of reproductive concerns discussed here, but also it denies any moral urgency to more general attempts to improve the quality of future people's lives.[34] But it's not clear why we should accept a moral approach with such consequences. In particular, a few moments' reflection on the benefits many of us enjoy as a result of the efforts of previous generations should reinforce my point.[35]

There are, of course, other obstacles to the project of protecting future people from serious physical problems. We as yet know very little about genetic traits. Furthermore, there may be insuperable moral objections to the kind of research necessary to find out more or to the procedures necessary to use that knowledge.[36] Still worse, it might turn out that some genes are inextricably linked with others that it may be important to keep in the gene pool; others may confer, like a single copy of the gene for sickle-cell anemia, a benefit. However, none of these problems entail that we should not, other things being equal, do what we can here to avoid creating people with serious health problems. I think that ordinary decency would therefore suggest that we at least make the effort to investigate our genetic history and, if necessary, attempt to avoid transmitting serious conditions.

[32] Ibid., chap. 1, and chap. 2, sec. 8.

[33] Those who imagine people waiting in line to be born, where the relevant moral rule presumably ought to be first come, first served, will be most apt to see the effort to prefer the birth of those more likely to live more satisfying lives as morally evil.

[34] For example, to the extent that women now have babies because of lack of access to contraception and abortion, or even, more broadly, because of the lack of satisfying alternative social roles, achieving women's equality will alter who gets born. Derek Parfit also points out the counterintuitive consequences with respect to pollution. *Reasons and Persons* (Oxford: Clarendon, 1984), part 4.

[35] For example, good social arrangements could now provide everyone with a kind of security and well-being that was unavailable to anybody just a few generations ago. No longer must we bear child after child only to watch them die; no longer need we fear such diseases as polio or smallpox. Although many scientific advances have proved to be mixed blessings, there is no doubt that many of us now have lives that offer unprecedented satisfaction and that many more could also enjoy such lives if we cared to make such a goal a social priority.

[36] Thus, for example, it may be inappropriate to spend such a large proportion of the science research budget on the human genome project, or it may open up possibilities too dangerous to handle at present. Even if it is successful, there may be good reasons to refrain from instituting the kind of mandatory screening programs that would capitalize most effectively on the knowledge gained by it. They might, for example, involve racism or other harmful stereotyped assumptions.

Arguing against this position, Saxton denies that the fact that disabled individuals suffer and even commit suicide is a reason to prevent their birth: after all, she argues, nondisabled people commit suicide, too. That nondisabled people also commit suicide is irrelevant, however. A good society does what it can to prevent or alleviate suffering on the part of its members. That there are many and diverse causes of such suffering is not a good reason to ignore any particular one. Her attitude toward some kinds of suffering seems oddly cavalier, almost as though it is good for us.

This question of morally appropriate challenges never seems far in the background here. Much of the writing about disability emphasizes the advantages of such challenge. For instance, Denise Karuth, in her moving and informative essay, "If I Were a Car, I Would Be a Lemon," writes that "the process of learning to live with a disability presents an opportunity to develop competencies in judgment, problem solving, and compassion that few of life's other experiences can equal" (p. 25). Perhaps. But as I read what it takes to manage her lot of blindness and multiple sclerosis—only some of which could be alleviated by maximal social support—I am skeptical about whether the lessons learned justify the suffering they require. There are wise and compassionate folk who have not had such difficulties, so it would surely be good to reduce the number who do to a minimum. The experiences of those who suffer from health catastrophes after birth will surely suffice.[37]

There may well be compensations for some disabilities. In *Seeing Voices*, Oliver Sacks takes us on a "journey into the world of the deaf." American Sign Language, it turns out, is a powerful and elegant means of communication, one that might in the future help communication not only with deaf persons, but also with chimps, babies, and those who speak languages other than our own. The world would clearly be a poorer place without ASL; now that it is here, it can enrich the lives of both those who are hearing-impaired and those who are not. It seems nonetheless doubtful that many deaf persons would refuse new ears.[38]

---

[37] It should not be inferred that what I say here implies that children grow best when everything is made easy for them. See my book *In Their Best Interest? The Case against Equal Rights for Children* (Ithaca: Cornell University Press, 1992). One might argue that reducing the number of people with disabilities would weaken the disability-rights movement, because advocates tend to have personal links with impaired individuals. That wouldn't be a very appealing objection, because it would be a paradigm case of using people as mere means. It's also dubious from a consequentialist viewpoint, because all that most families can do is to cope with their own child's immediate needs. The most promising development would be to recruit energetic workers who are free to devote themselves wholeheartedly to advancing the interests of people with impairments, much as the civil rights movement recruited students.

[38] The debate about cochlear implants erupted after this piece was written. Some deaf people have refused cochlear implants that could restore hearing for themselves or their

A somewhat different, but related, cluster of worries about preventing the birth of disabled individuals centers on issues of control. Asch asks what will happen when women who abort fetuses with problems they do not think they can cope with have other children who "develop characteristics [they] dislike or find overwhelming."[39] She goes on to suggest that such women may not recognize or may refuse to accept that childbearing should be undertaken only if "we are willing to face what we cannot control and to seek resources in themselves and the world to master it."[40] Now it may very well be that some women who knowingly choose to avoid bringing a child with a disability into the world have an unrealistic view of childbearing, as do, no doubt, many who go ahead. But the solution in both cases is early and universal education to pierce the rosy haze pronatalism still wraps around babies and having babies.[41] There is no reason to slight or belittle the judgment of those who attempt to avoid foreseeable problems, or to prejudge their ability to cope with unexpected ones.

It would be all too easy here to fall in line with the backlash's rejection of women's barely won right to control their bodies and lives. Only lately have women begun to be able to exert such control, and we should be wary of suggestions that there is something wrong with it—especially as it is still mostly women who are expected to sacrifice their other plans to care for others, and this without much support.[42] In any case, it is one thing to have to cope with difficulties that could not have been avoided; it is quite another when they could have been.[43] Given that difference, it in no way follows (or

---

children. They do so in part because they do not see deafness as a disability and in part because they fear that the deaf community will be impoverished if there are fewer young people entering it. The latter concern is understandable, and one would think that it would be possible to ensure that hearing children of the deaf would be taught to sign; it would be better still if signing came to be more universal among hearing people. The claim that deafness is not a disability is less appealing. Resolving this question is a delicate matter, but I would be inclined to defer to John Stuart Mill's test for deciding which of two states of affairs is more desirable, namely, consultation with those who have experienced both. I suspect that such persons would not choose to be deaf. Edward Dolnick, "Deafness as Culture," *The Atlantic* 272, no. 3 (September 1993), 37–51; John Stuart Mill, *Utilitarianism,* in *The Utilitarians* (New York: Dolphin Books, 1961), p. 401.

[39] Asch, "Can Aborting 'Imperfect' Children Be Immoral?," p. 320.

[40] Ibid.

[41] It is sad (and instructive) that anybody who tries to get childless students to think in realistic terms about children is immediately plastered with the reputation of "baby-basher," just as those who attempt to get them to think realistically about women's place in society become "male-bashers."

[42] Good parenting is by itself a demanding enterprise, one that is barely compatible under present circumstances with many jobs. Adding special needs to that mix is, in the case of many women, the straw that breaks the camel's back.

[43] Asch agrees that elective abortion should remain a legal option for women, even where she doubts the morality of abortion for disability. However, I fear that her position about the wrongness of most abortions for disability will cause some women to feel that they

is even empirically likely) that by attempting to prevent the birth of children with disabilities we encourage the kind of self-indulgence that refuses to come to terms with the demands of life.

Despite the importance of questions about the social costs of certain decisions about reproduction, the main focus here still needs to be on what happens to children, not the attitudes of others. Thus I am deeply troubled by Saxton's comment that she would "like to welcome any child born to me. I believe that I have the emotional, financial, and other resources to effectively care for a child. I know I can be a good mother and my husband a good father to any child."[44] Would that her warmth and generosity were more common! But although these traits would help children deal with their problems, wouldn't it be better to try to avoid the serious and foreseeable burdens in the first place?

EXISTING AND POSSIBLE PERSONS

As I write these last paragraphs, I can hear in my mind's ear the angry reaction build: she wants to kill us off—she's talking about getting rid of persons who have a right to life just to get rid of their problems. That would be true if what were at issue was killing those with serious health problems; that would of course also be a ludicrous misunderstanding of my position, comparable to the reception of Peter Singer's views in Austria.[45]

One of the most common themes in writing on this topic is the distressing possibility that if we attempt to avoid the birth of children with disease or disability, we will harm those who already exist. At the most practical level, some believe that acting so as to avoid such births will lead us to reduce the social resources now allocated to the disabled. At a more theoretical level, the judgment that life is better without such problems is taken as an insult to those now facing them.[46]

---

should not abort in that case, even where they would prefer to do so. That is why I think it is important to address this issue head on. See, for example, "Real Moral Dilemmas," and Adrienne Asch and Michelle Fine, "Shared Dreams: A Left Perspective on Disability Rights and Reproductive Rights," in *Women with Disabilities: Essays in Psychology, Culture, and Politics* (Philadelphia: Temple University Press, 1988).

[44] Saxton, "Born and Unborn," p. 310.

[45] See Helga Kuhse and Peter Singer, "From the Editors," *Bioethics* 5, no. 4 (October 1991): iv–v, for a brief account. A major conference at which he was to speak was threatened with disruption on the grounds that he and others who have argued in favor of euthanasia were "preparing the way for a resurgence of Nazi-style mass killing" (p. iv). Rejecting a proposal to withdraw its invitation to Singer, the conference's organizing committee instead canceled the conference.

[46] See, for example, Adrienne Asch, who writes in *Reproductive Laws* a propos of suits for wrongful birth and wrongful life: "claiming that life with disability is worse than no life at

The first worry would be legitimate if the only reason for attempting to prevent such births is the kind of esthetic preference for perfection to which I objected earlier, an outlook that does indeed fail to see any morally significant difference between existing and possible persons. But I mean to make, maintain, and rely on this difference.

It *is* unreasonable, in a world of limited resources and great need, to be required to allocate resources for those who did not have to need them. The obvious rejoinder is to point to the waste and corruption now apparent in the distribution of resources. Unfortunately, that does not make those resources available for human welfare. Even were such waste eradicated, it is quite likely that, given the overall world situation, every spare dime would be needed for fending off the suffering of already existing persons. Isn't it immoral knowingly to act so as to increase the demands on these resources, resources that could otherwise be used for projects such as feeding the starving or averting environmental disaster? Isn't attempting to avoid the birth of those who are likely to require extra resources, other things being equal, on a par with other attempts to share resources more equally? But from none of this does it follow that we should reduce the concern for those who already exist: on the contrary, it is in part *their* welfare that dictates such careful use of resources. This is not to say, as I suggested earlier, that any and all measures should be used to achieve the goal I am recommending, for some may themselves be wasteful of resources or have other morally dubious consequences. It may be wrong to refuse to undergo relatively noninvasive testing when there is evidence that you are at risk of passing some serious problem on to your child,[47] but it does not follow that you ought to be taking every conceivable step to avoid that outcome. Nor am I recommending anything like legally sanctioned invasions of women's bodies for prenatal testing or therapy.[48]

Asch warns of more subtle harm to the living from attempts to avoid the birth of disabled children. She asks whether "we want to send the message to all such people now living that there should be 'no more of your kind' in the future?"[49] This interpretation draws its force from the possibility that what is being said is that although you are a perfectly nice person, because of your imperfections and neediness, you still aren't worth the trouble and

---

all offends self-respecting disabled people and represents the extreme of what is dangerous about testing, diagnosing, and suing" (p. 95).

[47] If *knowing* that you will most likely come down with something dreadful, such as Huntington's disease, is too much for you to bear, then how can you impose such risk on your children?

[48] See Chapter 4, "Are Pregnant Women Fetal Containers?"

[49] Asch, "Can Aborting 'Imperfect' Children Be Immoral?," pp. 319–20.

we don't want to repeat you. That would be a devastating thing to hear. If this interpretation were correct, it would also reflect very badly on the speaker: one would hardly know where to start in on such a crude, instrumental view of human life.[50]

But I would dispute Asch's view that by attempting to avoid the birth of individuals with serious impairments that we either intend or in fact send such a message to the living. Wanting a world where fewer suffer implies doing what we can to alleviate the difficulties of those who now exist as well as doing what we can to relieve future people of them. This is an entirely different justification for the position in question, one that ought to be reassuring, not threatening. It is also important here once again to resist identifying disability with the disabled. My disability is not me, no matter how much it may affect my choices.[51] With this point firmly in mind, it should be possible mentally to separate my existence from the existence of my disability. Thus, I could rejoice, for instance, at the goal of eradicating nearsightedness, without taking that aim as an attempt to eradicate *me*, or people like me—even if achieving it means avoiding the birth of certain children.[52]

Contributing to the misunderstandings here, I think, is a fundamental uneasiness about our power to determine who shall be brought into being. Such uneasiness is an appropriate danger signal: it alerts us to the fact that we are embarking on a new and potentially harmful project. But we need to resist the urge to latch on to apparently plausible limits that may in fact be undesirable.[53]

---

[50] The beginning of a proper response would be to deny the moral framework that judges people according to a crude cost–benefit analysis, one that would conclude that some people don't "pay off." A livable moral framework must, on the contrary, concentrate on each person's opportunity to live a satisfying life; it recognizes our interdependence and takes for granted that we will all be helping each other at different times and in different ways. This way of looking at things leaves judgments about whether one's life is worth living to the individuals in question. However, it would not necessarily preclude an effort at avoiding some births for the kinds of reasons proposed here. This effort would be precluded by the response that virtually every possible life is worth living. However, that position might have some trouble showing why, other things being equal, we should not prefer to bring a nondisabled, rather than a disabled, individual into existence.

[51] Certain mental disabilities might be an exception to this claim.

[52] Since the advent of effective, comfortable, safe, and inexpensive contact lenses, simple nearsightedness is no longer a persuasive example for the middle class in Western industrialized nations. In other circumstances, such as in nontechnological societies where keen eyesight is essential for survival, it could still be a ghastly problem.

[53] Our reluctance deliberately to monkey with the future in certain ways (together with our apparently foolhardy willingness to do so in others) seems as yet inadequately explored. Bringing these fears out into the open would probably help us make wiser choices. See, for example, Jonathan Glover, *What Sort of People Should There Be?* (Middlesex, Eng.: Penguin, 1984).

I believe that such limits show up in the argument at the intersection of the philosopher's case against attempting to prevent the birth of unhealthy babies and the one advanced by disability-rights activists. It is the claim that if potential individuals would judge their lives worth living, then bringing them to life is no injury, and thus that there are no grounds for asserting on their behalf that it is wrong to create them.[54]

Derek Parfit is one of the philosophers who has been considering this problem.[55] He supposes that a child will have some defect—say, a withered arm—if she is conceived now; in three months, her mother could instead conceive a sound child, because the teratogenic drug that would cause the problem will have passed out of her system. But waiting would mean that the child with a withered arm (let us call her Minnie) would not exist; the child who would be born three months later would be someone else. So the price of existence, for Minnie, is a withered arm. Consequently, unless she agrees that nonexistence would be preferable to life with a bad arm, she is not wronged.

But this case rests in part on the assumption that a different egg and a different sperm necessarily produce a different person. And, of course, if we define ourselves as the product of a given egg and sperm, then it is indeed trivially true that different ones would not be us. We do know that some genetic rolls of the dice result in vastly different characteristics, but it seems quite likely that many would produce only tiny differences—grayish eyes instead of greenish, the ability to curl your tongue or not, a slightly bigger pancreas. On the other hand, however, nurture clearly plays a significant role in who we are. Not only does it affect our personality, but it also affects the expression of physical traits.[56] So a given environment is quite likely to mold even somewhat genetically diverse children into similar patterns. Conversely, different environments help create different people out of those with similar genetic endowments. For example, a friend of mine was born to poor, uneducated Druse villagers but was adopted at birth by Scottish missionaries and is now a professor of literature. Is there any serious sense in which we could say she is the same person she would have been had she

---

[54] This argument assumes that the only reason for refraining from bringing someone into existence is that it would wrong them; however, if there is no reason for preferring one possible future person over another, then we could still argue against bringing the unhealthy one into existence on the grounds of unnecessary burden to others, which tips the case against the unhealthy.

[55] Derek Parfit, "On Doing the Best for Our Children," in *Ethics and Population,* ed. M. D. Bayles (Cambridge: Schenkman, 1976); *Reasons and Persons,* part 4.

[56] Alison Jaggar points out that athletic girls tend to grow taller than nonathletic ones, because being physically active retards the onset of puberty, when growth slows. "Sex Inequality and Bias in Sex Differences Research," in *Science, Morality, and Feminist Theory,* ed. Marsha Hanen and Kai Nielsen, *Canadian Journal of Philosophy* supp. vol. 13 (1987): 34.

never left her original family? On a smaller scale, perhaps, we can be deeply changed by divorce, war, or accident. Thus the idea that the only significant determinant of who we are is the union of a particular egg and sperm seems rather unsatisfactory.

But suppose that premise were true; does it necessarily have any significance, moral or otherwise? Consider Minnie, the child of the mother who didn't wait. She is quite happy with life, although she would prefer not to have a withered arm. Suppose we suggest to her that *she* could not have been born whole; only somebody else would have been born instead.

A rational Minnie would be aware of the odds against *any* of us having our particular genetic and environmental constitution. If mom had failed to ovulate in July, the August-conceived you might have had curly hair instead of straight. If there was a crisis at work and dad was too tired to make love on Friday night, the Saturday-morning you might have a talent for running instead of race-walking. . . . In any case, the rational Minnie, although glad to be alive, would realize that if some other Minnie had been born instead, she herself wouldn't be looking enviously down from heaven saying "Drat, but for my mother's misplaced moral concern, that would be me."[57]

Furthermore, let us imagine that Minnie's mother *had* waited and that as a result, sound-bodied Minnie no. 2 was born instead of Minnie. Maybe Minnie no. 2 would have had other problems, but let us suppose that all else is equal, so that the only difference between them is that the two Minnies are "different" people—that is, conceived of different eggs and sperm. Even assuming that they are quite different, if Minnie no. 2 had been born instead of Minnie, is there any reason for thinking that she would be any less attached to her particular self than the original Minnie? Is there any reason for her to regret not having been the bad-armed Minnie? In short, if Minnie no. 2 is brought to life, why should she be any less glad to be who she is than Minnie would have been had she existed? Furthermore, wouldn't she be delighted that her mother had been thoughtful and had waited? Her delight at being alive is no less than Minnie's would have been, and she has two good arms to boot.

In short, if Minnie had been born instead, Minnie no. 2 wouldn't be here to be upset about that—and the converse. The other would just be one of trillions of unconceived possibilities out there. Furthermore, the realization that we ourselves might have been one of them seems to me to de-

---

[57] It is enormously important to recognize the limits of our thought experiments. As we try to think through the implications of various choices, we almost necessarily attribute to the "players" a kind of ghostly existence, as if they were waiting in the wings to be called out on stage. This conception tends to lead us astray and causes us to think inappropriately in terms of discrimination, hard feelings, and so forth.

mand some detachment from the conditions that led us to be here. Saxton asks whether she could in good conscience have a medical test that, if her mother had had access to it, would have led to her being aborted. Not only would that reasoning militate against legal abortion in general, but also it would demand that we commend fruitful acts of rape or incest. I myself would never have been born had World War II not occurred. Was it therefore a good thing?

The conclusion to be drawn from this thought exercise is surely that there is no good reason to conceive a child at special risk for disability when you would with little effort conceive one at only the usual odds. There are, in addition, good reasons for not doing so, based on the welfare of future persons. Parfit himself cannot, given his premises, find any way out of the dilemma he has described and concludes that we need to change the focus of our moral concern: "our reasons for acting should become *more impersonal*. Greater impersonality may seem threatening. But it would often be better for everyone."[58] By this he means that we ought to be more willing to judge that the prospect of people living in a harmed state should deter us from bringing it about, even if, according to the usual criteria, no one has been harmed.[59] That conclusion is compatible with a utilitarian approach that seeks greater happiness for each individual, rather than a highly populated world where individual lives are barely worth living.

Although Parfit's conclusion that we should lessen our fixation on individual rights and be more attentive to the overall picture is attractive, I am not quite ready to concede it as the whole story. Can it really be true that we do not wrong a child with serious impairments when we knowingly bring it into the world?[60] There is no space here for a full analysis of the issue, but one promising avenue would be to question further the extreme abstraction of some of the premises Parfit uses to generate his paradoxes,

[58] Parfit, *Reasons and Persons*, p. 443.
[59] This distinction is Feinberg's. (See *Harm to Others*, chap. 1, sec. 1.) Feinberg implicitly agrees with Parfit when he asserts that "It is, of course, possible to be wronged without being harmed ... and it is possible to blame A for bringing B into existence in an initially harmful condition, but that is still another thing than A harming B, which as we have seen ... requires worsening a person's prior condition, or at least making it worse that it would otherwise have been" (p. 99).
[60] This line of argument seems worth pursuing in part because of how odd it is to have to say that it would be wrong to inflict a given problem on an existing person, but not wrong to bring others to life if having it is the condition of their existence—when there is otherwise no particular good reason for "choosing" them. So if I failed to inoculate my child against, say, a bacterial version of Huntington's disease, I would be considered an irresponsible parent, even though the arguments in favor of conception of a child at risk for it downplay the misery of the disease. The differences in these two cases just seem insufficient to bear the moral weight required of them. That anybody has the disease is what's bad, not who they are or why they have it.

an abstraction that sometimes beguiles us into accepting implausible assumptions.[61] Reasoning with such bare-boned instruments denies us the context essential for developing livable moral views.

In general, the conjunction of abstract method and focus on harming individuals (as opposed to states of harm) in the way Parfit poses the question is most unfortunate because it implicitly promotes an unattractive ethic of moral minimalism that could hardly be distinguished from libertarianism. The underlying moral principle here seems to be that it is morally permissible to bring you to life so long as you can be expected to find your life worth living, because you are not thereby harmed (even if you have been born in a harmed state) and it is permissible to do anything that does not harm you.[62] What we owe others is thus reduced to not harming them, and the standard for not having harmed them is set very low. Generalizing these principles to other cases would lead to a great deal of misery. Why couldn't a government refuse to fund polio vaccination programs, for instance, on the grounds that even if a certain percentage of babies become paralyzed, they'll still be glad to be alive? Why pay for good schools when poor ones won't make kids wish they were dead?

PREVENTABLE AND UNPREVENTABLE HARMS

The stopper is supposed to be the morally relevant distinction between preventable harms and unpreventable ones. In this situation unpreventable harm is one that couldn't have been avoided without precluding your existence. But there is no particular reason for thinking that such a stringent criterion would be required in other cases. For instance, there might be no way for manufacturers to make "satisfactory" profits and reduce occupational hazards, and so the harm to workers would be neither preventable, nor, if their subsequent life still is worth living, wrong to them. Moreover,

---

[61] Thus, for example, he says that his wide average principle "could imply that, in the best possible history, only two people ever live." He comments: "most of us find this view too extreme. Most of us believe that there is value in quantity, but that this value has, in any period, an upper limit." Because the whole approach is so abstract, adding yet another abstract principle to counteract the counterintuitive consequence of the first becomes necessary. However, it would not be necessary if we thought seriously about what it would mean to imagine a two-person world. This rumination would, by itself, show that the wide average principle could never imply that a two-person history would be best. His descriptions of human interactions are uncomfortably reminiscent of that of billiard balls.

[62] There are also difficult epistemological problems because different people have different thresholds for suffering. Mistaken guesses about a given situation may create truly dreadful suffering as the individual comes to the conclusion that her life is not worth living, both on her part and on that of those who love her.

a different (and I think more realistic) view of personal identity, one that views some life experiences as constitutive of who you are, could undermine the crucial stopper effect still more. For if we recognize that some experiences can make you a different person, the impetus for social intervention, especially in children's lives, would be seriously undermined. At risk would be such desirable enterprises as Head Start and early nutrition programs.

However, my worry here goes still deeper. Although facts and logic constrain possible moral theories, they do not by themselves determine the values inherent in them. Thus how we approach ethics reflects our more general attitudes and dispositions. A narrow focus on not harming others, rather than enthusiasm for flourishing and happiness, will therefore both arise from but also help to perpetuate the relevant attitudes. Yet it is not from such a narrow, almost legalistic, conception of morality that flows the kind of generosity that will *of course* do everything to dissolve away the effects of disability and disease: it flows, instead, from a utilitarian preoccupation with doing whatever good one can. So to the extent that disability-rights activists borrow the morally minimalistic terms of Parfit's dilemma, they implicitly work against their own moral interests.

As I suggested earlier, it is good, other things being equal, for desires to be satisfied. It does not follow from this that we should accept desires uncritically, but merely that there is a prima facie case for satisfying them. In the case of the desire for genetically related children, other things are often not equal, however. It has in the past led to a great deal of misery when, for instance, a couple could not produce an appropriate heir, or when an inappropriate ("illegitimate") one was instead produced. Today, the first problem is leading women to try dangerous and expensive reproductive technologies in the search for a genetically related child when they could instead adopt a child in need of a good home. It can also motivate people to risk the health of future children, even though they could still enjoy the other aspects of having children by sacrificing all or part of the genetic link.

It is true that providing a decent quality of life for each of us would, by itself, go far toward avoiding the birth of children with serious health problems and that it is, for this and other reasons, morally obligatory. Efforts in this direction are not even on the political horizon and will not by themselves make every problematic case go away, so, how are we to face these issues in the meantime?

Having said that there is a serious strike against bringing certain children to life does not give us much specific guidance, and there is no space here to consider that issue in the detail it deserves.[63] It is well-known that a variety of options now exist for those who want to refrain from producing children with their own genetic material. Among them are Artificial Insemination by Donor and egg donation, as well as contract pregnancy and adoption. Although AID is widely used and, for the most part regarded as uncontroversial, egg donation and contract pregnancy are not.[64] The last word on these remains to be said; I have argued elsewhere at length that contract pregnancy, if stringently regulated, could be made a morally acceptable alternative to the usual method of childbearing.[65] Adoption, although more morally problematic and practically difficult than is often thought, may also be in many cases a reasonable option.

Unfortunately these compromises have only limited utility for some, most notably the poor. Not only do the poor face more than their share of the kinds of health problems that create risk for babies, but also they get less help with them. And the reproductive risk now posed for them by the AIDS epidemic is making their lives still more difficult. Given society's responsibility for so much of their plight, it hardly seems tenable to argue that they are now to forego one of their only sources of satisfaction, reproducing "their own," genetically related children. Yet, that does not protect their children. As John Arras points out in his sensitive paper on the topic, "the reproductive decisions of infected women have serious and problematic ethical implications for their offspring."[66] The interplay of social and individual responsibility here creates moral problems that cannot be adequately resolved by pointing the finger solely at individuals, even if doing that seems to be the only way to prevent immediate harm. However, the unfair price such individuals pay for stopping it underlines once again our ultimate social responsibility in many of these matters.

[63] I discuss some of these, such as the question of risk, in Chapter 1, "Genetic and Reproductive Risk: Can Having Children Be Immoral?"

[64] For views on these issues, see Helen B. Holmes and Laura M. Purdy, eds., *Feminist Perspectives in Medical Ethics* (Bloomington: Indiana University Press, 1992); Helen B. Holmes, ed., *Issues in Reproductive Technology I: An Anthology,* (New York: Garland, 1992); and Richard Hull, ed., *Ethical Issues in the New Reproductive Technologies* (Belmont, Calif.: Wadsworth, 1990).

[65] See Chapter 11, "Surrogate Mothering: Exploitation or Empowerment?," and Chapter 12, "Another Look at Contract Pregnancy."

[66] Arras, "AIDS and Reproductive Decisions."

CHAPTER 3

What Can Progress in Reproductive Technology Mean for Women?

Our society is in love with new reproductive arrangements and technologies.[1] It hardly seems possible to open a general interest publication like *Life* or *Time* without encountering an enthusiastic article on the latest reproductive wrinkle, and substantial social resources are being devoted to reproductive research. The medical establishment—and apparently the public—are welcoming these new developments without much awareness of their potential consequences.

However, the new technologies have been criticized both by conservative and progressive thinkers. Conservatives object to their interference with nature and tradition; these issues will not be considered here.[2] Progressives object to the naive technological optimism inherent in the mainstream view and raise questions about who will control the new technologies.

No one—not the scientific mainstream, not conservatives, not progressives—seems particularly concerned about the potential consequences of the new technologies for women. These consequences therefore cry out for feminist analysis. Among the most prominent feminist critics of the new

From *Journal of Medicine and Philosophy* (1996). Reprinted by permission of the editor.
[1] In the rest of this chapter I will, for the sake of simplicity, refer to these new social arrangements and technologies as "new technologies," even though contract pregnancy, or surrogacy, does not necessarily involve any new technology.
[2] See, for example, Donald DeMarco, *In My Mother's Womb: The Catholic Church's Defense of Natural Life* (Manassas, Va.: Trinity Communications, 1987).

technologies are members of FINRRAGE[3] and disability-rights activists,[4] and it is primarily their views that I evaluate here.[5]

Because these feminists generally see themselves as part of the progressive left, they tend to adopt its negative position about the technologies as a starting point and go on to detail their potential dangers for women. They emphasize how the technologies reinforce harmful biologically determinist stereotypes of women at the expense of a more accurate conception of women as human persons with a full range of interests. They remind us of how often medical science has failed to protect women's welfare. They also show why new choices do not necessarily spell progress and how the sexist social context in which the new technologies are being developed and practiced harms women,[6] especially women already disadvantaged by race and class.[7]

The central question I want to address here is the adequacy of this feminist response. In particular, I want to ask how well its alliance with the progressive movement serves women. I reject neither progressive worries nor these feminist extensions of them. But I do fear that by starting with the progressive critique, they inherit a devastating gender blindness that puts women at risk in unnoticed ways. Ironically, eradicating this gender blindness brings what I see as a reasonable feminist position somewhat closer to that of the scientific mainstream.

WOMEN AT RISK

Feminists who generally oppose the new technologies sometimes suggest that those who are more positive about them are naive liberals who are

---

[3] FINRRAGE stands for Feminist International Network of Resistance to Reproductive and Genetic Engineering; its members see new reproductive technologies as a new form of eugenics therefore essentially destructive of human welfare.

[4] Adrienne Asch and Marsha Saxton are among the most articulate leaders of the disability-rights movement.

[5] Influential feminist philosophers such as Susan Sherwin and Christine Overall are also quite negative about the new technologies. Their work provides us with some of the best argued and most persuasive reasons for caution. See, for example, Sherwin's *No Longer Patient: Feminist Ethics and Health Care* (Philadelphia: Temple University Press, 1992), and Overall's *Ethics and Human Reproduction: A Feminist Analysis* (Boston: Allen & Unwin, 1987), and *Human Reproduction: Principles, Practices, Policies* (Oxford: Oxford University Press, 1993). Feminists who are more positive about the beneficial potential of the new technologies are Lori Andrews, Harriet Baber, Anne Donchin, Michelle Stanworth, Christine Sistare, Mary Anne Warren, Dorothy Wertz, and myself. One of the few treatments of genetic services that raises the issue I discuss here is "A Critique of Some Feminist Challenges to Prenatal Diagnosis," by Dorothy C. Wertz and John C. Fletcher, *Journal of Women's Health* 2, no. 2, (1993): 173–88.

[6] See, for example, Sherwin, *No Longer Patient*; Christine Overall, *Ethics and Human Reproduction*; and Gwynne Basen, Margrit Eichler, and Abby Lippman, eds., *Misconceptions: The Social Construction of Choice and the New Reproductive and Genetic Technologies* (Hull, Quebec: Voyageur, 1993).

[7] See, for example, Helen B. Holmes, ed., *Issues in Reproductive Technology I: An Anthology*, (New York: Garland, 1992).

blind to the fundamental dangers they pose for women.[8] Despite this intellectual environment, I often find myself drawn to these more positive assessments of the new technologies.

One reason for wanting to legitimize a broader range of positions on the new technologies is the necessity for developing ethics for an imperfect world. Most societies still fail to recognize women's interests on an equal basis with those of men. The difficulty is to devise policies that both take into account this reality and help end sexism. Following rules that would make sense in a feminist world may lead to very different results in a sexist world. Yet following rules intended to maximize women's welfare in a sexist world may create barriers to the better society we hope to create. So practical feminist ethics must tiptoe through this minefield, neither selling the interests of contemporary women short nor discounting excessively those of future women. Given this situation, one might reasonably expect a wide variety of moral responses to particular issues, and such variety is necessary to help us fix on the best policies.[9]

Still more important, I think that the feminist rejection of the new technologies often fails to factor in existing inequities that could be alleviated by their judicious use. Sadly, the progressive movement has all too often been as oblivious to gender issues as the mainstream—that was, after all, a major impetus for the second wave of feminism; certainly its critique of the new technologies rarely displays much sensitivity to the problems women currently face. Some feminists remedy that situation, in part, by highlighting the new technologies' potential harm to women and conclude that because the technologies are so generally problematic for women, they should be rejected. However, it does not make sense to reject the technologies unless they are more harmful than the alternatives (including the status quo), for even a potentially risky course of action may nonetheless be better than a still more harmful alternative.[10] The failure to make this move is especially odd in light of the extensive feminist critiques of reproduction and childrearing.[11]

---

[8] See, for example, Overall's rejection of in vitro fertilization, "Access to *in Vitro* Fertilization: Costs, Care, and Consent," in *Human Reproduction*, p. 147.

[9] Such diversity is easily squelched by the all-too-common reaction that work that explores unpopular lines of argument "isn't really feminist."

[10] This is, of course, a consequentialist approach, one not shared by many feminists. However, if the new technologies are to be rejected because of their risks to women, consistency would seem to require that those risks be compared with those of other policies. Given what I believe are the extensive risks to women of the status quo, I doubt that the particular standard that one then goes on to apply would alter my conclusion. (Among the contenders would be that one ought to minimize harm to women and that to try to maximize women's welfare—within an overall context of justice.)

[11] See, for example, Susan Moller Okin, *Justice, Gender, and the Family* (New York: Basic Books, 1989), and Ann Oakley, *Women's Work* (New York: Pantheon, 1974).

The new technologies fall into three basic categories. One kind limits reproduction by preventing conception or ending pregnancy. Another kind promotes conception and includes such practices as contract pregnancy (surrogacy) and in vitro fertilization (IVF). A third kind attempts to determine the characteristics of children who are born and includes genetic counseling and screening programs. Feminists have fought hard to make safe, effective versions of contraception and abortion available, a fight that is, as we all know, by no means over. But prominent feminist thinkers have been quite negative both about techniques that promote conception and about so-called quality control genetic services.[12]

CONCEPTIVE TECHNOLOGIES

Why have these feminists been so negative about new conceptive approaches such as contract pregnancy and biological techniques such as IVF? Both topics now sport voluminous literatures whose pros and cons are mostly variations on the themes already mentioned here. Two special reasons cited by feminist critics for opposing conceptive innovations are the socially constructed nature of women's desire for children and the chauvinistic, perhaps even racist, nature of the desire for genetically related children. Opponents of conceptive technologies play up the pervasive pronatalism that persuades women that they will not be fulfilled without having children of their own and concludes that because the desire for genetically related children is socially conditioned anyway, it is not morally essential that it be satisfied. This position seems to assume that socially constructed desires are malleable and can, in any case, be denied relatively painlessly.

There is reason to doubt this assessment. On the one hand, it is obviously true that society is still intensely pronatalist.[13] It is quite likely that many women (and men) have children because "it is the thing to do," and only "misfits" fail to reproduce. Undoubtedly that same pronatalism, together with the pressures on women to provide genetically related children for their husbands, leads some infertile women to seek conceptive help. Because having children without a genuine desire for the experience of childrearing and a vivid understanding of the sacrifices required to be a good

---

[12] See John Robertson, *Children of Choice: Freedom and the New Reproductive Technologies* (Princeton: Princeton University Press, 1994), p. vii.

[13] See Ellen Peck and Judith Senderowitz, eds., *Pronatalism: The Myth of Mom & Apple Pie* (New York: Crowell, 1974), especially Leta S. Hollingworth, "Social Devices for Impelling Women to Bear and Rear Children," and Judith Blake, "Coercive Pronatalism and American Population Policy," which are, for the most part, as relevant today as when they were written.

parent in a society so unsupportive of human welfare will likely lead to much suffering, pronatalism should be eradicated. Women also need to be clear about the fact that they would often be better off, both individually and as a group, if fewer women reproduced.[14]

On the other hand, I believe that even in the absence of pronatalism, many women would continue to want children. As a voluntarily childless woman myself, I am as aware as anybody that life can be fulfilling without a child of one's own. Nonetheless, as one who has also participated in parenting, I also know that—for better or for worse—there is nothing else quite like it. A special closeness arises from being children's primary caretaker and witnessing their gradual development into persons. In addition, some individuals' ties to their children are the strongest and most enduring human connections they will ever make. So long as we think human survival desirable, these interests are likely to unite into a desire, sometimes an extremely intense desire, to be involved in childrearing.[15] For many people, a genetic link is an essential element in their desire for children. It is true that this wish is not particularly rational,[16] and it may sometimes be morally questionable.[17] Nonetheless, it can be a powerful desire. In addition, it is important to remember that some of the factors that thwart its satisfaction may be a result of morally dubious social policies.[18]

A combination of circumstances—the costs to women who cannot reproduce without conceptive aid, the genuine pleasures of childrearing in a world that provides few other satisfactions for many women, and the social genesis of a good deal of infertility—seems to me to justify cautious approval in principle of some conceptive innovations, if it is coupled with a

---

[14] See Rivka Polatnick, "Why Women Don't Rear Children: A Power Analysis," in *Mothering,* ed. Joyce Trebilcot (Totowa, N.J.: Rowman & Allanheld, 1983). Polatnick argues both that childrearing contributes to women's powerlessness and that women are forced to do most childrearing because they are relatively powerless. She supports her case with compelling social science studies. For a discussion of the benefits for individual women of being childless, see Susan S. Lang, *Women without Children: The Reasons, the Rewards, the Regrets* (New York: Pharos Books, 1991), chap. 6. The demands of childrearing also reduce the time available to women for political activism aimed at achieving gender justice.

[15] See Chapter 12, "Another Look at Contract Pregnancy."

[16] See Michael D. Bayles, *Reproductive Ethics* (Englewood Heights, N.J.: Prentice-Hall), chap. 1.

[17] See Purdy, "Genetic Diseases: Can Having Children Be Immoral?" in *Genetics Now,* ed. John L. Buckley (Washington, D.C.: University Press of America, 1978); a revised version will appear in *Biomedical Ethics,* ed. Thomas A. Mappes and David DeGrazia (New York: McGraw-Hill, 1996).

[18] Among them are career ladders that require women to wait until their less fertile years before reproducing, insufficiently stringent standards for contraceptive medical devices such as the Dalkon Shield, or standards for exposure to toxic substances that put susceptible people at risk of disease.

campaign against pronatalism. The main thrust of such concern about infertility should be preventive, and it need not imply approval or encouragement of existing halfway technologies such as IVF.[19] But that concern
must also acknowledge that existing desires count and make a commitment
to help.

GENETIC SERVICES

Equally unjustifiable as the negativism about conceptive aids[20] is the rejection of so-called quality control that uses genetic services to prevent the
birth of babies at risk for serious physical or mental illness or disability.[21]
Scientific efforts to predict potential problems of this sort are often rejected
as mere economy measures.[22] No doubt, avoiding the additional cost of ac-
commodating such individuals is a major motivation for the current interest in this area. Progressive thinkers routinely point to the enormous sums
the United States devotes to the defense establishment, arguing that this
reason for attempting to prevent the birth of children at risk for serious
health problems could be undermined by changing our budgetary priorities. But by now it should be obvious that no such change in priorities will
occur in the foreseeable future, even though that does not mean that we
should give up the fight for it. Spending on human welfare is at best a
zero-sum game:[23] the more is spent in one area, the less is available for another. Those who are concerned about justice and equality are well aware
of the enormous unmet needs in our society. They include food, shelter,
education, and preventive medical care. Among those with the greatest
unmet need are persons with health problems. Other things being equal, I
believe that existing persons should have first call on resources. Therefore,
if programs to prevent the birth of children who are likely to have serious

---

[19] Although prevention isn't necessarily cheaper than remedial measures, it is nonetheless
generally preferable. In this case, prevention also promotes other desirable goals, such as
healthier environments and a weakening of sexism. On the economics of prevention, see
Louise B. Russell, "The Role of Prevention in Health Reform," *New England Journal of Medicine*, 329, no. 5 (July 29, 1993): 352–54, and David Stipp, "Prevention May Be Costlier Than
a Cure," *Wall Street Journal*, July 16, 1994, pp. B1, B4.

[20] See, for instance, Gena Corea, *The Mother Machine: Reproductive Technologies from Artificial
Insemination to Artificial Wombs* (New York: Harper & Row, 1985).

[21] I use the phrase "health problems" to stand in for the long, awkward phrase "physical
or mental illness or disability," even though I am aware that they do not ordinarily have the
same precise meanings. For an example of feminist argumentation against using genetic
services, see Basen et al, eds., *Misconceptions*.

[22] See, for example, Lisa Blumberg, "Eugenics vs. Reproductive Choice," *Sojourner: The
Women's Forum* (January 1995): 17.

[23] In 1995 virtually *all* resources now devoted to human welfare are in question.

health problems cost less than the alternatives, there is a moral argument in their favor.[24]

Progressives and a significant number of feminists believe that other things are not equal, however: attempting to prevent the birth of children with serious health problems is immoral.[25] One major objection to this practice is possible harm to existing persons with disabilities. Another objection turns upon the harm that can be caused by the social programs necessary for achieving that goal. Feminist critics echo these concerns and raise, in addition, the potential for serious harm to women because of their intimate involvement in reproduction and because of the historical discounting of women's interests whenever they come into conflict with the interests of others. They also rightly point out that health, including children's health, could be improved more effectively by preventive social measures such as feeding programs, better prenatal care, environmental cleanups, and, more generally, by eradicating poverty.[26]

Most of these arguments raise legitimate issues.[27] Society needs to be alert to the danger of yet again ignoring the interests of disabled persons, even if, as I believed is true here, this particular worry is misconceived.[28] Attention to human welfare also demands thorough scrutiny of social programs (even those proposed to secure entirely desirable ends) for they are sometimes ineffective or meet their goals only by externalizing their costs unfairly. Given the sexism that pervades most human societies, they are especially likely to do so at women's expense.[29] Furthermore, it is obviously true that broader social welfare programs hold out more immediate hope of promoting human well-being, including health, and fighting for such programs should be the main focus of progressive political action. All these issues should cause us to think twice about embracing mainstream views.

---

[24] By this measure, naturally, only some programs would be justified.

[25] Again, Blumberg, "Eugenics vs. Reproductive Choice," is a good example. Philosophers (most notably Derek Parfit) have also argued that there is no moral reason to prevent the birth of children with any but the very worst prospects. See Parfit, *Reasons and Persons* (Oxford: Clarendon Press, 1984).

[26] See, for example, Mary Briody Mahowald, *Women and Children in Health Care: An Unequal Majority* (Oxford: Oxford University Press, 1993), chap. 13; "The Feminization of Poverty: Its Impact on Women's and Children's Health," and Sherwin, *No Longer Patient*, chap. 11, "Gender, Race, and Class in the Delivery of Health Care."

[27] I have serious doubts about the philosophical argument that we rarely harm future people by bringing them into existence and have argued against it in Chapter 2, "Loving Future People." Parfit himself concludes that his argument is not the whole story.

[28] For an extended argument about this issue, see Chapter 2, "Loving Future People."

[29] See Sherwin, *No Longer Patient*.

However, we also need to think again before embracing the progressive and feminist rejection of genetic services, for they do not seem to take into account the almost overwhelming problems many women now face.

This issue crystallized for met at a recent bioethics workshop entitled "The Burden of Knowledge: Moral Dilemmas in Prenatal Testing." The *pièce de résistance* was a video of the same title[30] that, according to the program, is intended to "help the public think about the ethical questions raised by prenatal testing. We meet women and couples who decide whether to use screened (sic) and diagnostic tests to access information about their fetuses. They share the outcomes of their decisions, thus helping the audience understand the benefits and the burdens of such tests. These personal experiences are interspersed with commentary from geneticists, genetic counselors, physicians, midwives, disability activists, and scholars."[31]

The video showed women as they dealt with the news that they might be carrying a fetus with serious health problems and interviewed them again after they either gave birth or aborted. Most of the women interviewed who were presented with bad news about their fetus chose to continue with their pregnancy. These women were portrayed as self-possessed, secure, competent individuals, who were ready to cope with any outcome. Without exception, they said they were happy with their choice and emphasized how much joy their children brought them. A couple of women who had chosen to abort were also interviewed. They were portrayed as insecure individuals, fearful of disability. When an audience member commented at this asymmetry, Deni Elliott responded that she and her coproducers wanted to counter the widespread belief that "disability is a disaster."

It is true that disability is not necessarily a disaster. There is a wide range of possible impairments, and many do not or need not seriously affect quality of life; it is important to disseminate that message to a society that seems obsessed with physical perfection. But sometimes disability *is* a disaster, and I believe that it is unfair to all concerned to obscure that possibility. I have argued elsewhere that it is not wrong to prevent the birth of children who can be expected to have serious health problems and that failing to do so is sometimes seriously immoral.[32] If these positions are sound, there is no good reason for proceeding with such births if they are in conflict with the interests of others. But they can be in serious conflict with such inter-

---

[30] The video was shown at the 1994 Annual Meeting of the Society for Health and Human Values (SHHV), in Pittsburgh, Pennsylvania. It was produced by Deni Elliott, who presented the video at the meeting.

[31] Ibid., program notes, p. 249.

[32] See Purdy, "Genetic Diseases: Can Having Children Be Immoral?" See also Chapter 1, "Genetics and Reproductive Risk: Can Having Children Be Immoral?" and Chapter 2, "Loving Future People."

ests. Who already does the bulk of caring work in this society, including childrearing? Women. And caring for a child with serious health problems can add immeasurably to a mother's burden.

Given the pervasive sexist assumption that women's role is to serve others, it is not surprising that the scientific establishment's case for using genetic services to prevent the birth of children with serious health problems emphasizes the burden to society and to the children themselves, leaving out any meaningful consideration of the potential benefits for women. Nor is it really surprising that this burden on women of caring for children with health problems is unnoticed by progressive thinkers, who are thus free to reject such genetic services without taking into account the consequences for women. But why does this fact not loom larger in feminist analysis?

It is not rare for, allegedly, feminist analyses to pay scant, if any, attention to the burdens now shouldered by women caring for children with health problems.[33] The thrust of these analyses focuses instead on resistance to a genetic establishment geared toward coercing women to accept "therapeutic" abortions and emphasizes a woman's right to choose to go forward even in the face of health risk for the future child. The literature also cites the quite real discomforts and dangers that may be involved in using genetic services. But where is a woman's right to be fully and realistically informed about the probable consequences of her decision to go forward with her pregnancy? Where is the feminist critique of pronatalism so prominent in treatments of conceptive aids? Surely these issues need to be right up front in feminist work, instead of submerged in some generalized "right to choose."[34]

This matter is particularly crucial because of the context in which women are having children. It is important to remember that motherhood often comes to women who have not actively chosen it. First, women may not have much say about when they will have sexual intercourse, and second,

---

[33] See Blumberg, "Eugenics vs. Reproductive Choice"; Marsha Saxton, "Born and Unborn: The Implications of Reproductive Technologies for People with Disabilities," in *Test-Tube Women: What Future for Motherhood?*, ed. Rita Arditti, Renate Duelli Klein, and Shelley Minden (London: Pandora, 1984); and Adrienne Asch, "Can Aborting 'Imperfect' Children Be Immoral?" in *Ethical Issues in Modern Medicine*, ed. John Arras and Nancy Rhoden (Mountain View, Calif.: Mayfield Press, 1989). One of the few articles to raise the issue in question seriously at all is Wertz and Fletcher, "A Critique of Some Feminist Challenges to Prenatal Diagnosis." One objection to attempting to prevent the birth of children at risk for serious health problems is to point to the obvious fact that women often find themselves devoting special care to children who develop unforeseen health problems after birth. Naturally, this situation cannot be avoided, but it does not follow that there is no benefit in attempting to reduce the number of cases where this is necessary. This issue also underlines the need for social mechanisms to share both risk and labor, even if genetic services are fully deployed.
[34] See Blumberg's "Eugenics vs. Reproductive Choice," which fails to raise the consequences for women of bearing children with serious health problems.

they may not have good access to contraception or to abortion services. In addition, as I pointed out earlier, pronatalism undoubtedly presses many women into motherhood they neither desire nor are suited for.

It is also important to remember the costs of motherhood for women, even women who are mothering "ordinary," healthy children. Despite twenty years of feminist argument and activism, daycare is still a luxury, not a right, even though most women must work. There is still no guaranteed health care. There is still significant discrimination against women in both education and workplaces. Women still earn, on average, far less than men. Divorce is still common, and so is unemployment. And, as of January 1995, a Republican congress is in place that vows to cut people—including women with children—off the welfare rolls if they have not found a job within two years.

Under these circumstances, raising even generally healthy children is a struggle for the poor. An increasing percentage of the population is poor in the United States, and single women with children constitute the largest proportion of poor people.[35] Raising children is also becoming more of a struggle for the middle class, as good jobs disappear into the global economy, women enter the labor market, and costs go up. Although men bear some of these burdens, the belief that women are responsible for childrearing means that they bear the brunt of the "second shift."[36]

In any case, women often become mothers unaware of the demands having children will make on them: there is no guarantee of informed consent for this decision, one of the most important decisions she will ever make. Feminists need to engage in an unrelenting campaign to remedy this situation and make sure that women are provided with the opportunity for thoroughgoing scrutiny of their own needs, desires, and plans *before* going ahead with a child. Such scrutiny must include a realistic assessment of the demands of motherhood. It must also include a clear-eyed assessment of each individual woman's inclinations, strengths, and resources—one that is sensitive to the danger of judging that one will be satisfied with the work of nurturing and the trade-offs it requires in terms of other activities only because that is what is socially expected of women.

When motherhood is not the result of this kind of informed decision, both children and women suffer. Children suffer because their mothers may not have the resources necessary for raising them well. Women suffer as well when they discover how unrealistic their expectations are and how their own needs and desires must be subordinated to those of their children.[37]

---

[35] See Mahowald, *Women and Children in Health Care*, pp. 219ff.

[36] See Arlie Hochschild, *The Second Shift* (New York: Avon, 1989).

[37] See Polatnick, "Why Men Don't Rear Children," especially the quotations on p. 34; and Lang, *Women without Children*, chap. 6, "Choosing to be Child Free," especially pp. 81–84.

This situation is exacerbated by the prospect of a child with special needs. One way of addressing the problem is to counsel women to accept their circumstances and learn to cope effectively. This attitude seems implicit in the position of disability-rights activists such as Marsha Saxton, who says she would "like to welcome any child born to me. I believe that I have the emotional, financial, and other resources to effectively care for a child. I know I can be a good mother and my husband a good father to any child."[38] If potential parents know they have the resources, both psychological and financial, to meet a child's needs, this is a truly admirable attitude. But presenting this attitude as the only morally permissible (or morally admirable) approach is indefensible. First, it is unfair because women in sexist societies are bombarded with the view that women (but not men) are nurturers by nature. This assumption, together with the (now usually subliminal) message that females lack the qualities necessary for other projects, undoubtedly leads many women erroneously to concur in this judgment. Others who know or suspect that they are better suited to different occupations must nonetheless struggle to overcome their own doubts. Second, some people will be led to count on outside resources that do not materialize.[39] Under these circumstances, many people, women particularly, will feel compelled to go ahead with children whose care they will experience as burdensome, whether they admit this fact or not.[40]

Both Saxton and Adrienne Asch oppose aborting fetuses that can be expected to result in children with serious health problems.[41] Asch goes on to ask what will happen when women who abort fetuses with problems they do not think they can face have other children who "develop characteristics [they] dislike or find overwhelming."[42] She goes on to suggest that such women may not recognize or may refuse to accept that childbearing should be undertaken only if "we are willing to face what we cannot control and to seek the resources in ourselves and the world to master it."[43]

---

[38] Saxton, "Born and Unborn," p. 310. A deteriorating economic picture, together with the threat of impoverishment that can follow divorce and insecure access to health services, make this confidence increasingly unrealistic for many women.

[39] Consider those whose health insurance is canceled or who are counting on social programs that may be defunded. Consider that the most recent estimate of Americans under 65 without health insurance is how 41 million persons. (See Trudy Lieberman, "How the G.O.P. Made 'Mediscare,'" *The Nation*, Nov. 6, 1995, p. 536.)

[40] It is important to remember that the same sexist and pronatalist influences that pressure women into choices for which they may not be suited also make it socially difficult to admit to dissatisfaction with the situation.

[41] See Marsha Saxton and Adrienne Asch, "Real Moral Dilemmas," *Christianity and Crisis* 46, no. 10 (July 14, 1986): 237–40. Asch thinks that it is permissible (though misguided) to refrain from conception to avoid a risk of disability; it is not clear how she defends this distinction between refraining from conception and aborting, given that she is pro-choice.

[42] Asch, "Can Aborting 'Imperfect' Children Be Immoral?," p. 320.

[43] Ibid.

Perhaps many women have an unrealistic view of the demands of motherhood and, in particular, of the demands of motherhood when a child has special needs.[44] However, attempting to foresee and avoid potential problems does not seem to me to be evidence that one will be unable to cope with unexpected ones.

I believe that a major goal of feminism should be to help women take more control of their lives. Girls and women *still* need to hear that they may have legitimate interests that are in conflict with the nurturing society expects of them in virtue of their sex. They need to hear that it may sometimes be morally desirable to refrain from having children. They also need to hear that it is morally desirable to exercise choice about the kinds of nurturing they will undertake, even if total control is impossible. Girls and women also need to be empowered to follow through on their decisions. Only then can they eradicate the slippery slope that so often deprives females of any significant say over their lives. Men have long taken for granted this measure of control about how they will live, and it contributes significantly to their well-being. Such control is sometimes repudiated as a middle-class "luxury," and perhaps it is. Surely feminism should aim to extend it to every woman, rich or poor, white, brown, or black. Suggesting that such control is unnecessary or morally dubious is to equate it unfairly with an egoism that subordinates all else to one's own desires. Naturally, women need to be aware of the moral dimension of their choices, but under present circumstances I believe that it is inappropriate to accuse them of incompetence or selfishness if they, after careful reflection, choose to avail themselves of certain conceptive or genetic services. The harm is especially grievous in the latter case because they may thereby sacrifice substantial control over the rest of their lives.

What does all this mean in terms of social policy? It is clear that a greater proportion of social resources should be redirected to broader programs that will reduce the incidence of health problems, including infertility. It is also clear that the new technologies need to be regulated to ensure insofar as possible that their benefits outweigh their potential harms and that such regulation must be sensitive to the often discounted interests of members of disadvantaged groups. In the meantime, women need to be offered the opportunity to make fully informed choices about how they will shape their

---

[44] There is evidence that *most* women have unrealistic views about mothering. Citing *The Motherhood Report*, Lang points out that 70 percent of the 1,100 mothers studied were "extraordinarily illusionistic. . . . Their unrealistic fantasies ran the gamut from slightly romanticized notions to fantasies of perfection: perfect children, perfect mothers, and perfect families." *Women without Children*, p. 82.

lives in a world that is all too ready to do it for them. It is up to feminism to help them think through the issues they face. It can do so only by inviting women to think realistically about their options and encouraging the very widest debate about the moral dimensions of those options.

CHAPTER 4

Are Pregnant Women
Fetal Containers?

Let me relieve your curiosity right away: yes, pregnant women are fetal containers.[1] That is, they have fetuses in their bodies. But the implication from this fact drawn by some people from the phrase—that women are nothing but cheap clay pots supporting infinitely precious flowers—is very far from being the case.[2]

Women carry fetuses in their bodies, it is true. It is equally true, however, that fetuses are part of women's bodies. The champions of fetus and woman in this latest round of the war about women's reproductive rights would argue that these claims are inconsistent. For one of the legacies of the abortion battle has been the assumption that if fetuses are part of women's bodies, they are not separate entities and women should therefore have the final say about what happens to them.

THE PROBLEM

Women, like men, want to control what happens to and in their bodies. Women's ability to do this is being threatened by proponents of the

From *Bioethics* 4, no. 4 (October 1990): 273–91. Reprinted by permission of Blackwell Publishers.

[1] This chapter was originally a paper given at the December 1989 meeting of the Society for Philosophy and Public Policy; I would like to thank commentators Joan Callahan and Mary Anne Warren for their helpful comments. I would also like to thank Dianne Romain for her criticism of an earlier version, as well as Denise McCoskey and the two anonymous readers for *Bioethics*, in which this chapter was then published.

[2] The flower pot theory is elucidated by Caroline Whitbeck, "Theories of Sex Difference," *Women and Values: Readings in Recent Feminist Philosophy*, ed. Marilyn Pearsall (Belmont, Calif., Wadsworth, 1986), p. 35.

view that their choices should be subordinated to the welfare of fetuses within them.

Respect for our right as moral agents to control our bodies, is a keystone of liberal society. The paradigm cases of such control consist of situations common to both women and men. Those, like pregnancy, that are experienced only by women, tend to be regarded as special cases and thrown into question. Such debate is perhaps innocuous when it involves moral claims. However, when, as here, it moves to the legal realm and can lead to coercion or punishment, its implications become much more serious.

Cases where women's decisions about their pregnancies have been overridden by doctors and judges are accumulating. Some involve drug use. For example, one woman was charged with child abuse last year after giving birth to her second cocaine-addicted baby; her child was placed in foster care. In another case, a woman was jailed for a week after she gave birth to a brain-damaged baby: she was accused, among other things, of drug abuse. In a third case, a woman arrested for cheque forgery was found to be using cocaine; a judge sent her to jail for four months to protect her fetus.[3] Others involve involuntary caesareans. In one such case, a Nigerian woman's husband was thrown out of the hospital and she was strapped to the table for the surgery.[4] In another, a terminally ill cancer patient was forced to submit to surgery in order to give a marginally viable fetus a chance at life; both were dead in two days.[5] And so forth. Relatively little publicity has accompanied such cases.[6] Yet if the same things were being done to the average middle-class white man on the street, there would be public outrage. Is there then some morally relevant difference between that man in the street and pregnant women that would justify such different legal treatment?

THE FETUS'S PLACE

Fetuses live in women's bodies. This means that what happens both in and to those bodies can adversely affect fetuses and that the only way to get at a fetus is through the body that houses it.

It is now well-known that fetuses can be harmed by a variety of causes that operate before or after conception. Genetic defects, exposure to radiation or toxic substances, maternal ill health, and birth itself can lead to a dis-

[3] Andrea Sachs, "Here Come the Pregnancy Police," *Time*, May 22, 1989, p. 101.
[4] Janet Gallagher, "Prenatal Invasions and Interventions: What's Wrong with Fetal Rights," *Harvard Women's Law Journal* 10 (1987): 9.
[5] See Mary Mahowald, "Beyond Abortion: Refusal of Caesarean Section," *Bioethics* 3, no. 2 (April 1989): 106.
[6] See for instance, Gallagher "Prenatal Invasions," p. 10.

eased or handicapped baby. Research has helped us to understand and deal with some of the difficulties afflicting fetal development and birth, and this area is currently the subject of intensive scrutiny and experimentation. The list of worries is long.

Consider, just for a start, maternal infections such as rubella, herpes, syphilis, and AIDS. Pregnant women may also suffer from a variety of diseases, such as diabetes, thyroid disease, hypertension, and cancer; they may also be exposed to toxic chemicals, such as anesthetic gases, chemotherapeutic drugs, benzene, and dioxin.[7]

Because fetuses are so vulnerable, protecting them requires a comprehensive approach. Women must avoid harmful substances, act to meet fetal needs, and, at times, submit to bodily invasions. They must exercise self-discipline about so-called lifestyle choices, keeping away from substances such as alcohol, tobacco, drugs—and no doubt hot fudge sundaes. They also need to stay away from toxic environments, including work and living places. It is also important that they get good prenatal care, eat a healthy diet, and exercise appropriately. Finally, they must make good judgments about recommended medical treatment for themselves and their fetuses.[8]

This list demonstrates how entwined fetal interests are with women's lives and at how many points those interests might diverge. Furthermore, the more thoroughgoing our understanding of the process of pregnancy and the bolder our technology, the more acute the potential conflicts.

The existence of such conflict is denied by many of those who are thinking about the problem. Some writers conflate fetuses and children, unable to see any morally relevant differences between them: they seem oblivious to the fact that fetuses live in women's bodies. The implications of that fact are therefore ignored or dismissed.[9] They fail to recognize that women's rights might sometimes trump considerations about fetal welfare.

---

[7] For a more detailed look at fetal hazards, see Margery W. Shaw, "Conditional Prospective Rights of the Fetus," *The Journal of Legal Medicine* 5, no. 1 (March 1984): 63–116.

[8] For a fuller description of the effects on women of recognizing fetal rights, see John Robertson, "The Right to Procreate and in Utero Fetal Therapy," *The Journal of Legal Medicine* 3, no. 3 (1982): 355.

[9] Among the writers who appear to be unaware of the implications of their recommendations, see Margery W. Shaw and E. W. Keyserlingk, "A Right of the Unborn Child to Prenatal Care—The Civil Law Perspective," *Revue de Droit* 13 (Winter 1982): 49–90. For others who dismiss women's rights to bodily integrity and determination, see Eike-Henner W. Kluge, "When Caesarean Section Operations Imposed by a Court are Justified," *Journal of Medical Ethics* 14 (1988): 206–11; Jeffrey Parness, "The Abuse and Neglect of the Human Unborn: Protecting Potential Life," *Family Law Quarterly* 20 (1986): 197–212, and "The Duty to Prevent Handicaps: Laws Promoting the Prevention of Handicaps to Newborns," *Western New England Law Review* 5 (1983): 431–64; Robertson, "The Right to Procreate"; and Michael A. Shakey, "Criminal Liability of a Prospective Mother for Prenatal Neglect of Viable Fetus," *Whittier Law Review* 9 (Summer 1987): 363–91.

We should not forget that the sacrifices exacted by a well-run pregnancy may be considerable; they deserve recognition and perhaps even compensation; some may be too great to require at all. Foregoing small pleasures like an occasional drink is just the beginning. Imagine a bad cold, let alone more serious illness, without pain relief. Imagine, too, foregoing the therapy that will cure your disease, or being denied, as was Angela Carder, the only drugs that may prolong your life. What is it like to be a cocaine addict voluntarily—or involuntarily—going cold turkey? Imagine losing a good job because it endangers your fetus. Imagine knowing that you need unavailable prenatal care or that its lack increases the probability that you will need dangerous treatment. Picture being required to undergo risky therapy for the sole benefit of another. Our anger rightly flares in response to those who take these situations for granted.

Yet it seems to me that those in the opposing camp are not altogether free of the same tendency to deny the reality of conflict or dismiss rather too quickly fetuses' interests.

Barbara Katz Rothman, for instance, writes that

> The perception of the fetus as a person separate from the mother draws its roots from patriarchal ideology, and can be documented at least as far back as the early use of the microscope to see the homunculus. But until recently, the effects of this ideology on the management of pregnancy could only be indirect. For all practical purposes, the mother and fetus had to be treated as one unit while the fetus lay hidden inside the mother.[10]

She goes on to argue that medical technology emphasizes and makes concrete patriarchal notions about the relationship between woman and fetus. Woman and fetus are seen as conceptually separate, joined only by an unimportant physical bond. A woman-centered view of pregnancy is, on the contrary, holistic: "the baby [is] not planted within the mother, but flesh of her flesh, part of her."[11] In consequence, the vision of warring interests and rights collapses.

What takes its place? Rothman suggests an analogy between persons at various ages and the relationship between woman and fetus: "our old selves, our aging selves, are part of our young selves, and yet become someone very different. Can I in my old age come to sue myself for behavior I engaged in when younger?"[12]

---

[10] Barbara Katz Rothman, *Recreating Motherhood: Ideology and Technology in a Patriarchal Society* (New York: Norton, 1989), p. 157.
[11] Ibid., p. 161.
[12] Ibid.

Now it may well be true that a patriarchal lens colors our view of pregnancy, obscuring the fact that fetuses are part of women's bodies. However, it does not follow that diverse interests cannot coexist in one bit of flesh. Consider Siamese twins: the surgery necessary to separate them may mutilate or kill one or both. Do we really want to say that the loss is an illusion, that there can be no conflict of interest here?

Likewise, it is undeniable that decisions a woman makes now may affect the child she later bears. Where she chooses—perhaps for good reason—to ignore physicians' recommendations, any resulting baby will share the consequences with her. A choice that is good for her may harm her fetus; one person enjoys a benefit whereas the other (eventually) bears a burden. Just societies attempt to minimize such situations.

This contrasts with Rothman's image of the self. We may feel less or more connected with our earlier selves throughout life, but we are nonetheless one person. If we are lucky, others cared enough to help us temper our youthful exuberance and rebellion with some attention to long-term consequences. To the extent that we did not, we may now be paying the costs of long-gone pleasures. But the pleasures—even if we now regret them—were *ours*, not someone else's. A woman might enjoy her nightly beer, but it is not she who reaps fetal alcohol syndrome. So the fact of being one flesh now does not preclude two different fates.[13]

Christine Overall attempts to diminish the impact of this conclusion by arguing that maternal and fetal interests tend to be in harmony: what is good for the one is also good for the other. This may often be true, but it does not help us when women, for whatever reason, fail to act in their own interest or when those interests truly diverge.[14]

THE SOCIAL CONTEXT OF CONFLICT

How can we begin to sort out the moral problems created by this situation? Surely we should start with the assumption that women have at least the same basic rights as other people. Universalizability requires that to the extent situations are parallel, women's interests should garner the same degree of respect as anybody else's. Where treatment diverges, it must be possible to point to a morally relevant difference in the situation. And the connection between that difference and the treatment must be tightly ar-

[13] I come to this conclusion with great regret, given Mary Anne Warren's attractive proposal that *"there is room for only one person with full and equal rights inside a single human skin."* "The Moral Significance of Birth," in *Feminist Perspectives in Medical Ethics,* Helen B. Holmes and Laura M. Purdy, eds. (Bloomington: Indiana University Press, 1992), p. 213.
[14] Christine Overall, *Ethics and Human Reproduction* (Boston: Allen & Unwin, 1987), pp. 99–100.

gued and show the same respect for women as middle-class white men would expect.

The question before us is a special case of the most general moral question: what do we owe others? More particularly, what do we owe others who do not yet exist? And, most particularly, what legally enforceable duties toward such future persons can be exacted of us?

Several different levels of obligation are recognized, depending on the nature of the relationship between the individuals in question. Various types of agreements (marriage, for instance), as well as biological relationships (such as parenthood) raise our expectations of what is morally owed; the law tends to reflect this understanding.

The closest analogy to the relationship between woman and fetus is the one between relatives. It is therefore more than a little interesting that a court refused to order involuntary bone marrow surgery on Shimp in order to increase the probability of his leukemic cousin McFall's survival.[15]

Perhaps the proper rejoinder is that Shimp and McFall were merely cousins—surely the closer relationship between woman and fetus can justify greater demands on the former. But, as Kolder, Gallagher, and Parsons argue, "the closest legal analogy would be an organ 'donation' ordered over the explicit refusal of a competent adult, and such an order would be profoundly at odds with our legal tradition."[16] George Annas notes that "no mother has ever been legally required to undergo surgery or general anesthesia (e.g., bone marrow or kidney transplant) to save the life of her dying child. It would be ironic, to say the least, if she could be forced to submit to more invasive surgical procedures for the sake of her fetus than for her child."[17]

Annas assumes that a woman's duty toward her fetus must be no more demanding—in fact, less so—than a parent's duty toward her child. Fetuses, after all, are not yet persons, and the call of persons on us is stronger than that of nonpersons. Those who insist that women owe their fetuses at least the equivalent of transplants, are, on the contrary, assuming that women owe their fetuses *more* than their children.

Pregnancy is, of course, unlike any other relationship in human experience: analogies go only so far, and then we venture on to new territory. The

---

[15] See Nancy K. Rhoden, "The Judge in the Delivery Room: The Emergence of Court-Ordered Cesareans," *California Law Review* 74, no. 6 (1986): 1977.

[16] Veronika E. B. Kolder, Janet Gallagher, and Michael T. Parsons, "Court-Ordered Obstetrical Interventions," *The New England Journal of Medicine* 316, no. 19 (May 7, 1987): 1194.

[17] George J. Annas, "Forced Cesareans: The Most Unkindest Cut of All," *Hastings Center Report* (June 1982): 17. Rhoden offers an interesting analogy for our consideration: suppose a "recalcitrant father were very obese and securely wedged in the door, and gaining access to the sick child to provide treatment required cutting through the father." "The Judge in the Delivery Room," p. 1968.

uniquely close relationship between woman and fetus has been taken to have serious moral implications. Those who are prepared to subordinate the welfare of women to that of their fetuses see this close relationship as justification for demands on women that exceed those required for children. However, proponents of this view don't seem to feel the need for argument showing just how and why this is the case; nor do they address the question of limits.

That this uniquely close relationship has compelling moral consequences is also taken for granted by those who think it justifies women's overriding say about their fetuses. But the case is little more developed than the previous one.

This as-yet-undefined characteristic that takes reasoning about pregnancy out of the realm of the relatively settled assumptions about parents and children seems to me to be disturbingly amorphous. Perhaps that is why we are seeing such contradictory implications drawn from it. Future research may help us to see the matter more clearly, but for now I think it would be a good deal safer to retreat to better explored ground.

The following points seem to me to be relevant to our discussion. First, dependence is a pervasive characteristic of human society. Second, because of their location and state, fetuses are dependent on women in an unusually fundamental and continuous way. Third, fetuses are not moral persons. Fourth, they will probably become such persons some time after birth.

I take it that we have a moral duty to take some steps to meet the needs of those who are dependent on us. I also take it that the morally relevant feature of pregnancy is not that fetuses are not now moral persons, but that they will be affected after birth by what happens now. So I think that Annas is wrong to assume that women might owe fetuses less than children here because they are not persons. But I think that there are no grounds for holding that woman owe them more than children, either.

If we ought to try to prevent disease or handicap in our children, the same duty holds for our fetuses, even if they are not yet persons. To achieve that end, no more and no less sacrifice ought to be legally expected of us in the two cases. Thus if parents are not required to submit to bodily invasions to save a dying child, then a woman should not be expected to do so for the benefit of a fetus; the converse is also true.

Personhood becomes relevant only where preventing death is at issue. Because fetuses are not persons, it may be morally permissible to abort them. This means that a woman could avoid some demands by aborting her fetus, whereas she cannot kill a child. In this way, pregnancy requires less of her than parenthood.

Other factors may also help us to differentiate between pregnancy and parenthood. One is that the fetus's probability of survival to personhood is somewhat lower. Another is that in some cases we are much less certain of how a fetus will be affected by a given state of affairs. This uncertainty increases the burden of proof on those who would override a pregnant woman's decision about what to do.

Given the foregoing, if judges refuse to order bodily invasions of parents for their children's benefit, they certainly should not be ordering them of women for their fetus's benefit. And they are refusing to order such invasions of parents. Consider, for instance, *In re George*, a case where a leukemic adoptee wanted access to his adoption records in order to see whether he could find a good bone marrow donor. The judge contacted his father, who was unwilling either to acknowledge paternity or be tested for compatibility. The judge would not even give the petitioner his father's name.[18] It should also be noted that the invasions so far contemplated (and denied) by the courts have been of substantially lesser magnitude then the caesareans now being ordered for women.

Not only are the orders legally inconsistent with precedent, but also the manner of their making violates established procedures. Despite a general legal trend toward increased respect for our right to determine what shall happen to us and our bodies, women are deprived of the safeguards routinely afforded the unconscious, criminals, and individuals with mental problems. Indeed, "court-ordered medical treatment—even of the incompetent or of those whose legal rights are limited—is imposed only after detailed fact finding conducted through full adversarial hearings with scrupulous attention to procedural rights."[19] The reference to incompetents is not inapposite, as some cases overriding competent women's decisions rely for precedent on those where she is judged incompetent, suggesting that pregnancy renders women incompetent or constitutes a waiver of autonomy.[20] Yet proposed surgical searches of criminal defendants, sterilization of the mentally retarded, or even mind-altering drug therapy for mental patients are supposed to be conducted only after a full legal hearing.[21]

These violations tend to be protected from appellate review because the case is moot or because the losing party is unable or unwilling to pursue such a remedy. Moreover, the time constraints on cases of this kind limit the potential for amicus briefs filed by outside experts. These factors, Gallagher contends, have serious repercussions on the resulting law: "the procedural shortcomings rampant in these cases are not mere technical deficiencies. They undermine the authority of the decisions themselves, posing serious

[18] Rhoden, "The Judge in the Delivery Room," p. 1978.
[19] Gallagher, "Prenatal Invasions," p. 20.
[20] Ibid., p. 37. See also Rosalind Ekman Ladd, "Women in Labor: Some Issues About Informed Consent," in *Feminist Perspectives in Medical Ethics*, ed. Holmes and Purdy.
[21] Ibid., p. 20.

questions as to whether judges can, in the absence of genuine notice, adequate representation, explicit standards of proof, and right of appeal, realistically frame principled and useful legal responses to the dilemmas with which they are being confronted."[22]

George Annas elaborates on the inadequate social context of such emergency decision making, arguing that

> In the vast majority of cases, judges were called on an emergency basis and ordered interventions within hours. The judge usually went to the hospital. Physicians should know what most lawyers and almost all judges know: When a judge arrives at a hospital in response to an emergency call, he or she is acting much more like a lay person than a jurist. Without time to analyze the issues, without representation for the pregnant woman, without briefing or thoughtful reflection on the situation, in almost total ignorance of the relevant law, and in an unfamiliar setting faced by a relatively calm physician and a woman who can easily be labelled "hysterical," the judge will almost always order whatever the physician advises.[23]

These procedures might help to explain why of the twenty-one cases where involuntary treatment orders had been sought as of May 1987, orders were successfully obtained in 86 percent of the cases and were received within six hours in 88 percent of them. That especially powerless women are at risk is suggested by the additional fact that 81 percent of the women were black, Asian, or Hispanic.[24]

The casual nature of these decision procedures, as well as the gravity of the intrusion, differentiates these cases from others cited by Robertson in their defense.[25] Overturning an adult's decision about a matter affecting her own body legally requires physicians to "meet an exacting standard of proof: establishing both the necessity of the procedure and the fact that no less drastic means are available. Their burden increases with the degree of invasiveness, risk, or indignity involved."[26] Even cursory scrutiny of existing cases suggests that physicians' decisions are not subjected to even the most minimally demanding version of this charge.

Until medicine becomes less of an art and more of a science, it is not clear whether it is possible even in principle to meet that standard of proof. Disagreements about the best way to handle many situations abound. For ex-

[22] Ibid., p. 49.
[23] George J. Annas, "Protecting the Liberty of Pregnant Patients," *New England Journal of Medicine* 316, no. 19 (May 7, 1987): 1213.
[24] Kolder, Gallagher, and Parsons, "Court Ordered Obstetrical Interventions," p. 1193.
[25] Robertson, "The Right to Procreate," pp. 353–54.
[26] Gallagher, "Prenatal Invasions," pp. 20–21.

ample, there is serious debate about whether caesareans are indicated when a woman is pregnant with triplets.[27] it is also well-known that caesarean rates generally vary widely, suggesting that decisions to cut are influenced by nonmedical factors.[28]

Even where there is broad agreement about the necessity for treatment, judgments are not certain. For example, a condition known as "placenta previa," where the placenta blocks the exit of the uterus, is widely considered a clear indication for a caesarean section. However, although ultrasonography is usually accurate in diagnosing this condition, it is not foolproof: less dangerous partial cases may be difficult to distinguish from complete ones. Furthermore, the placenta can move before delivery.[29] In fact, despite dire predictions for both woman and baby, a substantial percentage of the women for whom caesareans were ordered subsequently gave birth to healthy babies without surgery. Thus, of the cases surveyed by Kolder, Gallagher, and Parsons, there were fifteen court orders for caesareans; in two of those cases the patient agreed in the end to have the operation; yet in six other cases, vaginal birth proved harmless.[30] Yet this reality has not prevented a judge from ordering "that if the pregnant woman did not admit herself to the hospital by a specified time and date, she would be picked up and transported there by the police and would have to submit to 'whatever the medical personnel deemed appropriate, including caesarean section and medication.' "[31]

In general, the widely varying opinions about treatment and the unreliable nature of the technologies, such as fetal monitoring, on which those criteria for action are based appropriately give rise to considerable skepticism about physician recommendations. It is well-known, for example, that fetal monitoring yields ambiguous results and there is much disagreement about its interpretation. Worse still, the Apgar scores used to rate fetal monitoring are themselves plagued by false positives, so that large numbers of children with low scores later do well. Even if such monitoring were accurate, however, many false positives would occur because of the special problems involved in screening for rare conditions. Many such practices, including

---

[27] Ibid., p. 9. This information comes from Veronika E. B. Kolder, *Women's Health Law: A Feminist Perspective*, August 1–2, 1985, unpublished manuscript on file at the *Harvard Women's Law Journal*.

[28] Gallagher, "Prenatal Invasions," pp. 50–51.

[29] Rhoden discusses this problem and others, "The Judge in the Delivery Room," pp. 2011–17.

[30] Kolder, Gallagher, and Parsons, "Court-Ordered Obstetrical Interventions," pp. 1193, 1195.

[31] Gallagher, "Prenatal Invasions," p. 47. In this particular case, the woman fled into hiding with her entire family and two weeks later gave birth normally to a healthy, nine-pound, two-ounce baby. This matter of caesareans is far from trivial.

keeping women prone during labor, have a tendency to precipitate the need for further intervention.[32] It is not just ignorance, but education, that might cause a woman to think twice about doing as her doctor orders.

Another important related issue is that many decisions made by physicians are value judgments, not medical decisions at all. For example, Rhoden notes that physicians' approach to risk may not be the only reasonable one. Thus American obstetricians tend to adopt a maximin approach that "focuses on the worst possible outcome in a situation of uncertainty (here, fetal death or damage), and takes action to prevent that outcome, regardless of the outcome's actual probability of occurrence."[33] Not only is this strategy not the only reasonable one, but also the judgment that fetal death is the worst possible outcome is a moral judgment, not a medical one: we might prefer the conclusion that the worst outcome is maternal morbidity or mortality. The problem is exacerbated by the fact that most doctors have little or no training in moral reasoning, and even if they do, we may not

---

An interesting sidelight on the safety of caesareans is provided by a nineteenth-century medical historian who comments that a "pregnant woman in labour had a 50 percent chance of survival post-caesarean if she performed her own surgery, or if gored by a bull, compared to a 10 percent reported survival rate if attended to by a New York surgeon" (cited by Rhoden, "The Judge in the Delivery Room," p. 1955, n. 22).

This historical tidbit is now outdated, but the risks of caesareans compared to natural childbirth remain considerable. Gallagher cites figures showing that the operation still involves a much higher risk of the woman's death: it is from three to thirty times the rate associated with vaginal delivery. Furthermore, all the subjects had much more pain, weakness, and difficulty holding and caring for their new babies. The latter would support studies that suggest that caesareans make it more difficult for mother and baby to bond. Many more women also get sick—10 to 65 percent of the women developed infections like intrauterine cystitis, peritonitis, abscess, gangrene, sepsis, urinary tract infections, and respiratory infections; women delivering normally experience five to ten times less infection (Gallagher, "Prenatal Invasions," p. 50, nn. 210–213). Among its risks, a caesarean apparently sextuples the risk of developing placenta previa in subsequent pregnancies (Rhoden, "The Judge in the Delivery Room," p. 1958, n. 51).

Caesarean delivery is not completely unproblematic for babies either. Apart from the aforementioned consequences of possible difficult bonding, they are more at risk physically, too. Gallagher cites a National Institutes of Health Caesarean Birth Task Force report that stated that the most serious worry is respiratory distress, especially when previous caesareans render a new, earlier operation necessary. It may be that vaginal delivery performs a helpful function by compressing the lungs ("Prenatal Invasions," p. 50, nn. 212, 213).

Gallagher argues that decreased rates of perinatal mortality cannot necessarily be attributed to the increasing rate of caesareans. She quotes Dr. Helen Marieskind who lists more plausible contributing factors such as improved sanitation and nutrition, increased access to health care, and use of contraception and abortion (p. 50).

[32] Rhoden, "The Judge in the Delivery Room," pp. 2011–17; Gallagher, "Prenatal Invasions," p. 51.

[33] Rhoden, "The Judge in the Delivery Room," p. 2017. She gives several specific examples of such strategies.

share their values. In any case, the medical establishment's track record on women's interests is mixed at best.

Finally, this analysis has so far assumed that the overall social context is just. This is not true: unfair assumptions about women and their importance are embedded in judgments about what actions constitute "least restrictive alternatives" and "least drastic intrusions" required for overriding principles about bodily integrity and privacy and blind us to alternatives.

Take, for instance, the question of medical care. First, a narrow case: studies show that birthing women monitored by nurses with stethoscopes and those monitored with fetal monitors had equally healthy babies, although the former had fewer caesareans.[34] Hence such human monitoring ought to be required where we otherwise risk invading women's bodies—even if it costs more.

More generally, perinatal mortality is most commonly caused by prematurity.[35] Prematurity is well-known to be strongly associated with poor prenatal care. Yet, 23 percent of pregnant women received late or no prenatal care in 1982. Such women, writes Lee Schott, "are three times more likely to have babies with low birth weight, the single most important contributor to infant mortality. Low birthweight babies are also susceptible to a host of medical problems and disabilities."[36] Poverty, lack of education, minority status, and geographical location are serious barriers to such care. For instance, according to Schott, it now costs in the United States of America an average of $5,000 to have a child. This amount may be more than a family without health insurance can pay. In 1978 twenty-six million Americans did not have insurance; in 1984, thirty-seven million did not have it, an increase of more than 30 percent. This means that some 36 percent of the women of childbearing age do not have insurance.[37]

Current medical welfare programs are not always sufficient to guarantee adequate care. Poor and minority women face special obstacles: they may have difficulty getting time off work, paying for childcare, arranging transportation to a clinic; they may also be subjected to indignities and outrages such as involuntary sterilization once there. As federal funds are repeatedly cut, care may become completely unavailable. By 1985, the percentage of poor people receiving Medicaid had dropped to 46 percent, down from 66 percent in 1975. Even if a woman has Medicaid, however, she is by no means guaranteed care: in some areas there are no obstetrics physicians who accept Medicaid patients; overall, only 56 percent of such physicians do so.[38]

---

[34] See Rothman, *Recreating Motherhood,* pp. 157–58.
[35] Rhoden, "The Judge in the Delivery Room," p. 2013.
[36] Lee A. Schott, "The Pamela Rae Stewart Case and Fetal Harm: Prosecution or Prevention?," *Harvard Women's Law Journal* 11 (1988): 241–42.
[37] Ibid., p. 242.
[38] Ibid., pp. 242–43.

Under these circumstances, invading women's bodies to impose last-minute, heroic care is stupid, mean, and unfair. It is reminiscent of proposals to dose us with contraceptives to lower the birth rate, before eradicating the pronatalist pressures and occupational discrimination that contribute significantly to overpopulation in the first place. Until we as a society act to make good, inexpensive, convenient, and respectful care a priority, punishing women for lack of prenatal care reeks of hypocrisy. It is especially inappropriate in a society where no one is required to provide the poor with care if they lack funds. Consequently, a woman may be denied life-saving treatment, yet later be subjected to life-threatening risk to attempt to save her fetus.[39] This state of affairs is all the more angering because it is cheaper to furnish good prenatal care than caesareans, jail, neonatal intensive care, or lifetime care for damaged babies. According to Schott, full prenatal care costs about $600 per patient; the cost of neonatal intensive care for a low-birthweight baby costs about $10,000 to $15,000.[40] Such care can, of course, cost vastly more, and these figures, in any case, take into account neither lifetime costs of disability nor pain and suffering.

Toxic exposures in the workplace raise similar considerations. Many women of childbearing age are now exposed to dangerous substances. Should they all be required to remove themselves from these environments, even at the cost of losing their job? Most women work because they must, and a well-paying safe job may be hard to find; many jobs are in any case inaccessible to the poor and uneducated. Eradicating discrimination against women in general and recognizing the special contribution and needs of pregnant women would relieve them of these difficult choices.

This particular problem would also disappear if employers were required to clean up workplaces. Some employers object that the expense of doing so is prohibitive. But then they are just passing on the cost of doing safe business to women, who are among those members of society least able to bear it as they earn the least. The dilemma facing women is therefore not inevitable: it is caused by employers' desire to save money and society's willingness to let them do so at women's expense. Alleged concern about fetuses rings hollow when people attempt to pass the entire burden of protecting them on to women.[41] Such "concern" is especially suspect when it keeps women from only high-paying jobs, not the traditionally feminine ones that may well pose equally serious risks. Lack of interest in possible damage to sperm simply reinforces this suspicion.

---

[39] See George J. Annas, "AIDS, Judges, and the Right to Medical Care," *Hastings Center Report* 18, no. 4 (August–September 1988): 21.

[40] Schott, "The Pamela Rae Stewart Case," p. 242.

[41] Of course, if women are impoverished by these policies, fetuses will ultimately also suffer.

The focus on getting women out of certain workplaces is especially odd when we discover that there have been no lawsuits by children with birth defects caused by occupational exposures of their parents. Furthermore, there are good reasons for believing that none are likely to be successful:

Scientifically conclusive evidence that a particular workplace exposure caused or contributed to an injury is rare . . . a court of law or a worker's compensation board may be unwilling to rely solely, or even substantially, on the results of epidemiologic or toxicologic investigations to support claims for compensation. . . . Therefore, for the most part, reproductively damaged workers have very limited access to redress against their employers through the courts.[42]

Odder still is the fact that, so far, more men than women have filed legal charges of reproductive damage caused by occupational exposures.[43] Environmental pollution raises similar issues.

Some environmental exposures arise from personal habits. Like men, women drink, smoke, and take drugs. It is now obvious that these substances affect fetuses. Disease and serious handicap are among the consequences for babies.[44] Shielding them from these substances is therefore highly desirable. What about the pregnant women who use them? Nonaddicted women can reasonably be expected to stop if they are pregnant or trying to get pregnant, although the moral basis for such responsibility is shaky while corporations still spew dangerous pollutants into the air.[45] However, at present we depend mostly on moral exhortation, backed up with coercion. This approach is notoriously ineffective, yet society is unwilling to make the changes that would help people to reduce their reliance on such crutches and find alternative pleasures that are less harmful. Steps could be taken to lessen the likelihood that young women (and men) would adopt these habits in the first place. How about banning the cigarette and alcohol advertising that helps to ensnare them? And, instead of subsidizing tobacco growers, the government could help to fund wholesome alternative sources of fun, such as swimming pools, ski camps, and cultural centers. This issue is symptomatic of the general reluctance to undertake

[42] Office of Technology Assessment, cited by Donna M. Randall, "Fetal Protection Policies: A Threat to Employee Rights?," *Employee Responsibilities and Rights Journal* 1, no. 2 (1988): 124.
[43] Ibid.
[44] See Marty Jessup and Robert Roth, "Clinical and Legal Perspectives on Prenatal Drug and Alcohol Use: Guidelines for Individual and Community Response," *Medicine and Law* 7, no. 4 (November 4, 1988): 377–89.
[45] See Gallagher, "Prenatal Invasions," pp. 56–57, n. 242.

fundamental reform that would help to eradicate problems at their root instead of punishing those caught in difficult situations. Schott demonstrates convincingly in her article on the Pamela Rae Stewart case that the apparently self-centered and callous behavior emphasized by the media can be shown to be reasonable in the circumstances; such circumstances could have been in large part prevented by better physician–patient communication and a more supportive society.

This point suggests the importance of raising some very basic questions about our society. Why is addiction growing? Why, in the eyes of so many, is being smashed or stoned a prerequisite for having a good time? I suspect that our social and political principles and arrangements have a great deal to do with what is happening. It seems that we have available to us relatively few sources of genuine pleasure and satisfaction. Furthermore, even those who are relatively well off are constantly enticed by goods they cannot have. Few of us have any real sense of economic security. Among industrialized countries, the United States is among the least developed in terms of social programs, and the growth of drug use in the 1980s coincides with reductions in those already inadequate programs; poverty is increasing. Furthermore, the philosophy of individualism, egoism, and self-sufficiency coupled with a system of hierarchy and privilege that for the most part excludes women and men of color is singularly hostile to human welfare. Austere and unsympathetic, this worldview prefers narrowly defined notions of freedom and justice to concerns about human happiness. It also tends to hold those on the bottom responsible for their acts, no matter how difficult the circumstances, and prefers punishment to making social and political arrangements that help people to act morally in the first place. Consider, for example, the dearth of drug treatment programs for pregnant women: there are six-month waiting lists for the few clinics that accept them in California.[46] Given the powerful grip drugs can have on people, how can we justifiably punish such women for not quitting when they get so little help?

If there is any truth in these speculations, then we are going to be faced with a choice between increasingly harsh and inequitable treatment of women or fundamental social change. The general social bias against fair consideration of women's interests already evident in much of medicine is likely, in the absence of such change, to lead to further high-handed treatment if contemporary trends continue. For example, physicians did an involuntary caesarean on a woman *without* seeking a court order in 1984.[47] That same year a hospital sought and got a court order granting it tempo-

---

[46] *Time*, May 22, 1989, p. 105.
[47] Gallagher, "Prenatal Invasions," p. 46.

rary custody of a Nigerian woman's triplet fetuses and authorization of a caesarean section against her will. Yet the woman had not even been informed of the court order.[48]

Taken to their logical conclusion, current attitudes and practices could lead to still more fundamental subordination of women in the interests (or alleged interests) of others. Schott suggests that:

> for a pregnant woman, the existence of a fetal harm law would make nearly every action potentially criminal. Her day-to-day movements, diet, sexual practices, recreation and other activities would be subjected to the exacting and suspicious scrutiny of doctors, the public and possibly a jury. A woman might find it difficult to explain the forces influencing her actions, and to convince a jury that she was not motivated by hostility to her fetus.[49]

These developments would broadcast a clear message about the relative weight of pregnant women's interests in comparison with those of fetuses. Peeping out from under such judgments would be the assumption that women in general are self-centered, thoughtless individuals who cannot be expected to behave morally.[50]

These possibilities are less far-fetched than they might seem at first blush. When Kolder et al. examined the attitudes of heads of fellowship programs in maternal-fetal medicine they discovered the following statistics. First, in a sample of 57, 46 percent thought that women who endanger a fetus by refusing medical advice should be held against their will "so that compliance could be ensured." Second, 47 percent wanted additional potentially lifesaving procedures ordered by courts if women refuse them. Last, but not least, 26 percent "advocated state surveillance of women in the third trimester who stay outside the hospital system." Because of erratic patterns of answers, only 24 percent consistently supported women's right to refuse medical advice.[51] *The Handmaid's Tale* looms ever closer!

In conclusion, court orders violating a woman's decisions about her own care are dubious at best. Both the procedures leading to the orders and the orders themselves constitute and perpetuate a legal double standard for pregnant women. The facts on which these decisions are based are less certain than they seem, and the nonmedical judgments involved are, at best, ones about which reasonable people might disagree; at worst, they are biased against women. All of this constitutes another proof that women are

[48] Ibid., p. 9.
[49] Lee A. Schott, "The Pamela Rae Stewart Case," p. 239.
[50] Ibid., p. 239.
[51] Kolder, Gallagher, and Parsons, "Court-Ordered Obstetrical Interventions," pp. 1193–94.

still second-class citizens who are tacitly excluded from supposedly universal rights whenever convenient. Americans have more say over what will happen to their bodies after death than many women do over their bodies while they are alive. Yet, as Rhoden points out, "by way of comparison, an organ taken from a cadaver can save a life just as an emergency caesarean can."[52]

Hence it is seriously unjust to subject women to the kinds of treatment lately visited on them. Although women in difficult circumstances have a moral duty to do what they can for their fetuses, society ought not to hold them responsible for situations that are in large part due to its own moral inadequacies. It is especially dubious for society to do so when it shows so little concern for the well-being of existing children.[53]

I do not say any of this lightly: I have argued elsewhere—and still believe—that it is seriously wrong knowingly to bring a diseased or handicapped child into the world.[54] Other things being equal, I think that a woman's right to control her body can in some cases be less morally compelling than her child's interest in not going through life with major damage.

Should this moral state of affairs ever be reflected in a legal duty to submit to medical coercion or punishment for having refused to follow medical advice? Recognizing any limit on women's right to control their bodies would be cause for considerable anxiety. A good deal of our current social and political edifice appears to have been constructed on the premise that even the most vital of women's interests deserve little consideration. Thus for example, it is still far from clear that all are persuaded that marital prerogative or privacy do not justify wife beating or rape. The research for this paper was eye-opening with respect to the contempt with which some of women's most basic interests can be treated. Because women's interests are in constant danger of being undervalued, I believe that in cases of conflict our inclination should be to grant them priority. It would follow from this that no legal duty to submit to medical advice should be recognized.

Suppose, though, that we manage to create a humane and fair society, one where women's interests are fully recognized, where discrimination based on race, class, sexual orientation, and the like are eradicated and much greater concern for human welfare informs social and political arrangements.

We might want to consider expecting more of each other, both morally and legally. One form such expectations might take would be to assume

---

[52] Rhoden, "The Judge in the Delivery Room," p. 1982.
[53] I am indebted to Joan Callahan for reminding me of this point.
[54] See Purdy, "Genetic Diseases: Can Having Children Be Immoral?," in *Genetics Now*, ed. John L. Buckley (Washington, D.C.: University Press of America, 1978).

that people should be willing to sacrifice expendable parts of their bodies (bone marrow, paired organs) to save the lives of others. A still more demanding expectation would be that people make such sacrifices to prevent serious illness or handicap on the part of others. Although the first of these would not affect pregnant women especially because fetuses are not persons, the second would have a disproportionate impact on such women, despite the fact that for all the reasons suggested in this article, a humane world would invite many fewer conflicts of interest between women and their fetuses.

Perhaps for this, or some other reason, we would reject the prospect of enforcing such expectations legally; perhaps medical science will advance sufficiently to render the point moot. If not, might we then have to countenance the possibility of a legal duty on women's part to submit to medical care? As many commentators have noticed, a duty of this kind might be counterproductive, leading women to avoid the medical establishment altogether. In that case, only extreme and unacceptable invasions of our civil liberties could then guarantee women's compliance.[55] Women might also maintain control of their bodies by being willing to see seriously damaged newborns die or be killed.

A more caring society would be very desirable: its coming should be encouraged by all those who are dissatisfied with the chill of the classical liberal approach to relationships. It is time for thinking about what forms such caring might reasonably take, together with their implications for our contemporary values. In the meantime, the contrast between this vision and our current world should be enough to fuel the fight against the invasions of women's bodies now occurring.

[55] Thanks to Mary Anne Warren for this point.

PART II

ABORTION AND THE RIGHT

NOT TO REPRODUCE

The right to reproduce has generally been considered relatively unproblematic, although as we have seen, it deserves far more analysis than it has yet received. Because the right to reproduce is a right that one may exercise or not, as one pleases, rather than a duty that must be satisfied, it implies a corollary right *not* to reproduce.

However, pronatalism is common in human cultures, and as yet, most fail to recognize a firm right not to reproduce. Although there seems to be reason for believing that effective contraceptives and abortifacients have been available before the twentieth century, it is only relatively recently that safe and effective techniques have become widely available to those who wish to avoid the birth of a child. Unfortunately, even in developed Western countries, birth control measures are still inaccessible to many persons. In other nations, access is still limited by poverty, culture, government, or religion.

In the United States, any reasonably well-educated and determined individual can get access to contraception; ignorance, fear, or poverty can pose almost insurmountable obstacles. The same factors can make it difficult or impossible to obtain an abortion. Access to both contraception and abortion became significantly more difficult during the 1980s, as the Reagan and Bush administrations tried to impress on the nation a sexual morality that advocated chastity except in marriage when a child was desired, together with a return to well-defined sex roles. It seems doubtful that this message reduced the amount of sexual intercourse, but it did undoubtedly create ambivalence about contraception and abortion, especially among the poor and uneducated.

The rhetoric supporting this policy has abated, and the Clinton administration has taken measures to increase access to contraception and abortion. However, both psychological and physical access will again be at risk if another extremist Republican administration wins the 1996 presidential election or if the currently Republican-dominated Congress has its way. It therefore remains important to continue to discuss the right not to reproduce.

Despite continued opposition from the Catholic Church to contraception, it did not occur to me until the early 1980s, when I started seeing comments such as "Birth control is moral insanity!" reported in the newspaper, that it would be a good idea to add contraception to the list of topics covered in my course on ethics. The only coherent literature I could find was Catholic, however, and my students kept pulling the rug out from our analysis of *Humanae Vitae* by telling the class that their priest had told them they should just follow their conscience about contraception. So the sessions on contraception had a hard time getting off the ground. The same thing kept happening in Philosophy of Law, as my students ran roughshod over the arguments opposing free access to contraception and abortion in the run of Supreme Court cases that gradually cleared the way for a universal, negative right to obtain and use contraception and to *Roe v. Wade*.

Given the widespread popular acceptance of the right to use contraception, do any substantial moral questions remain? It seems to me that all those I can think of are, in fact, relatively peripheral. Some, such as the development and testing of new techniques, involve the ethics of experimentation. Others, such as the coerced sterilization and the potential use of Norplant as a penal instrument, involve primarily the right to reproduce. Still others, such as the failure to develop truly effective, safe, comfortable, convenient, and inexpensive methods implicate the market mechanisms that drive the health care establishment in the United States.

However, abortion, despite the prospect of a relatively private abortion pill (RU486), is still a devastatingly divisive issue in the United States. All of the essays in this section focus on some element of the abortion debate. Chapter 5, "Is Abortion Murder?" (with Michael Tooley) was first published in 1974 and provides a utilitarian analysis of abortion. Chapter 6, "Abortion, Potentiality, and Conferred Claims: A Response to Langerak," takes on one version of the ubiquitous argument that it is wrong to kill fetuses because they are potentially moral persons with a right to life. In Chapter 7, "Abortion and the Argument from Convenience," I evaluate the claim that because most abortions are just a matter of convenience, they are unjustified. In Chapter 8, I argue that abortion is not just a matter of convenience. Finally, included is an article on the difficulties raised by the fact that two individuals create any pregnancy. Published in 1976, Chapter 9, "Abortion and the Husband's Rights: A Response to Theo," argues that a husband ought not to be able to veto a wife's abortion. Unfortunately, this matter is still very much a live issue, with opponents of abortion routinely adding such provisions to abortion bills in state legislatures.

Conspicuously missing from this group of papers on the moral aspects of abortion is any discussion of the vexed question of abortion funding. Because I see the right not to reproduce as so central to the well-being of women and children, it has never seemed to me that there were any substantial moral issues here worth investigating. The only objection to government-funded abortions for poor women appears to be that opponents of abortion do not think that they ought to have to pay for what they see as immoral purposes. I would have more sympathy with their complaint were they to press for the general principle that nobody should have to contribute tax dollars for purposes they judge immoral. After all, the bulk of my tax dollars probably go for endeavors that from my point of view range from the morally dubious to the morally despicable; but nobody is arguing for my right not to pay for them. Furthermore, as the pro-choice camp has been pointing out for years, alleged concern for fetuses rings hollow when accompanied by vetoes of the social programs that could provide the only hope the children those fetuses become of living anything like a decent life.

CHAPTER 5

Is Abortion Murder?

by Laura M. Purdy and Michael Tooley

This essay deals with the morality of abortion. We argue that abortion is morally unobjectionable and that society benefits if abortion is available on demand. We begin by setting out a preliminary case in support of the practice of abortion. Then we examine moral objections and show why these objections are unsound. We conclude by considering what properties something needs in order to have a serious right to life, and we show that a human fetus does not possess those properties. Thus because there is no moral objection to abortion, the practice must be viewed as both permissible and desirable, in the light of the advantages outlined in the first section of our article.

PRELIMINARY CONSIDERATIONS IN SUPPORT OF ABORTION

One way of approaching the abortion question is to envision two possible societies, one where strict anti-abortion laws are in force, the other where abortion is unrestricted. In imagining these two societies, we suppose that all other factors are the same, and that the societies otherwise resemble the United States in their social arrangements.

To flesh out these images, we must make some empirical assumptions, which philosophers are no more qualified to evaluate than is the ordinary educated individual, as it is not the main business of philosophy to ascertain facts. However, such assumptions cannot be avoided in moral and po-

From *Abortion: Pro and Con*, edited by Robert L. Perkins (Cambridge, Mass.: Schenkman Books, 1974). Reprinted here by permission of Michael Tooley and Schenkman Books, Inc.

litical philosophy, unless one is uninterested in the outcomes of various courses of action. There is room for disagreement on the issues discussed in this section for we depend on sciences that are as yet incomplete and on common sense. But although the accuracy of the following pictures is contingent on future investigation, the major features of the pictures seem plausible in the light of present knowledge and theory.

The first society is much like that which has existed in the United States up until the present, where abortion has been generally unavailable, either because of restrictive legislation or because of de facto unobtainability. The second society is very different. In it, abortion is freely available. We contend that, as a result, individuals in that society suffer less unhappiness than those in the first society.

Let us consider, in concrete terms, why this is the case. First of all, men and women in our second world can enjoy sex more, because anxiety regarding contraceptive failure will no longer exist. Moreover, pregnancies can be timed so that no child is neglected, reducing stress on all concerned. As a result, couples can plan on temporary or permanent childlessness when necessary or desirable to achieve life goals. In addition, if pregnancy threatens the health—either physical or mental—of the mother, or of other parties or unduly strains the marriage, it can be safely terminated. Last, and most important perhaps, illegal abortions, now a significant factor in the maternal death rate, can be replaced by legal abortions, thus saving the lives of very many women.

That abortion on demand would reduce frustration and unhappiness among the young is equally evident. When abortion is readily available, we can prevent the birth of babies who would otherwise enter the world with gross physical or mental abnormalities and who would face short and unhappy lives. We can also ensure that only wanted children will be born. Because parents who sincerely desire a child are more apt to provide for its physical, intellectual, and emotional needs, it is probable that children will be better cared for than at present. This change should be especially significant in light of our growing awareness of the problem of child abuse.

It also seems reasonable to believe that members of society who do not belong to families availing themselves of abortion will benefit. It is generally frustrated and unhappy individuals who turn to crime, violent or otherwise. Happy people, if not necessarily constructive citizens, are at least not destructive ones. Thus readily available abortions, by eliminating sources of frustration and unhappiness, should improve the social environment for everyone. Second, abortion, by making childbearing completely voluntary, will help to keep the population in check. The importance of this with respect to education and the environment, and thus the impact on the general quality of life, need not be labored.

It seems reasonable to conclude then, on the basis of our present knowledge, that the second society will be much happier than the first. At this point two questions arise. The first is empirical: "Is abortion on demand in fact the *best* way to satisfy the needs and desires of members of society? Might not some third type of society be superior to both of the possibilities we have so far considered, as measured in terms of the happiness of its members?" The second is moral: "Even if members of the second society are on the whole happier than members of the first, does it follow that the second society is morally preferable to the first? Are there not other factors that should be taken into account, such as the rights of the unborn, that tell in favor of the first society?"

We will consider the moral issues raised by the second question in the next two sections. Our discussion in this section will be confined to the first question.

The issue, then, is this. May there not be alternative social arrangements, not involving abortion, that would result in even greater happiness? Those who are wary of the practice of abortion on demand sometimes suggest that the same ends can be achieved as follows. First, society should ensure that everyone has access to safe and completely reliable methods of contraception. Second, there should be legislation to cope with the social welfare problems that are created or aggravated by unwanted or defective children.

This alternative presupposes the existence of a foolproof contraceptive that has no undesirable side effects. At present no such device exists. It is true that if a perfect method of contraception were developed, it would dissolve much of the abortion problem. However, at least two problems would remain. First, pregnancy, even though initially desired, sometimes has a serious negative effect on the mother or other people. We will still need abortion to handle cases of this sort. Second, some fetuses turn out to be grossly deformed or otherwise seriously defective. If abortion is not available, what is likely to happen to such defective children? Proper care is expensive, and if the societies we are envisaging do resemble the present-day United States, then we know that to do the job adequately will be thought to impose too great a sacrifice on parents and taxpayers. This fact cannot be swept under the rug; it must enter any realistic assessment of the available options. As the real alternative to abortion here, the defective person will face life in an uncaring environment, where physical needs will be only barely met, and where emotional needs will generally go unfulfilled. Only if drastic changes in social legislation were to occur would such individuals have the opportunity to lead a protected life and to develop fully their potentialities. Thus it is not possible to achieve, by contraception and social legislation, all of the benefits that can be realized by abortion.

We must now consider two important objections to our position. The first is that in evaluating the happiness of society, one should take into account the happiness of the fetus, and we have failed to do this.[1] We have considered only the happiness of other members of society, so that, even though abortion may increase the happiness of these other members, it certainly does not satisfy the fetus's desires and so contribute to its happiness.

Our response to this is that it is a mistake to attribute to a fetus a significant range of desires. A fetus may have a few very rudimentary desires, such as a desire not to feel pain, but it is incapable of having most of the desires that adult humans can have.

How can we support this claim that a fetus is capable of having only very elementary desires? Perhaps the place to start is by drawing a distinction between having a desire for some state and being programmed to act so as to increase the likelihood that the state in question will be attained. Thus, imagine a machine constructed so that when its batteries run down, it searches for an electrical outlet to recharge its batteries. The machine is programmed to behave in ways that tend to bring about certain states, but one could not literally speak of the machine having a *desire* to recharge its batteries. Similarly, imagine a more complex machine that can "recognize" certain situations as threats to its survival and take action that decreases the likelihood of its being destroyed. Even if such a machine were capable of a wide range of complex and effective survival behavior, it would not make sense to speak of it having a desire for continued existence. Moreover, all plant behavior and that of lower animals provide other examples in which there is complex programmed behavior directed toward some goal, but where the organism has no corresponding desire.

What, then, is required before one can attribute desires to something? Our view is that, first, it is not possible to attribute desires to something unless it is capable of *consciousness*. So if a machine is not conscious, one cannot attribute any desires to it, no matter how sophisticated its behavior. Second, the *specific* desires a thing can have are limited by the concepts it possesses. The justification for this claim is as follows. The fundamental way of describing a given desire is as a desire that a certain proposition be true.[2] But

---

[1] For the sake of brevity, we use the term *fetus* in an extended sense to refer to an organism in either the embryonic or fetal stage of development.

[2] In everyday life one often speaks of desiring things, such as an apple or a newspaper. Such talk is elliptical, the context together with one's ordinary beliefs serving to make it clear that one wants to eat the apple and read the newspaper. Thus if one wanted to provide a completely explicit description of an individual's desires, one would use sentences such as "John wants it to be the case that he is eating an apple in the next few minutes." This is why the fundamental way of describing a given desire is not as a desire for some object, but as a desire that a certain proposition be true.

one cannot desire that a certain proposition be true unless one understands it, and because one cannot understand it without possessing the concepts involved in it, it follows that the desires one can have are limited by the concepts one possesses.

A slightly different way of developing this point is this: if something is to have any desires at all, it must possess consciousness. But to have a specific desire it is not enough to be conscious and to be disposed to bring about certain states. The migration of birds, for example, enables them to achieve a certain end, and it certainly seems likely that they are to some extent conscious. Yet it is implausible to attribute to them a desire for those states that their migratory behavior makes possible. What is needed is a specific connection between consciousness and the goal toward which the behavior is directed. One speaks of a desire only where the organism is capable of recognizing that a behavior is directed toward certain ends: where the organism is incapable of being aware of the object of its behavior, one does not attribute the corresponding desire to it. To be aware of a certain state as the aim of one's behavior presupposes that one possesses concepts that can be employed to characterize that state.

Given this account of the conditions an organism must satisfy if it is to have desires, the justification for our claim that a fetus has at best extremely simple desires should be clear. In the early stages of the development of a human organism it has no mental life at all, that is, no consciousness, and hence no desires. At later stages, it is reasonable to think that the fetus has some sensations, but its mental life is still very limited. Thus if one compares, say, a human fetus with a chimpanzee fetus, there are no grounds for holding that the mental life of the former is significantly richer than that of the latter. This means that one should not attribute desires to a human fetus that one would be unwilling to attribute to a chimpanzee fetus. The upshot is that one cannot consistently object to abortion in the case of humans on the grounds that the destruction of the fetus violates some desires that the fetus has, unless one would also object to abortion in the case of chimpanzees.

Moreover, there seem to be no grounds for attributing complex desires to fetuses, human or otherwise. In particular, it seems absurd to attribute to any fetus a desire for continued existence, because to have such a desire it would have to have a conception of what it is to be a continuing subject of experiences and other mental states.

Are there any desires that a fetus has that might be violated by abortion? It appears reasonable to say that fetuses can feel pleasure and pain. Thus abortion might violate a fetus's desire to avoid pain. As it is certainly undesirable to inflict suffering upon any living organism, abortion should be carried out so as to inflict as little pain as possible on the fetus. If this is done, we do not think that the fetus has any desires that are violated by abortion.

To sum up, our response to the first objection is this: we certainly agree that in choosing policies and institutions, one should take into account everyone affected. So in particular, if the fetus had desires that were adversely affected by abortion, it would be unfair not to take those desires into account. But we have argued that, as a matter of fact, the fetus is incapable of having desires that will go unsatisfied if it is destroyed, providing that action is carried out painlessly.

This brings us to the second objection. It involves the suggestion that although the consequences of isolated acts of abortion do benefit society, this would not be true if abortion were to become a *generally accepted practice*. It is precisely the latter issue that we are interested in.

It has often been suggested that general acceptance of abortion would have disastrous consequences; however, no convincing evidence has been offered in support of this contention. Anti-abortionists usually attempt to sway unreflective people with vague claims that abortion will lead to the "denigration of humanity" or to an "erosion of respect for the sanctity of life." Such emotion-laden appeals are in the same intellectual category as politicians' rhetoric about patriotism and the family. Both are designed to encourage unthinking acceptance of a position that would fare ill if exposed to impartial, rational scrutiny.

It is possible, however, to divest the claim of its illicit emotional appeal. When this is done, the underlying suggestion appears to be that if one permits the killing of some humans, that is, fetuses, then respect for human life will decrease, so that other classes of humans, such as the handicapped and the elderly, become candidates for elimination. But this conclusion rests on intellectual and moral confusion. Specifically, it rests on a failure to get clear about the conditions something must satisfy if it is to have a serious right to life. To advocate abortion is *not* to suggest that one allow violations of one's moral principles when it happens to be socially convenient. The pro-abortionist's position is that the *fundamental* principle involved here is that it is seriously wrong to kill not human beings, but *persons*. It is seriously wrong to kill a human being *because* he or she is a person, not because he or she is a human being. And our contention is that fetuses are not persons, but only *potential* persons. Once one realizes that it is persons who have a right to life and that abortion is morally unobjectionable because fetuses are not persons, there is no danger that one will conclude that it is morally acceptable to kill other humans, such as handicapped and elderly ones, who are persons. When the moral principles relevant to abortion are clear, it is apparent that general acceptance of the practice should not have any undesirable consequences of the sort envisioned by the anti-abortionist.

This completes our defense of the claim that where abortion is viewed as morally permissible and is available on demand, people are happier than they would otherwise be. We can now proceed to consider the views of those who hold that abortion should be prohibited even if to do so results in significant frustration and unhappiness. Most anti-abortionists feel that there are moral considerations involved in the issue of abortion that far outweigh considerations of human happiness. In view of what is at stake, this is not a claim to be lightly advanced. By lobbying for the prohibition of abortion, the anti-abortionist is in effect assuming responsibility for the consequences of those actions. As we have emphasized, these consequences are deeply disturbing. If anti-abortionists prohibit abortion, they will be responsible for untold human misery. They will be responsible for lessened enjoyment of sex; for frustration caused by inconvenient pregnancies and childbearing; for ill health, either physical or mental, of mothers or other persons; for deaths of women resulting from pregnancies and illegal abortions; for child abuse; for crimes committed by frustrated or improperly socialized individuals; and for the stunted life of everyone if overpopulation seriously curbs our freedoms or lowers the quality of life. Ardent anti-abortionists must shoulder the burden of responsibility for these things because, had they acted otherwise, these things would not have existed. What considerations, then, can the anti-abortionists point to that outweigh the suffering produced by the prohibition of abortion?

In reply to the accusation that the responsibility for this catalogue of woes lies on their shoulders, anti-abortionists will argue that these evils are necessary in order to avoid a much greater evil. Fetuses have a right to life. They have a right to be born and to have the opportunity to become adults. To destroy them by abortion is seriously wrong, and in comparison with it the miseries enumerated pale into insignificance. Fetuses are human beings, and to kill a human being is murder.

REFUTATION OF "PRO-LIFE" OBJECTIONS TO ABORTION

The "pro-lifer's" contention is that the fetus has a serious right to life, comparable to that of a normal adult human being. This claim deserves very careful consideration, because if the fetus did have a serious right to life, then indeed it would be necessary to suffer the evils that we enumerated. It would be no more justifiable to kill a fetus to avoid threats to someone's health, to eliminate frustration and unhappiness, or to curb population growth, than it would be to kill an adult. Abortion would be justified, if at all, only to save the life of the mother.

In the next two sections we will show that there is no satisfactory support for the claim that the fetus has a right to life. On the contrary, there are excellent reasons for holding that it does not. Before developing our case, however, it is worthwhile to comment on the framework of our discussion, even though this requires a brief digression into metaethics.

There is an important distinction between *deontological* ethical systems and *consequentialist* ones. Some moral principles deal with rights or duties, while others are concerned with the intrinsic desirability of different states. A central question in metaethics is whether there is any relation between these two types of principles. Consequentialists hold that the best action is the one that maximizes the existence of intrinsically desirable states. This enables them to derive all principles dealing with rights and duties from principles specifying what states are intrinsically desirable together with empirical information about the consequences of actions. In contrast, the deontological view is that such derivation of principles dealing with rights and duties is not possible.

Anti-abortionists almost always approach the issue of abortion from the latter perspective. They treat rights in general, and the right to life in particular, as incapable of being derived from more fundamental principles dealing with the intrinsic desirability of various states of affairs. If pressed to defend their principles, they may contend that they are "self-evident." Alternatively, they may appeal to "moral intuition"—thereby implying that those who disagree with them are morally blind. Another common stratagem is to cite their favorite religious authority. None of these invocations is conducive to rational discussion of the issues.

In contrast, if one adopts a consequentialist approach to ethics, the question of abortion can be dealt with in a much more fruitful way. Whereas deontological ethical theories involve a number of unrelated principles dealing with obligations and rights, consequentialism bases its ethical claims on a very few principles specifying what states are intrinsically valuable. Because consequentialists cannot view the right to life as underived, they must offer some account of it, and in doing this, they will be able to determine whether a human fetus has a right to life.

The following discussion will be formulated in terms of rights, despite the fact that we are inclined to think that a consequentialist outlook is correct and that a discussion of abortion and the right to life in a consequentialist framework would lead to a deeper understanding of the issues. For this is an essay in ethics, and we want our arguments to be neutral with respect to metaethical controversies.

Let us now examine the critical contention that a fetus has a serious right to life. What *grounds* do anti-abortionists offer in support of this claim? A survey of anti-abortion literature provides us with the following considerations:

(1)   A fetus resembles an adult human.
(2)   A fetus is alive.
(3)   A fetus is a distinct individual.
(4)   A fetus inside a human mother is itself human.

We will show that none of these considerations constitutes adequate grounds for attributing a right to life to the fetus.

The following typical passage illustrates the first appeal:

> At the moment of conception, of course, the new life does not look like a baby. But within a very few weeks visible changes occur, and the new life *does* begin to look like a baby. From about two weeks onwards, the unborn child can respond to moments of stress. The heart is pumping between the eighteenth and twenty-fifth day. By the fourth week the backbone is complete. By eight weeks the child has all his organs—legs, arms, feet, hands— he looks like a human being.[3]

This reference to the physical resemblance of the fetus to adults has considerable emotional impact, and it is no accident that it figures prominently in "pro-life" attacks on abortion. Descriptions such as that are reinforced by pictures of "unborn children" and by bottled fetuses "murdered" by abortionists.

Do anti-abortionists really believe that such resemblance is morally relevant? It is hard to believe that they do. If pig fetuses resembled adult humans, would it be seriously wrong to kill pig fetuses? Or if human fetuses looked like frogs, not adult humans, would abortions be morally permissible? Surely not. The anti-abortionist is opposed to abortion at any time after conception, and it is simply false to say that a fertilized human egg cell looks like an adult human being.

Why then the great emphasis on resemblance? Perhaps resemblance seems relevant because it appears to support the claim that the fetus is a human being. But if "human being" simply means an organism belonging to the biological species *homo sapiens*, the claim that a fetus developing inside a human mother is a human being is trivial. If to call something a human being is to assert something more than this, namely, that it also has a right to life, then the fact that the fetus resembles adult human beings in *certain physical* respects does not show that it has a right to life. As we will argue later, psychological properties, not physical ones, determine whether something has a right to life.

---

[3] See The Committee for Human Life, "The Question of Abortion," in *Declaration of U.S. Policy of Population Stabilization by Voluntary Means* (Washington, D.C.: 1972), U.S. Government Printing Office, p. 352.

In our opinion the appeal to resemblance is an attempt to gain support by appealing to the emotions of people instead of by presenting carefully reasoned argument. Sometimes anti-abortionists protest that there is nothing in principle wrong with such emotional appeal. Is it ethically objectionable to use films of atrocities to impress on people the immorality of actions occurring in war? Surely not. But then how can it be ethically objectionable to use pictures of murdered fetuses in order to rally support against abortion?

This response is quite confused. In one case there is clear agreement about the relevant moral principles, and one is simply pointing out that events prohibited by those principles are occurring. In the other there is puzzlement, or disagreement, about what moral principles apply. To sway emotions, anti-abortionists, rather than offering rational argument in support of their views are using considerations that are irrelevant to whether the fetus has a right to life. The situation would be comparable if a vegetarian, rather than arguing for the view that it is wrong to kill animals, were to go about showing gory pictures of slaughtered animals.

We can dismiss the second condition—that since the fetus is alive, it is wrong to kill it—rather quickly. Expressions such as "respect for the sanctity of life," "pro-life movement," and so on, suggest this line of thought, although only in very unsophisticated discussions is this claim explicitly advanced. There are all sorts of living things we do not hesitate to kill, from viruses and bacteria up to complex animals such as chickens and cows. The reply may be that although it is not wrong to destroy life in general, it is wrong to destroy human life. We will consider this view shortly.

A third consideration advanced by anti-abortionists is that the fetus is a distinct individual.[4] This suggestion must be clarified before it can be evaluated. The fetus is not distinct in the sense of being physically unconnected to other organisms. Nor is it a separate individual in the sense that it is capable of existing independently of other organisms, at least for most of its development. The idea is presumably that although the fetus depends on another organism, much like an ordinary parasite, it is still a biological unity that contains within itself factors that determine the direction of its development.

As it stands, this consideration has no force. Animals belonging to nonhuman species are distinct individuals in this sense, and most people have no moral qualms about destroying them.[5] So it is not sufficient to claim that

---

[4] See *Declaration of U.S. Policy of Population Stabilization by Voluntary Means*, p. 331.

[5] It is quite possible, however, that people ought to have moral qualms about killing nonhuman animals, for it may well be that adult members of other species have a serious right to life. For a brief discussion of this question, see Michael Tooley, "Abortion and Infanticide," in *Philosophy & Public Affairs* 2, no. 1 (Fall 1972): 64–65.

the fetus is a distinct organism. If there is a point here, it must be that it is a distinct *human* organism.

Thus most of the "pro-life" arguments seem to boil down to the fourth and final claim—that a fetus developing inside a human mother is a member of *homo sapiens*, and this feature confers on it a right to life. The first part of the claim is uncontroversial. A fetus developing inside a human mother is certainly an organism belonging to *homo sapiens*. What is incorrect is the contention that membership in a particular biological species in itself endows an organism with a right to life.

We can show this as follows. Some things, normal adult human beings for example, have a right to life. Other living things, such as carrots and flies, apparently do not. How is this difference to be explained and justified? If we grant some things a right to life, while denying others such a right, there must be some morally relevant difference between the two classes of objects. What might this be?

Because most people, rightly or wrongly, tend to hold that only human animals have a serious right to life, it is tempting to suppose that membership in the biological species *homo sapiens* is the relevant property. Most anti-abortionists succumb to this temptation. However, a little reflection shows that this is not a justifiable answer.

First of all, membership in a species is defined by the ability to interbreed and produce fertile offspring. Suppose then we discover Yahoos—animals that look like us, and with whom we can interbreed, but whose brains are much smaller, and whose intellectual qualities are comparable to those of chickens. They could not perform any of the intellectual tasks, such as language learning and problem solving, of which human beings are capable. It is difficult to see why we should treat Yahoos any differently from chickens. Yet they would belong to our species. Hence it cannot be that an organism has a serious right to life because of membership in a particular species. Another way of seeing this is to notice that there might be individuals to whom we would ascribe a right to life, even though they were not humans. If there were a God, he would probably not belong to our species, yet surely it would be wrong to kill him without good reason. Science fiction provides us with many examples. Olaf Stapledon's Sirius is a dog as intelligent and as capable of moral behavior as most humans.[6] When prejudiced individuals hound him to death, we feel enraged and saddened, for his destruction is as wrong, and for the same reason, as that of an adult human being.

Why do we ascribe a right to life not merely to normal adult humans, but also to deities, and to animals such as Sirius? Surely it is because they have

[6] Olaf Stapledon, *Sirius* (Secker and Warburg, 1944).

certain characteristics in common. These cannot be tied up with physical appearance or with membership in some biological species. The normally relevant properties are *psychological* ones.

It seems then, that the anti-abortionist is wrong to hold that it is a *basic* moral principle that human beings have a right to life. If a given organism enjoys a right to life, it does so not because it is a member of biological species *homo sapiens*, but because it has psychological traits, as yet unspecified, possessed by normal adult human beings. Once we recognize this, the question is whether fetuses have these psychological traits, or whether it is true only that they will *later* come to possess them. If the latter is the case, there seems to be no reason to think that fetuses have a serious right to life.

Is it possible to justify the contention that a human fetus does not possess the psychological traits that adult humans have and that confer on them a serious right to life? We believe that it is. The clearest way of doing this is to determine, as we will do in the next section, precisely what the relevant psychological properties are. But even without doing that we can argue that a fetus lacks the relevant properties. One can ask whether there is any reason for holding that the mental life of a human fetus is significantly different from that of a nonhuman fetus such as a chimpanzee. We contend that there is no evidence that this is so. Therefore, unless one is prepared to hold that it is seriously wrong to kill nonhuman fetuses, it seems that one cannot maintain that it is seriously wrong to destroy human fetuses.

There is, however, a last line of argument open to the extreme anti-abortionist. Even if a human fetus does not possess the relevant psychological characteristics, it is possible to contend that the fetus has a right to life in virtue of the fact that it will *later* come to develop those properties. Thus "pro-lifers" might try to defend their position by appealing to the following *potentiality principle*:

> If there are any properties possessed by normal adult human beings which endow any organism possessing them with a serious right to life, then at least one of those properties is such that it is wrong to kill any organism that potentially possesses that property, simply in virtue of the organism's potentiality. (An organism possesses a property potentially if it will come to have it in the normal course of its development.)

This principle is exposed to three telling objections. The first is that if one accepts the potentiality principle, one ought to accept the generalized version that differs from it in only two respects. First, in the generalized version the term "organism" is replaced by the expression "system of causally interrelated objects," on the grounds that it is not morally relevant whether the potentiality resides in a single organism or in a system of individuals that are so interrelated that they will causally give rise to something possessing the property in question, if not interfered with. Second, the generalized version prohibits *any* action that prevents a system from developing the morally relevant property that it potentially possesses, rather than only prohibiting actions that destroy the possessor of the potentialities. To refuse to accept the latter change would force one to admit that a two-step abortion is morally permissible, where one first destroys the potential in the fetus to develop later the relevant psychological features and then kills the fetus. And surely no "pro-lifer" wants to be driven to this conclusion.

If one accepts the generalized potentiality principle, one must conclude that some methods of contraception are as seriously wrong as abortion, because they involve actions that prevent certain systems (human spermatazoa and unfertilized egg cells) from developing potentialities they otherwise would have developed. It is true that some anti-abortionists will find this a cheering conclusion. But there are many more conservatives on abortion who would want to reject the view that artificial contraception can be wrong. Such a combination of positions cannot be defended. One must either accept the claim that some methods of contraception are seriously wrong or else abandon the potentiality principle, and with it the conservative position on abortion.

Our second argument shows that the potentiality principle, even in its ungeneralized form, leads to even more disturbing consequences. Before we can state this argument we must defend the following moral symmetry principle:

> Let C be any causal process that normally leads to some outcome E. Let A be any action that initiates process C, and B be any action, involving no risk to the agent and a minimal expenditure of energy, which stops process C before E occurs. Assume further that actions A and B do not have any other morally significant consequences, and that E is the only part or outcome of process C that is morally significant in itself. Then there is no moral difference between intentionally performing action B and intentionally refraining from action A, assuming identical motivation in the two cases.

Some philosophers would reject such a symmetry principle, arguing that it is worse to kill someone deliberately than to refrain from saving her or his life. We feel that this objection is unsound and that its initial plausibility rests on a failure to consider the motivation likely to be associated with the two kinds of actions. To kill a person deliberately usually indicates that one *wanted* the person dead, whereas this is not usually true when one merely refrains from saving someone's life. But our moral symmetry principle deals only with cases in which the motivation is the same. One should consider situations such as the following. Jones wants to kill Smith and has acquired a grenade for that purpose. He has pulled out the pin and is about to throw it at Smith. Compare now the following courses of action. In the first, Jones throws his grenade at Smith and it explodes, killing Smith. In the second, just as Jones's arm is moving forward, he notices that someone else has thrown a grenade at Smith. The grenade lands on a trap door near Smith. Jones realizes that there is a button at his fingertips that, if pushed, will open the trap door and save Smith's life. Jones does not throw his grenade, since he sees that Smith is going to be killed anyway, and he can save his grenade for another day. Wanting to see Smith killed, he intentionally refrains from pushing the button. The grenade goes off, killing Smith. Are we to say that there is a significant difference between the wrongness of Jones's behavior in these two cases? It seems unintuitive to do so. Hence, initial appearances notwithstanding, our moral symmetry principle appears to be perfectly reasonable.

Given this principle, we can now set out our second objection to the potentiality principle. One need simply take as process C the development of a fertilized human egg cell, prior to the time when it acquires those psychological properties that confer a serious right to life. Process C will thus encompass the life of the organism before birth, since we saw earlier that there is no reason to believe that a fetus possesses the morally relevant properties. Action B can then be any action of destroying the fetus. Any action that leads to conception, and thus initiates process C, can be chosen as action A, providing that its only morally significant consequence is that it leads to process C. The symmetry principle then asserts that, given identical motivation, there is no moral difference between intentionally performing action B and intentionally refraining from action A. That is to say, there is no moral difference between abortion and intentionally refraining from procreation. Hence if the extreme conservative view of abortion were correct, one would be forced to conclude that conception at every possible opportunity was a serious duty! Few indeed would accept this consequence. It is therefore necessary to reject the potentiality principle.

Our third argument against the potentiality principle turns on the following example. Suppose that technology has advanced to the point where it is possible to construct humans in the laboratory out of inorganic compounds. Suppose further that it is possible to freeze living beings and then to thaw them out without damaging them, and to program beliefs, desires, and personality traits into organisms by bringing about certain brain states. Given these techniques, imagine now that we construct an adult human in the laboratory. We program in a set of beliefs, desires, and personality traits. If we then thaw it out, we will have a conscious adult human with a distinct personality. But what if, because of all this work, we have developed ravenous appetites, and rather than thawing it out, we grind it up for hamburgers? Our action might be economically unwise, and subject to culinary objections, but would it be open to moral criticism? In particular, would we be guilty of murdering an innocent person? We think most people would agree that the answer to this question is no. Until the organism has been brought to consciousness, and until it envisages a future for itself and has desires about such a future, there is nothing prima facie wrong about destroying it. Thus it is false that something can have a serious right to life in virtue of its potentialities. So we can bid adieu to the potentiality principle, and with it, the final "pro-life" objection to abortion.

WHEN DOES AN ORGANISM HAVE A RIGHT TO LIFE?

We have shown that there is no reason to believe a human fetus possesses those psychological traits that confer a right to life. But we have not yet indicated precisely what those properties are. We will discuss this now in our final section.

Our view is as follows: an organism can have a right to life only if it now possesses, or possessed at some time in the past, the capacity to have a desire for continued existence. An organism cannot satisfy this requirement unless it is a person, that is, a continuing subject of experiences and other mental states, and unless it has the capacity for self-consciousness—where an organism is self-conscious only if it recognizes that it is itself a person.

The basis for our contention is the claim that there is a conceptual connection between, on the one hand, the rights an individual can have and the circumstances under which they can be violated, and, on the other, the desires he can have. A right is something that can be violated and, in general, to violate an individual's right to something is to frustrate the corresponding desire. Suppose, for example, that someone owns a car. Then you are under a prima facie obligation not to take it from him. However, the obligation is not unconditional: if he does not care whether you drive off with his car, then prima facie you do not violate his right by doing so.

A precise formulation of the conceptual connection in question would require considerable care. The most important point is that violation of an individual's right to something does not always involve thwarting a *present* desire, that is, a desire that exists at the same time as the action that violates the right. Sometimes the violation of a right involves thwarting a *past* desire. The most dramatic illustration is provided by the rights of dead persons, because here the individual whose right is being transgressed no longer exists. A more common example is that of people who are temporarily unconscious. An unconscious person does not have any desires. Yet his or her rights can certainly be infringed on. This presents no problem when one takes past desires into account. The reason that it is wrong to kill a temporarily unconscious adult is that in the period before he became unconscious, he had a desire to go on living—a desire which it is possible to satisfy.

Violation of an individual's right may also involve frustrating a *future* desire. The most vivid example of this is the case of rights of future generations. Most people would hold that for those living today to use up all of the world's resources would violate the rights of future individuals. Here, as in the case of the rights of a dead person, the violation of an individual's rights occurs at a time when the individual does not even exist.

However, it is very important to notice that what is relevant are the desires that individuals will *actually have* at some time in the future. The desires that individuals would have *if* they were to exist at certain times at which, as a matter of fact, they will not exist, are not relevant. The need for this restriction is brought out by the example used at the end of the previous section of this article. If one were to consider the desires that something would have if it were to exist at a later time, it would be wrong to destroy the frozen human being we had constructed in the laboratory. Even though it has never been conscious, if it were thawed out, it would not want to be destroyed. Rights of future generations provide a second example. Suppose we know with certainty that no future generation will ever exist. Then there is no objection to using up the world's resources now. But if one were obliged to take into account the desires future individuals would have if they were to exist, it would be wrong to use up the world's resources.

A complete account of the connection between rights and desires would also have to take into consideration unusual cases, where an individual is in an emotionally unbalanced state, or where a person's desires have been affected by lack of relevant information, or by his being subjected to abnormal physiological or psychological factors. We shall ignore these and confine ourselves to paradigm cases of violations of an individual's rights.[7] When this is done, we can say that first, an individual cannot have a right to something unless there can be actions that would violate it. Second, an action cannot violate an individual's right to something unless it wrongs him by depriving him of the thing in question. And third, an action can wrong an individual by depriving him of something only if it violates his desire for that thing. The desire is generally a present desire, but it may be a past or future desire. It follows that a person cannot have a right to something unless he is at some time capable of having the corresponding desire.

[7] For an account of rights that takes into consideration these cases, see Michael Tooley, "In Defense of Abortion and Infanticide," in *The Problem of Abortion*, ed. Joel Feinberg (Belmont, Calif.: Wadsworth, 1973).

Let us now apply this to the case of the right to life. The expression "right to life" misleads one into thinking that the right concerns the continued existence of a biological organism. The following example shows that this interpretation is inadequate. Suppose that we could completely reprogram an adult human so that it has (apparent) memories, beliefs, desires, and personality traits radically different from those associated with it before the reprogramming. (Billy Graham is reprogrammed as a replica of Bertrand Russell.) In such a case, however beneficial the change might be, it is true that *someone* has been destroyed, that someone's right to life has been violated, even though no biological organism has been killed. So the right to life cannot be construed as merely the right of a biological organism to continue to exist.

How then can the right in question be more accurately described? A natural suggestion is that the expression "right to life" refers to the right of a person—a subject of experiences and other mental states—to continue to exist. However, this interpretation begs the question against certain possible positions. It might be that while persons have a right to continue to exist, so do other things that are only potentially persons. A right to life on this view would be either the right of a person to continue to exist or the right of something that is only potentially a person to become a person.

We concluded that something cannot have a specific right unless it is capable at some time of having the corresponding desire. It follows from this together with the more accurate analysis of the right to life that something cannot have a right to life unless it is capable at some time either of having a desire to continue to exist as a person, or of having a desire to become a person. If something has not been capable of having either of these desires in the past, and is not now capable, then if it is now destroyed, it will never have possessed the capacity in question. Hence an organism cannot have a right to life unless it is now capable, or was capable at some time in the past, of having a desire to continue to exist as a person or a desire to become a person.

But recall now the discussion of desires in the first section. We showed that one's desires are limited by the concepts one possesses. Therefore one cannot have a desire to continue to exist as a person or a desire to become a person unless one has the concept of a person. The question we must now ask is whether something that is not itself a person could have the concept of such an entity. It seems plausible to hold that it could not. This means that something that is not a person cannot have a desire to become a person. Hence the right to life is confined to persons.

This brings us to our final requirement: an organism cannot have a right to life unless it is capable of self-consciousness, where an organism is self-conscious only if it recognizes that it is itself a continuing subject of experiences and other mental states. To justify this requirement, let us ask whether a person can fail to recognize that it is a person. If the answer were negative, it would follow from the requirement just established that an organism cannot have a right to life unless it possesses self-consciousness.

It is unclear, however, that something necessarily possesses self-consciousness if it is a person. Perhaps a person might fail to notice this fact about himself. Even if this is possible, it seems reasonable to believe that if something is a person, then it is ipso facto *capable* of acquiring the concept of a person and of recognizing that it is itself a person. Thus even if something can have a right to life without having been self-conscious, it appears that it cannot have such a right without ever having possessed the capacity for self-consciousness.

Thus, the psychological characteristics that bestow a right to life on an organism are these: it must be a person, capable of self-consciousness, of envisaging a future for itself, and of having desires about its own future states.

We began by setting out a preliminary case for abortion. Then we examined attempts by anti-abortionists to overturn that case by arguing that abortion is wrong because it violates the fetus's right to life. We showed that the arguments anti-abortionists offer in support of this claim are unsound and that the contention itself is false. Our central point was that neither an organism's potentialities, nor membership in a particular species, serves to confer a right to life. An organism has a right to life only if it has certain psychological traits possessed by normal adult human beings, but not by fetuses.

Next we considered what properties endow an organism with a right to life. We defended the view that something can have a right to life only if it possesses, or has possessed, the capacity to have a desire for continued existence. We then argued that to satisfy this requirement, an entity must be a person capable of self-consciousness.

The issue of abortion thus ceases to be puzzling. A human fetus does not have a right to life because it does not have the capacity for self-consciousness; it cannot conceive of itself as a continuing subject of experiences; it cannot envisage a future for itself, nor have desires about such a future. A fetus is not a person, but only a potential person. Hence there is no moral objection to abortion. To prohibit it is to inflict unjustified suffering and death upon society.

CHAPTER 6

Abortion, Potentiality, and Conferred Claims: A Response to Langerak

Although moderate positions on abortion rights are both intuitively plausible and politically convenient, it has proved difficult to justify them coherently. In "Abortion, Potentiality, and Conferred Claims,"[1] Edward Langerak argues that the potentiality principle (P) provides a reason for thinking that (1) it is not merely the social consequences that make abortion morally problematic, but something about the fetus itself. He defines P as the claim that "if, in the normal course of its development, a being will acquire a person's claim to life, then by virtue of that fact it already has some claim to life" (p. 2). He believes that P cannot by itself account for the fact that (2) late abortions are more morally problematic than early ones, but that what he calls a "conferred claims" approach is consistent with P, can account for (2), even though it cannot by itself account for (1).

I think that Langerak is right that P would go far toward justifying a moderate approach to abortion if it could be defended. I am less sure of the relevance of the conferred claims approach.

Is P justified? In support of P, Langerak argues that there is a morally relevant difference between a possible and a potential person. Thus, when Michael Tooley asserts that it would be no more wrong to kill the kitten af-

---

[1] This article was written in response to a paper Edward Langerak gave at the December 1979 Eastern Division APA meetings. He also published a longer and somewhat different version of it in the October 1979 *Hastings Center Report*. I believe that both papers are vulnerable to the objections I raise here.

ter injection than before, he is begging the question.[2] I agree that we need to examine the two states to see whether there are grounds for differing moral judgments about them. To defend his view that there is a moral difference here, Langerak argues that an organism that is very likely to turn into a valuable organism later thereby acquires some value now. Thus a potential person, a fetus, acquires some value from its proximity to full personhood, value that a merely possible person does not have.

It seems to me that there is some danger of a slippery slope back to the fertilized cell, and perhaps even beyond, because one might apply the same rule to possible and potential organisms.

My main criticism, however, is that Langerak does not supply us with any good reasons for accepting P in the first place. He provides two examples of cases where people acquire power or "instrumental value" as a result of our expectations about their future. On the basis of these examples we are expected to conclude that the same can be said of the "intrinsic value" of fetuses. Let us look at these claims in more detail.

The first case is that of a president-elect, a potential president. It is claimed that the president-elect has increased power and respect in virtue of the high probability of his becoming president.

One need not concede the thesis that the potential president is powerful now because he will be powerful later. It would be much more plausible, I think, to argue that he was already very powerful *before* he was elected (how else does one get elected?) and that the power he is enjoying is largely an extension of his earlier power. But I do not think that this objection gets at the crucial problem here, which is that the logic of power is different from that of moral value, and so it is hard to see how showing that a certain claim is true of power makes it also true of moral value. It is rather like claiming that because eggs get hard when boiled that wax does so too. So the question of the power of potential presidents has no bearing on the moral value of potential persons.

If moral worth involves meeting certain criteria, then it is plausible to believe that if you do not meet the criteria, you do not have the corresponding moral worth. Arguing that you get something else (like power) in virtue of expected events or states of affairs does not show that you always get (or

---

[2] See Michael Tooley, "A Defense of Abortion and Infanticide," in *The Problem of Abortion*, ed. Joel Feinberg (Belmont, Calif.: Wadsworth, 1973), pp. 86–88. Tooley asks us to imagine that there is a substance that, when injected into kittens, would cause them to have all the psychological capacities of adult humans. He argues that it would not be wrong to kill such a kitten after it had been injected with this substance but before it had developed these capacities.

ought to get) benefits or status *now* because of what you will do or be in the future. Moral worth here seems to operate more like esthetic worth: a promising soloist is not necessarily a better dancer now because she is likely to become a prima ballerina later—whatever recognition she gets should be based on her current performances, not her probable future ones.

Langerak's second example concerns a medical student, who, it is claimed, has increased "instrumental value" because in the normal course of events he will acquire the instrumental value of a physician.

The first problem with this case is the notion of "instrumental value": I do not see quite what it can mean here, so I look at the case directly to see what it might plausibly be taken to mean.

Why do we value medical students? Some people value them for their promise of power. Medical students can reasonably expect to be well-off and secure, qualities that are attractive to certain potential spouses and to those who prefer the company of such individuals to that of ditch diggers or impoverished professors. But this kind of value cannot do the job here, for reasons already mentioned.

What other value might medical students have? If they have any special value, it seems to me that it has to do with what they already know about medicine, not the fact that they will know a lot about medicine in the future. Thus a medical student might be good to have around in an emergency or to satisfy our curiosity about medical subjects. But this cannot help Langerak either, for the fetus's alleged claim to value is based only on qualities it would have if it continued to develop, not those it already has—the analogy breaks down.

Thus neither of Langerak's examples is adequate. Perhaps better ones could be found: this remains to be seen. But for now, we have no good reason to believe that a potential person is valuable because the person is likely to become valuable. Therefore the burden of proof remains with those who see a serious moral distinction between a possible and a potential person.

Let us now turn to the conferred claims approach, which is to account for (2), our sense that early abortions are significantly less problematic than late ones. This notion seems to demand that at some point society ought to confer a stronger claim to life on relatively mature fetuses than they would have on their own in virtue of P. This principle is based on social consequences: killing an organism, X, which is quite like organism Y, although X has a weaker inherent claim to life than Y, will endanger the life of Y.

This is a claim about human psychology that has yet to be proven; it also raises an empirical question concerning the actual cut-off point beyond which such killing would be innocuous. Langerak admits not knowing the answer to this question, but asserts that first-trimester abortions are outside the danger zone.

I doubt that extreme conservatives would find this claim persuasive, but that is not my main concern here. Although I am reluctant to lump fertilized eggs and nine-month fetuses together in the same moral basket, even if neither meets the criteria for personhood, I am not sure that a satisfactory way to prevent this can be found. But suppose it is: what then?

It would mean, one supposes, that to get a later abortion, a woman must have a good reason for wanting one. But surely this is virtually always true. Women are not, in general, capricious creatures who invest seven or eight or nine months in a pregnancy and then want out at the drop of a hat. So it is almost certain that a good reason will be forthcoming. Perhaps the fetus has been found to be seriously defective or it is threatening the woman's life or health; perhaps her circumstances have changed in such a way that she no longer feels able to care for a child—her companion died or left her, another child or relative became crippled; perhaps she sought an abortion earlier and was unable to obtain one; perhaps she has slowly come to the firm conclusion that she does not want a child

In some of these cases she might be glad if the child could be salvaged, either to be raised by her or put up for adoption. Where she is not, does she have the right to see the fetus dead? This depends on how we justify conferring a right to life on late fetuses and on our moral evaluation of her anguish at knowing it to be alive. Where claims are only conferred, however, and not inherent, I would argue that this anguish should be taken very seriously. Hence a conferred claims approach would not necessarily provide even late fetuses with enough of a claim to make any practical difference, although it might help to explain our uneasiness about late abortions.

In conclusion, I believe that P remains highly debatable, and that the conferred claims approach probably ought not to make any practical difference in abortion policy. Hence Langerak has not succeeded in producing a satisfactory defense of the moderate position on abortion.

CHAPTER 7

Abortion and the Argument from Convenience

As the era of constitutionally guaranteed abortion rights enters its third decade in the United States, the war against abortion mounted by its opponents has grown ever fiercer. Enraged by the failure of peaceful protest to end legal access to abortion altogether,[1] and encouraged by Republican administrations hostile to abortion rights, protestors have moved on to ever more violent approaches, picketing abortion clinics, threatening abortion providers, and finally committing murder. Disagreement about abortion is an ongoing disruptive theme in local and national politics.

Is there a middle ground where reasonable people of good will might meet? A number of writers have been exploring this possibility recently.[2] And it might seem that there is already consensus among all but extremists about the desirability of access to abortion in cases of rape, incest, fetal deformity, and threat to the life or health of the pregnant woman. Unfortunately, this approach fails to satisfy those who believe that abortion truly is murder. Nor does it satisfy some feminists who believe that this apparently reasonable compromise leaves women as second-class citizens.

My aim here is to explore further this feminist contention that nothing short of full access to abortion services, the so-called abortion on demand,

---

[1] Despite the very real victories in limiting access, such as reducing public funding for poor women, tacking burdensome restrictions on state abortion laws, and reducing the accessibility of abortion by intimidating abortion providers.

[2] Most notably, Nancy (Ann) Davis, "The Abortion Debate: The Search for Common Ground, part 1," *Ethics* 103 (April 1993): 516–39 and part 2, *Ethics* 103 (July 1993): 731–78; and Ronald Dworkin, *Life's Dominion: An Argument about Abortion, Euthanasia, and Individual Freedom* (New York: Knopf, 1993).

suffices. For if that is true, then compromise on abortion is incompatible with equality for women.

The particular issue I examine here is whether most abortions would be unjustifiable if they were carried out just for women's "convenience," as opponents of abortion often assert. Is this a reasonable inference? To test it, let us suppose that one were to concede for the sake of argument the first claim that many abortions are a matter of convenience. Would it follow that these abortions are immoral and ought to be prohibited?

No. Consistent social policy requires us first to determine whether society condones similar deaths in other contexts. If it does, then abortion cannot justifiably be prohibited unless some other morally relevant difference can be found between these cases.

The argument against convenience is reminiscent of Judith Thomson's strategy in "A Defense of Abortion,"[3] and is subject to the same problem: both cases rest on the view that promoting other values can be more important than preserving human life. My formulation, like hers, can be dealt with in two ways. One approach is to face its implications and resolve to treat these convenience-based deaths consistently. Thus society could retain its nonchalance about convenience-based deaths, but only if it sanctioned convenience-based abortions. Or, it could mend its ways with respect to other convenience-based deaths, at the cost of denying women many of the abortions they want. The alternative approach would be to question the comparison between common societal practices that lead to human deaths and fetal deaths caused by these allegedly convenience-based abortions. Those who oppose such abortions would tend to argue that killing fetuses is more wicked than, say, adopting transportation policies known to cause many deaths. Those who want to defend them could either attempt to show that fetal deaths are less wicked than traffic fatalities, other things being equal, or that these abortions are not a matter of convenience.

As we all know, there is a voluminous literature on the question of the moral status of fetuses, and I do not propose to recapitulate it here. I believe that allegedly convenience-based abortions would be justifiable at present even if fetuses were full-fledged moral persons. This position is supported in part by the fact that it is obviously absurd to define women's desire to control such a fundamental aspect of their lives as a matter of convenience,[4] and in part by the disregard for human life displayed ever more frequently

---

[3] See Judith Jarvis Thomson, "A Defense of Abortion," in *The Problem of Abortion*, ed. Joel Feinberg (Belmont, Calif.: Wadsworth, 1973). She argues that we have no duty to exert ourselves to save the lives of others when we have no special relationship with them.

[4] I go on to defend this position in Chapter 8, "Abortion, Forced Labor, and War."

by both institutions and individuals in this society.[5] However, I do not want to argue that case here. Instead, let us go forward with a moderate understanding of fetuses as neither moral persons nor mere excisable tissue, but as objects of serious moral concern. It follows that fetuses may be killed, but only for good reason.

Why is this conception of fetuses a reasonable one for the purposes of this article? Ronald Dworkin has recently argued quite convincingly that our understanding of the debate about abortion erroneously assumes that the opponents have contradictory beliefs about fetal interests and rights. He contends instead that the real disagreement is about how to respect a widely shared belief that human life is sacred or inviolable. His conclusion explains the otherwise puzzling inconsistencies in attitudes about abortion repeatedly unearthed by polls, particularly with respect to whether abortion should be legal or not. His case is shored up by both the willingness of many conservatives to countenance some abortions and the ambivalence about abortion often expressed by those who situate themselves firmly in the pro-choice camp.[6] If Dworkin's analysis of the abortion debate is accurate, my claims about the argument from convenience should be all the more convincing.

CONVENIENCE AND DEATH

Convenience, according to *Merriam Webster's Collegiate Dictionary, Tenth Edition,* is an appliance, device, or service conducive to comfort, or easy performance. The emphasis is on ease and comfort. So, if x is convenient, x makes it possible to do easily and without discomfort something that could otherwise be done, but only with more difficulty. The implication is that convenience is nice, but optional; thus it would seem to be immoral to pursue convenience if others are seriously harmed.

It is evident, however, that society tolerates, indeed, encourages, a wide variety of practices that trade well-being and, quite often, life itself, for convenience. One might argue, for example, that most wars are undertaken for the convenience of some segments of society, yet wars are notoriously

---

[5] A large part of the population must now live with daily threats of deadly violence from other individuals. Government organizations and businesses also knowingly make decisions that threaten the lives of citizens. A less sinister, but no less frightening, manifestation of the disregard for human life is reckless driving: people routinely endanger the lives of others in order to spare themselves the trouble of hitting the brake pedal, changing lanes, or to save themselves a few moments' driving time. The recent rescinding of the 55-mile-per-hour speed limit may result in six thousand to nine thousand more deaths a year.

[6] See Dworkin, *Life's Dominion,* esp. chaps. 1 and 2.

bloody. But I will not use war as an example here, because discussion of the causes and motivations of war inevitably raises fundamental political questions too tangled to consider now.[7]

There are less controversial ways of making the same point. Take, for example, the automobile-based transportation system. We know that trams, buses, trains, and even airplanes are far safer per passenger mile traveled than are cars.[8] In addition, automobiles cause serious pollution that damages human health and the environment.[9] The alternatives to automobiles have side effects, too. However, in every category, they are smaller than the ones associated with cars.[10]

Many lives would undoubtedly be saved if excellent public transportation systems replaced the automobile-based system now existing in the United States.[11] However, at its best, this system is wonderfully convenient—more convenient than any existing public transportation system I am familiar with.[12]

---

[7] It would probably be quite easy to show how unfounded were the claims used to justify many lesser wars initiated by the United States, together with how the actions undertaken furthered certain business interests.

[8] For further information, see Steve Nadis and James J. MacKenzie, *Car Trouble* (Boston: Beacon Press, 1993), esp. chap. 1. Particularly troubling is the intersection of two social problems, problem drinking and unsafe driving. See H. Laurence Ross, *Confronting Drunk Driving* (New Haven: Yale University Press, 1992). Ross argues for a wide variety of ways to reduce the toll of drunk driving. They include alcohol policies that reduce dangerous drinking, transportation policies that reduce dangerous driving, and ways to save lives in spite of drunk driving.

[9] See Nadis and MacKenzie, *Car Trouble,* esp. chaps. 1 and 2. They go into the true costs of an automobile-based transportation system at some length. In addition to the aforementioned damage to human health it causes, air pollution also leads to a variety of problems, including ozone depletion and the emission of greenhouse gases. Manufacturing cars also consumes enormous natural resources, and disposing of them creates enormous quantities of hazardous junk. Using cars encourages us to pave over good land and to create living spaces that undermine community. Our dependence on cars also influences foreign policy in undesirable ways. Many of these outcomes lead to additional deaths, quite apart from the more obvious ones caused by traffic accidents.

[10] Not only are other forms of public transportation safer than cars, but they outperform cars in both pollution control and fuel efficiency. Buses emit 25 percent less nitrogen oxide, 80 percent less carbon monoxide, and 90 fewer hydrocarbons than cars. Trains do still better: they emit 77 percent less nitrogen oxide, and 99 percent less carbon monoxide and hydrocarbons. As Nadis and MacKenzie point out in *Car Trouble,* "a transit train with 22 persons per car consumes 43 percent less energy than an automobile with a single driver; a transit bus with 11 riders on board takes 45 percent less energy" (p. 120). Subways, surface trains, and buses also carry far more people than a highway lane full of single-occupant cars.

[11] I ignore here for simplicity's sake morbidity and concentrate on mortality.

[12] It hardly needs saying that much of the time the automobile-based system does not function at its best and that if the full costs of the system were taken into account, people would be much less enthusiastic about it. Some of the best European public transportation systems are quite good; putting together still better ones is surely feasible.

As a person who lived many years without a car, I am intensely aware of the guilty pleasures of having my own car. I no longer have to wait endlessly at frozen bus stops, scramble for alternative transportation during off hours or strikes, align my schedule with that of the system. Now my arms never ache from the ever weightier bags and parcels that accumulate in shopping expeditions, because I can stow them in the car and walk unencumbered into each new shop. Having a car means that I can live out in nature, in a forested rural neighborhood not well served by public transportation. And, I can go to a health club anytime for a stress-reducing workout. In short, because I live in a small town where there are few traffic jams and more or less adequate parking, having a car adds enormously to the comfort and convenience of my life.

But does the car add any fundamentally important value to my life? No. I could do the things I want to do most without it. It wouldn't be as convenient, I wouldn't be as comfortable, I couldn't accomplish quite as much. But the extras, although I enjoy them a lot, are just that: extras. And although I am not prepared to give up my car under the present circumstances, it seems clear that most people would be far better off if we could reduce our dependence on cars.

In fact, it is arguable that doing so is a matter of justice. Living with the current system requires us to put up with a lottery that kills at least 40,000 people a year. If those lives were as valuable as sanctity-of-life rhetoric suggests, the appeal to convenience would be unceremoniously rejected.

Society tolerates other enterprises that promise convenience for some, despite the risk of death for others. Consider, for example, the tobacco industry. The government continues to subsidize the tobacco industry and to permit widespread advertising for a product that has been estimated to kill 400,000 people a year in the United States alone.[13] Or what about guns? We, as a society, tolerate nearly universal access to extremely efficient means of killing: the number of deaths attributable to guns now rivals those from traffic fatalities. No doubt some would occur by other means if guns were less available; however, it is plausible to believe that many would not. Yet even the feeblest attempts at gun control have been rejected until recently.[14]

---

[13] And the bad news keeps coming in. For example, recently a newspaper reported that smokers increase their risk for colorectal cancer, a risk that stays with them even if they later quit smoking. "Studies Link Cigarette Smoking to Colon, Rectal Cancer," *Ithaca Journal*, February 2, 1994, p. 5A.

[14] For an interesting consideration of the Second Amendment, see Sanford Levinson, "The Embarrassing Second Amendment," and Wendy Brown, "Guns, Cowboys, Philadelphia Mayors, and Civic Republicanism: On Sanford Levinson's *The Embarrassing Second Amendment*," both in *Yale Law Journal* 99, no. 1 (December 1989): 637–59 and 661–67, respectively.

What, too, of the practice—common both in business and state enter-prises—of lax safety practices that maim or kill,[15] or of letting products known to be dangerous into the marketplace? One example of the latter is the notorious Pinto case, where Ford decided against spending an extra $11 per car to remedy a serious hazard.[16] Another is the story of the automobile industry's footdragging on safety measures such as airbags.[17]

One could go on and on in this vein. What about the excess mortality in groups ill-served by the health care system? What about famine deaths abroad caused by self-serving foreign policy? But the basic point should by now be clear: if life is as priceless a good as some would have us be-lieve, why do we, as a society, tolerate such cavalier waste in these kinds of circumstances?

Putting together a watertight argument in each of these cases would take more space than is available here. Such examples may involve eco-nomics, constitutional rights, or issues of paternalism. Each also involves factual determinations and discussion of mid-level moral principles. Nonetheless, the point that should be emerging is that if these matters were treated analogously with abortion, the argument would be that none of these competing values trumps the value of the deaths that could be averted by undertaking new policies.

Some of these deaths might even be averted at no extra expense by changing attitudes. For example, education might encourage people to choose public transportation where possible. It might also help them to find satisfaction in exercise rather than cigarettes. People could be taught to channel their violent impulses into constructive pursuits, too. And educa-tion could help us labor cooperatively for safer workplaces.

However, reducing many of these dangers would require us to allocate resources differently. For example, society might increase its support of Amtrak while reducing highway subsidies. It could train tobacco farmers to grow other crops instead of giving them subsidies. It could subsidize

---

[15] For a helpful introduction to some of these issues, see Anthony Bale, "Women's Toxic Ex-perience," in *Women, Health, and Medicine in America,* ed. Rima D. Apple (New Brunswick, N.J.: Rutgers University Press, 1992).

[16] For a short account, see Richard T. De George, *Business Ethics,* 3d ed. (New York: Macmil-lan, 1990), pp. 193–95.

[17] See Nadis and MacKenzie, *Car Trouble,* p. 54. They point out that the provision of airbags in cars was delayed twenty years by the auto industry, which spent more than twenty mil-lion dollars fighting against them. Certainly, some ten years ago when I was car hunting, the only car equipped with airbags was the Mercedes Benz, which is out of the range most people can afford. In general, it is estimated that by 1982, vehicle safety standards intro-duced since 1968 had saved some 80,000 lives in the United States. Joan Claybrooke, Jacque-line Gillan, and Ann Strainchamps, *Reagan on the Road: The Crash of the U.S. Auto Safety Program* (Washington, D.C.: Public Citizen, 1982), p. i.

vocational education and create government job programs to provide a living wage to those who would otherwise turn to a life of crime. It could enforce existing safety regulations by hiring more inspectors, and so forth.

Many people will also want to argue that in addition to the specific differences between each of these particular cases and fetal abortion deaths, there are more generally applicable morally relevant differences. First, and most obvious, the former usually involve *statistical* deaths. Statistical deaths are those that we know from experience are likely to occur if we pursue a given course of action. But such statistical deaths are morally different from the killing of a particular fetus. Second, most of these deaths occur in the pursuit of other goals, and so nobody intends them. With abortion, however, the death of the fetus is intended and actively pursued. Third, statistical deaths, unlike abortion deaths, occur with some degree of consent on the part of those at risk. Fourth, these deaths, unlike fetal deaths, do not involve one individual making decisions that harm others. And fifth, unlike fetal deaths, these deaths are not killings, but rather instances of letting die.

These are all debatable assumptions there is no space to explore fully here. But the following brief considerations should raise serious questions about their worth. First, is the fact that a given death is "merely" statistical morally relevant? One might try to argue that since the death is less certain than one caused directly by an abortion, those who make the decisions leading to it are less morally responsible. Perhaps. But often enough there is sufficient evidence to be quite certain that a given course of action will have fatal consequences for some people. For example, by now, we know that if no changes are made in transportation, at least 40,000 more people will be dead a year from now. That knowledge would certainly be central for any consequentialist moral theory, and it's hard to see how a nonconsequentialist theory that recognizes the sanctity of life could discount it: it is hard to imagine what consideration could bear the moral weight of such a large number of deaths. And, when we look carefully at the facts, the fetal deaths that result from setting a particular abortion policy are more like these statistical deaths than is at first evident. We don't know which fetuses will die, and our knowledge of any particular fetus that is to die is, in any case, extremely limited: we know only that it is the fetus inside a given woman.

And although it is true that no one wants those who die in traffic accidents dead, the same could justifiably be said of aborted fetuses. In the first case, society wants a convenient transportation system, one that happens, in fact, to lead to a large number of deaths. In the second, women aim at freedom from pregnancy and motherhood. In both cases, people would no doubt gladly change these undesirable consequences if the desired ends could be achieved without them.

Can doubt be as easily cast on the objection based on consent? Fetuses do not consent to being aborted, of course, whereas those anonymous individuals who die as a result of social policies may be thought to have consented both to the relevant policies and the specific situations that led to their deaths.

Naturally, fetuses do not consent to their deaths. What is in question here is the extent to which participants in other risky practices are informed and consenting. This disagreement can quite reliably be correlated with the traditional split between political conservatives and progressives. Conservatives tend to see individuals as egoistic rational calculators, making most decisions on the basis of their own perceived self-interest. Progressives are more likely to notice how decision making is molded by circumstances that cause people to make choices that are really neither in their self-interest nor in that of society as a whole. There is no space here to analyze any case fully, but it is clear that the latter outlook is, in at least some important cases, more accurate.[18]

For example, conservatives tend to stress that the dangerous transportation system has developed as a result of individual choices by people who knowingly incur its risks. However, a look at the history of its development and the choices that face those now currently participating in it would suggest otherwise. On the one hand, there is reason to believe that the system did not emerge from informed, democratic public debate but, rather, as a result of pressures created by those who stood to benefit financially from the reliance on cars.[19] On the other, given the existing alternatives, those who now participate have very limited choices. As H. Laurence Ross comments:

> The dependence of Americans on the private automobile is extreme, and in some situations virtually total. Except in the largest cities, alternatives to

[18] As Ross points out, "to 'see' events as outgrowths of more complex social institutions requires a particular way of understanding, a paradigm less individualistic than the psychological. It is less reassuring than the tacit belief that accidents are the outcome of immoral people rather than of complex, morally ambiguous, even morally acceptable actions and persons" (*Confronting Drunk Driving*, p. xii). He goes on to point out that the more individualistic paradigms are not only "intuitive" in American culture, but they also cost less: "by placing all responsibility on individuals we avoid the political and economic conflicts attendant on examining our institutions, our culture, and our technological assumptions. While punishment and law enforcement are expensive, they avoid the trauma of changing our social system" (p. xii).

[19] See Nadis and MacKenzie, *Car Trouble*, p. 5. They point out that "starting in the 1930s, National City Lines, a company backed by General Motors, Standard Oil, Phillips Petroleum, Firestone Tire and Rubber, Mack Truck, and other auto interests, systematically bought up and closed down more than 100 electric trolley lines in 45 cities across the country. In 1949, a federal jury convicted GM and the other companies of conspiring to replace electric transportation systems with buses and to monopolize the sale of buses. (These corporations were fined a trifling $5,000 each for their actions.) But the long-term damage had already been done. In 1947, when the destruction of mass transit was just beginning, 40 percent of U.S. workers relied on public transportation to get to their jobs. In 1963, only 14 percent did. . . [T]oday less than 5 percent of the working population commutes by way of public transportation."

automobile transportation are inconvenient, expensive, unpleasant, dangerous, or nonexistent. . . . The extent of our automobile dependence is suggested by the fact that the possession of a driver's license is nearly universal. Indeed, it can be said that the license serves as a kind of national identity card. Moreover, the availability of cars has transformed even the physical structure of American society so that driving has become to all intents and purposes a necessity.[20]

These claims square with my own experiences, as well as my observations of others who are unable, for various reasons, to drive: it would be no exaggeration to say that they are, in many ways, as limited in their choices as are the wheelchair bound. Under these circumstances, it is dubious whether the choice to drive can often be truly voluntary.

The same might reasonably be said of those insecure young people who, seduced by Joe Camel, have been exposed to 200 puffs of nicotine by the time they have finished their first pack of cigarettes.[21] Nicotine now turns out to be so addictive that there is some talk of the FDA banning it.[22] Nicotine affects the brain's pleasure centers in a positive way and improves alertness, efficiency, reaction times, and learning.[23]

Can the decision to start smoking truly be described as informed? Most people start early in life at a time when they are ill-prepared to undertake the appropriate cost–benefit analysis. The probability that their decision is uninformed is increased by ubiquitous tobacco ads, as well as the virtual media blackout on the dangers of smoking.[24] Yet smoking is implicated in more than 400,000 deaths a year in the United States alone.

These are, of course, just two cases, albeit important ones. Others must be evaluated on an individual basis. But what they suggest is that, despite popular beliefs, there is good reason for thinking that many convenience-based deaths are not informed, and/or not voluntary. They are thus more

---

[20] Ross, *Confronting Drunk Driving*, p. 5.

[21] Ruth Winter, *The Scientific Case against Smoking* (New York: Crown, 1980), p. 5.

[22] See, for example, "Fighting and Switching," *Newsweek*, March 21, 1994, pp. 52–53.

[23] Winter, *The Scientific Case against Smoking*, pp. 2–3.

[24] For information about the risks of smoking, see G. E. Shelton, "Smoking Cessation Modalities: A Comparison for Healthcare Professionals," *Cancer Practice* 1, no. 1 (May–June 1993): 49–55. Both the absolute number of deaths and the percentage of deaths related to smoking are impressive: one enormous study found half of all deaths to be associated with cigarette smoking. L. H. Kuller, J. K. Ockhene, E. Meilahn, D. N. Wentworth, K. H. Svendsen, and J. D. Neaton, "Cigarette Smoking and Mortality. MRFIT Research Group," *Preventive Medicine* 20, no. 5 (September 1991):638–54. Another study found that 30 percent of all cancers could be prevented if no one smoked and that for some cancers (oral cavity, esophagus, lung, and bronchi), 90 percent could be eliminated. P. A. Newcomb and P. P. Carbone, "The Health Consequences of Smoking. Cancer," *The Medical Clinics of North America* 76, no. 2 (March 1992): 305–31.

comparable to the allegedly convenience-based fetal deaths caused by abortion than they may at first seem. For if individuals' participation in activities or situations is not informed or voluntary, they are being put at risk of death by the decisions of others who benefit from those constrained choices.

The question is, what follows? It seems to me many such issues fall properly in the province of democratic decision making. Perhaps then some societies will decide that having a given bridge is worth the probable loss of three construction workers or that getting chicken for 2 cents a pound cheaper is worth the risks inherent in antibiotic-laced chicken feed. However, such decisions are morally dubious unless all the relevant issues are fully aired and the resulting burdens are shared as equally as possible. These conditions often fail to be met in our society.

Decision-making contexts that fail to meet these criteria devalue human life. Facing them squarely shows that society's rhetoric about its value has some meaning. Many in our society have wanted it both ways. Where it costs them nothing, they are all for the sanctity of human life (and other "mom and apple pie" values), but when the steps necessary to protect life reduce their profits or violate their conception of proper social arrangements, they seem quite willing to risk the lives of others. As a society, we tolerate such behavior, excusing it with a variety of subterfuges that keep us psychologically comfortable in the face of practices that do devalue life and other allegedly valued goods.[25]

One source of comfort is a philosophical establishment that often seems unable or unwilling to notice or challenge the moral status quo. One escape route is to disappear into the thickets of abstraction, disparaging or downgrading the kind of work that risks threatening fundamental social assumptions. Another is to focus on fine distinctions without ever subjecting the big picture to the same careful analysis.

I believe that much of the philosophical effort engaged in the killing/letting die discussion falls into the second category: the emphasis has been on ferreting out subtle distinctions between cases rather than on showing where they are irrelevant or overshadowed by other considerations.[26] In the kinds of cases we are discussing here, those distinctions may have little, if

---

[25] For an illuminating discussion of this issue, see Guido Calabresi and Philip Bobbitt, *Tragic Choices* (New York: Norton, 1978), as well as Calabresi's "Reflections on Medical Experimentation in Humans," in *Experimentation with Human Subjects,* ed. Paul A. Freund (New York: George Braziller, The Daedalus Library, 1969), pp. 178–96.

[26] For an excellent recent discussion of these issues, see Tom L. Beauchamp and James F. Childress, *Principles of Biomedical Ethics,* 4th ed. (New York: Oxford University Press, 1994), chap. 4. For additional argument, see Shelly Kagan, *The Limits of Morality* (Oxford: Clarendon, 1989).

any, force. For instance, the line between killing and letting die may be un-reliable, shifting according to the context within which the decision is ex-amined. So when a company deliberately chooses to omit a safety feature from a product in order to save money, do we focus on the fact that the deaths arise from an omission or on the fact that the moving force here was an active decision? Surely *that* difference is not what determines whether a death is more or less blameworthy. Nor does the fact (important in some cases) that in letting die, responsibility for the death is spread to an outside agent. So if a company knowingly exposes its employees to carcinogens, could it really mitigate its responsibility by saying that the benzene is the killer, not the policy?[27] These kinds of distinctions seem especially ques-tionable where those at risk are, unlike fetuses, paradigm cases of full-fledged moral persons.

My suspicion that philosophers are guilty of neglecting the overall pic-ture is reinforced by the fact that the convenience-based deaths I have dis-cussed are at first blush more obviously worrisome than fetal deaths. After all, they involve fully self-conscious individuals who are embedded in a web of social relationships. Not only are victims often unhappily aware that their lives are ending prematurely, but also their deaths may well involve serious suffering on the part of those who love them. So one would think that there would be at least as many attempts to show that these deaths are as culpable as those of fetuses, than of the contrary thesis. Yet that is not the case. Furthermore, any attempt such as mine to argue for the seriousness of these other convenience-based deaths is likely to be dismissed as "politi-cally motivated," whereas the case that is more comfortable for the status quo proceeds without any such comment.[28]

Philosophy is guilty on another related count. I have objected to its ten-dency to focus on details at the expense of the big picture. Both popular and philosophical discussion has a way of focusing on dead fetuses rather than the overall context of abortion decisions. Feminist treatments of abortion have raised this issue again and again.[29] Yet the point rarely seems to stick.

---

[27] For a wonderful discussion of these issues, see W. K. Clifford, "The Ethics of Belief," in *Lectures and Essays* (London: Macmillan, 1879). The law is also, naturally, a particularly rich source of food for thought about them.

[28] Not only are these accusations inconsistently applied, but they often confuse moral claims for political ones. Doing good ethics requires us to take account of all aspects of the situation, including existing power relationships. See "Good Bioethics Must Be Feminist Bioethics," reprinted as part of Chapter 1. A still further point to ponder here is the tendency on the part of moral philosophers to prefer a moral theory that can be applied consistently, no matter how unattractive its daily demands, over serviceable theories even if they falter in desert-island cases. I am inclined to believe that this attitude constitutes a kind of intel-lectual elitism that subordinates welfare to neatness.

[29] For a helpful discussion, see Susan Sherwin, *No Longer Patient* (Philadelphia: Temple Uni-versity Press, 1992), chap. 5.

One central feminist point is that women are expected to accomplish the impossible. In general, women have fewer resources than men of the same class, yet they are expected to do far more with them because of their primary responsibility for childrearing. So many women seek abortions because they would otherwise be unable to cope with these conditions.[30] Because even these powerful defenses of abortion (abortion from desperation, we might call them) tend to be rejected by a society that does not wish to acknowledge its own unreasonable demands, women have been kept on the defensive, and even feminist discussions of abortion have reflected that fact by emphasizing the altruism motivating many abortions.[31] In particular, they have emphasized women's reluctance to bear babies whose care will undermine their ability to care for others.

This is a real concern, especially at a time when more or less severe forms of child neglect are widespread. It is crucial for women to insist on, and society to take seriously, what solemn undertakings childbearing and childrearing are. Many children are not getting either the material resources they need or enough time with responsible adults. There is not always room for one more in a family, not if people care about being good parents.

Attention to this kind of context would begin to bring our society's conception of abortion more in line with its views about other death-producing activities. So why does the discussion continue to focus monomaniacally on dead fetuses? If the defense of convenience-based deaths in general is to point to a justifying context, why is the same strategy considered suspect or ignored altogether in much of the abortion debate?

This point is relevant in another way, too. Opponents of abortion often sound as if their only concern is the welfare of fetuses. But that is untrue in most cases. Those who favor women's access to abortion have pointed out ad nauseam that if abortion opponents truly cared about fetuses, they would support a variety of social measures designed to ensure both that fewer unwanted fetuses were conceived in the first place and the welfare of born individuals.

There is a still stronger way to put this point. Moral positions on particular issues come in packages. It is not possible just to hold the isolated belief that killing fetuses is unjustifiable; what is really believed is some view about killing fetuses *plus* a set of beliefs about the appropriate trade-offs involved in acting on that belief. In short, inextricably bound up with the

---

[30] Perhaps it bears saying once again that women often have, in any case, little say over when they will have sexual intercourse. Yet they are held responsible for any resulting child.
[31] Even Caroline Whitbeck's excellent "The Moral Implications of Regarding Women as People: New Perspectives on Pregnancy and Personhood" has some tendencies in this direction. In *Abortion and the Status of the Fetus,* ed. William B. Bondeson et al. (Dordrecht: D. Riedel Publishing Company, 1983).

evaluation of killing fetuses is an evaluation of how the costs of stopping such killing should be borne.

Reducing the need for abortions would be expensive, both financially and, for some people, in terms of losing valued social arrangements. For example, reducing unwanted conception in teenagers would probably include setting up excellent sex education programs, universal access to contraception, and the kind of gender equality that empowers girls to say no to sex they don't want and to make sure that contraception is used in sexual encounters they do want. These are changes incompatible with the value systems of many anti-abortion activists. Likewise, reducing pregnancies due to contraceptive failure requires making the development of safe, convenient, effective, and universally available contraception a priority. And, to reduce the number of abortions necessary for women's health, it would be necessary to take expensive measures to improve women's health in the first place. To address the need for abortion for fetal defect would require society to provide universal pre-conception counseling and care for impaired children and adults. Providing the financial and social support women need to raise more children well would require enormous social changes.

Although such measures would not altogether eradicate women's desire for access to abortion, they would lead to vastly fewer abortions. If reducing the number of abortions is the highest priority of opponents of abortion, why do so few fight for them?

My suspicion is that relatively few anti-abortion activists expect to suffer personally from a ban on abortions. If they are women, they may see themselves primarily as nurturers and are, in any case, prepared to assign this role to all other women, regardless of their own life plans. Members of either sex may adhere to moral and political views that cause them to see with equanimity the financial or other inequities that caring for additional children thrusts on women. In the most general terms, restricting legal abortion now is consonant with their other values, such as the belief that premarital sex is wrong, whereas contributing to the effort to spread the burden of such a restriction does violate those values. But this understanding of the situation is much different—and much less appealing—than the position they profess to hold.

In short, unwillingness to share the burden of abortion restrictions implicitly says that reducing the slaughter of fetuses is *not, after all,* the primary value here. The overriding value is, on the contrary, shifting the cost of restrictive policies to others. Recognizing that fact changes the complexion of the abortion debate drastically.

I started out by asking whether conceding that many abortions are desired for the sake of convenience would require us to conclude that they are immoral and thus ought to be prohibited. I have argued that society tolerates many deaths that can be attributed to convenience, deaths that are at least as culpable as fetal deaths in abortions allegedly desired for the sake of convenience. However, the moral similarity of in these deaths is obscured by a variety of powerful social mechanisms. So at present it would be inconsistent to call for prohibiting convenience-based abortions.

But it is also obvious from what I have said so far that many of these other convenience-based deaths are morally suspect. What then of abortions that appear to fall into the same category? At the beginning of this article I said that I wanted to see what would follow from granting the premise that many abortions are performed for the sake of convenience. I think I have shown that it is by no means clear that allegedly convenience-based abortions should be prohibited. Of course, I conceded that most abortions are based on convenience only for the sake of argument. It is, on the contrary, extraordinarily bizarre to think that continuing an unwanted pregnancy and giving birth against one's will constitute mere inconveniences. Indeed, the values preserved by full access to abortion are jealously guarded in other contexts. However, that is an argument for another day.

CHAPTER 8

Abortion, Forced Labor, and War

Opponents of abortion often assert that abortions are carried out just for women's "convenience." Suppose that, for the sake of argument, one were to concede this claim. Would it follow, as opponents of abortion assume, that these abortions are immoral and ought to be prohibited? No. Attention to consistent social policy requires us first to determine whether similar deaths are condoned in other contexts. If so, then abortion cannot justifiably be prohibited unless some morally relevant difference is found between these cases.[1]

A careful look at social policy reveals a surprisingly high tolerance for practices that routinely cause deaths. Some, such as building bridges to speed traffic, are appropriately described as a matter of convenience. Others, such as growing tobacco for profit, are only charitably so described.

One glaring example of society's willingness to trade death for convenience is the automobile-based transportation system. Although the current system is, at best, wonderfully convenient, it leads to at least 40,000 deaths from accidents every year in the United States alone. Many lives would undoubtedly be saved if an excellent public transportation system were created instead.

In such mortal trade-offs, education alone could prevent deaths; in others, changing the situation would require that resources be allocated differently. We, as a society, often prefer to keep costs low even if that results in more deaths. Yet in the case of abortion, it is argued that preventing fetal deaths is worth any price.

---

[1] I have argued this issue more at length elsewhere. See Chapter 7, "Abortion and the Argument from Convenience."

So what morally relevant difference justifies this disparity? It could be argued that the first type of death, unlike fetal death, (1) are just "statistical" deaths; (2) are foreseen but not intended; or (3) involve informed consent on the part of those at risk. But none of these objections can withstand critical scrutiny. They turn out to be intellectual subterfuges that keep us psychologically comfortable in the face of practices that truly devalue life.

The morally troubling point here is that these deaths are excused by pointing to a justifying context. Yet when the same kind of justifying context is proposed for abortion, it is rejected because life is so sacred that no competing values outweigh it. This state of affairs constitutes a costly double standard for women who bear most of the resulting burdens.

Now many abortions would be unnecessary if society were organized somewhat differently. Some of these alternative arrangements would be expensive, although all would provide worthwhile benefits on top of their power to reduce the need for abortions. But opponents of abortion can prohibit abortion and shift its burdens to women by rejecting the alternatives as "too expensive." In short, they can eat their cake and have it too. If they, instead of women, bore the burden, one wonders whether they would judge the benefit to be worth the cost. For the real social perception of the value of life emerges every time a safety standard or a vaccination program is rejected as "too expensive."

Until this double standard is eradicated, it would be inconsistent to call for an end to abortions for convenience. But suppose society set itself the goal of preventing other convenience-based deaths? It seems reasonable to suppose that this turn of events would include a new willingness to undertake changes that would substantially lessen women's need for abortions.[2] So there would be relatively few cases where women would want abortions for the kinds of reasons that are now labeled matters of convenience. Would women have to give those up?

No. I will argue here that the values preserved by full access to abortion are not of the relatively trivial sort implied by the word "convenience" that has been attached to them by opponents of abortion. They are, in fact, much more significant.

TYPES OF ABORTION

Many people are prepared to concede that some abortions are justifiable. Among justifiable abortions are those that avert or remedy threats to a woman's life or health or to end pregnancies that result from rape or incest. More liberal moderates may also countenance abortion for fetal deformity,

---

[2] See Chapter 7, "Abortion and the Argument from Convenience," for a list of such measures.

poverty, or heavy family responsibilities. It is generally understood that these are not mere matters of convenience. Just what principles permit these cases to slip by the gatekeepers?

What they seem to have in common is that a woman's access to abortion has important benefits for others. Pregnancies that threaten a woman's life or health risk burdening fathers or society at large with the care of existing children and/or of the woman herself. Rape looks quite different. Reasonable people agree that rape is a particularly horrible form of assault, although many still believe that women themselves are at fault when they are raped. Why then is the exception for rape so widely accepted? One plausible line of reasoning is that rape followed by pregnancy embarrasses the man who is supposed to be in charge of a particular woman. Incest may also involve rape; in addition, it may produce children with serious problems; the same is true of fetuses thought to have biological defects. They, like the children of women in extreme poverty, may well become costly social burdens.

Focusing on the benefits, not for women, but for those around them, is characteristic of "moderate" treatments of abortion. As Rosalind Petchesky points out, even feminist positions tend to be influenced by "the association of fetus with 'baby' and the aborting woman with 'bad mother' . . . and the assumption that sex for pleasure is 'wrong' (for women) and the women who indulge in it have to pay a price."[3] These ways of looking at women and sex "obscure the ways in which abortion is a basic need of women, which is different from either a 'necessity' (unchosen) or a 'choice' (unnecessary)."[4]

Petchesky believes, and I agree, that even a feminist utopia would not eradicate the women's desire for abortions. As I have argued elsewhere,[5] it is a mistake to think that only patriarchy and capitalism stand in the way of women rearing every child they conceive. Although women clearly need much more help than they are getting, and they do often abort or give up their babies because they cannot cope with existing social conditions, the way these claims create a standard could make it quite difficult for a pregnant women to refuse motherhood.

However, not even an unimaginably supportive society will take all the burden of motherhood from women. That would be especially true if abortion for fetal disease or disability were frowned upon or prohibited. There will always be women whose other projects are incompatible with the demands of motherhood, and it is surely best for both woman and child if such a reluctantly pregnant woman either aborts or lets others do the rear-

---

[3] Rosalind Pollack Petchesky, *Abortion and Woman's Choice: The State, Sexuality, and Reproductive Freedom* (Boston: Northeastern University Press, 1985), p. 386.
[4] Ibid., pp. 384–85.
[5] See Chapter 12, "Another Look at Contract Pregnancy."

ing. Even if the perfect contraceptive may considerably reduce this problem, it will not, given human nature, make it go away altogether. In any case, do we really want a society where women cannot change their minds about a given pregnancy?

As Kristen Luker notes, "this round of the abortion debate is so passionate and hard-fought *because it is a referendum on the place and meaning of motherhood.*"[6] But is the issue motherhood? Or womanhood? In her discussion of abortion activists in Fargo, Nancy (Ann) Davis writes: "both sets of women seemed to accept the conventional wisdom that it is the special capacity to nurture that sets females apart . . . once one considers the possibility that the 'essential female characteristic' (that is, nurturance) is not strongly tied to biological reproduction . . . the question 'Why should nurturance—or indeed, any particular characteristic or set of allegedly female, cultural characteristics—be seen as the basis of female gender-identity?' seems inescapable."[7] Davis goes on to suggest that all but the most radical approaches "leave intact the suspect essentialist presumption that there is some special quality or qualities that make women female and the view that it is a matter of unalterable fact rather than a matter of (possibly oppressive, certainly changeable) social custom or institutional fact what those special qualities are deemed to be."[8]

People have long raised questions about whether typical gender traits are necessary or beneficial. As John Stuart Mill pointed out over a hundred years ago, the pressures of socialization are so pervasive that it is impossible to know what women would be like in their absence. And, as feminists have been pointing out for some time, much of women's oppression can be traced to their nurturing role.[9]

If this kind of essentialism were true, then justice would require that society reward female nurturing as much as more traditionally masculine activities. But that approach ignores the vast psychological differences among women and assumes that women have more in common with females of other species than with men.[10] That these assumptions are widespread

[6] Kristen Luker, *Abortion and the Politics of Motherhood* (Berkeley: University of California Press, 1984), p. 193.

[7] Nancy (Ann) Davis, "The Abortion Debate: The Search for Common Ground, Part I", *Ethics* 103 (April 1993): 533–34.

[8] Ibid., p. 534.

[9] See John Stuart Mill, "The Subjection of Women," in *Essays on Sex Equality*, ed. Alice S. Rossi (Chicago: University of Chicago Press, 1970). Nurturing is by no means the only source of oppression, as psychological studies have been showing for some time. (Studies show that "healthy" females have what would be considered "unhealthy" human (e.g., male) traits.)

[10] Not that it is always the females of other species that do most of the nurturing, as feminist biologists have been noticing lately. But, of course, in many species it is the female who bears most of this burden.

helps explain why the notion of equal rights for women still seems so alien to most people.

Yet it is only in this context of equality that the full consequences of unwanted childbearing can be evaluated. For only such a perspective makes it possible to compare the sacrifices required by it with men's expectations of freedom. In this light, unwanted childbearing looks a lot less like a labor of love than the kind of threat that impels men to war.

Because public life is still so male centered, there is little social recognition of what it means to become a mother. Laurence Tribe puts it beautifully: "Pregnancy does not merely 'inconvenience' the woman for a time; it gradually turns her into a mother and makes her one for all time."[11] Indeed,

> Having a child is a permanent commitment. Yet the decision is often a blind one, and the outcome is unpredictable ... there is no way of knowing whether a child will be a source of love, comfort, and inexpressible joy or worry, pain, and torment.
>
> Whichever it is, and it's usually a blend of them all, a child becomes part of a woman's life forever. To be a mother is a lifelong task. The decision to become a mother is fraught with implications. . . . In many ways, to have or not have a child will be the deciding factor in hundreds, perhaps thousands, of other little decisions down the road—what job you'll take, what house you'll buy, what neighborhood you'll live in, how you spend your days, your money, your weekends, holidays, vacations, where and when you'll travel, who your friends are, who's in your kinship network, and so on.[12]

For poor women, of course, having children has still more fundamental consequences.

The financial cost of children is suggestive of the demands of childrearing. According to the U.S. Dept. of Agriculture, raising a "no-frills" kid to the age of eighteen costs some $100,000; college adds another $100,000. Middle-class children cost more still, and neither of these figures includes opportunity costs for women who choose to be housewives. Other costs are substantial. Studies show that married women without children have three months more discretionary time a year than do mothers, months of twelve-hour, five-day weeks. Husbands average 20 percent of the domestic work, up from 8 percent in 1965. Thus there is a huge imbalance in the child-related work done by women and by men. Worse yet, despite

---

[11] Laurence H. Tribe, *Abortion: The Clash of Absolutes* (New York: Norton, 1990), p. 104.

[12] Susan S. Lang, *Women without Children: The Reasons, the Rewards, the Regrets* (New York: Pharos Books, 1991), pp. 3–4. She goes on to point out that studies show that "parenthood . . . tends to wreak havoc on a marriage. . . . Study after study confirms that the negative impact of children on marital happiness is pervasive, regardless of race, religion, education, and wives' employment" (p. 81).

women's burden, many children are suffering because of insufficient adult attention.[13]

Some human rights legislation addresses the question of how such social burdens should be allocated. Consider the International Labor Organization (ILO) Forced Labor Convention of 1930.[14] It prohibits forced labor except in a series of narrowly restricted cases.[15] In particular, forced labor is not to be used as a means of political repression, economic development, or "as a means of racial, social, national or religious discrimination."[16] Forced labor cannot be used to benefit private parties. Furthermore, the work to be done must be important and in the direct interest of the community from which the workers are to be drawn, the work or service must be "of present or imminent necessity," it must not "lay too heavy a burden upon the present population," and it must have "been impossible to obtain voluntary labour for carrying out the work or rendering the service by the offer of rates of wages and conditions of labour not less favourable than those prevailing in the area concerned for similar work or service."[17] It is instructive that "the maximum period for which any person may be taken for forced or compulsory labor of all kinds in any one period of twelve months shall not exceed sixty days," that "the normal working hours of any person from whom forced or compulsory labour is exacted shall be the same as those prevailing in the case of voluntary labour, and the hours worked in excess of the normal working hours shall be remunerated at the rates prevailing in the case of overtime for voluntary labour," and that "a weekly day of rest shall be granted to all persons from whom forced or compulsory labour of any kind is exacted."[18] Furthermore, wages are to be paid "to each worker individually and not to his tribal chief or to any other authority."[19]

---

13 Ibid., pp. 206–9; Laura M. Purdy, *In Their Best Interest?* (Ithaca: Cornell University Press, 1992).

14 Edward Lawson, *Encyclopedia of Human Rights* (New York: Taylor and Francis, 1991), pp. 802–8.

15 Excluded from the prohibition are (1) work exacted in the course of compulsory military service laws for work of a purely military nature; (2) work that "forms part of the normal civic obligations of the citizens of a fully self-governing country"; (3) public work resulting from criminal conviction; (4) work required by a major emergency; and (5) "minor communal services of a kind which, being performed by the members of the community in the direct interest of the said community, can therefore be considered as normal civic obligations incumbent upon the members of the community, provided that the members of the community or their direct representatives shall have the right to be consulted in regard to the need for such services" (ibid., p. 802).

16 Lawson, "Slavery and the Slave Trade," in *Encyclopedia of Human Rights*, p. 1351.

17 Lawson, *Encyclopedia of Human Rights*, p. 803.

18 Ibid.

19 Interestingly, although "ordinary rations [may be] given as a part of wages, deductions from wages shall not be made either for the payment of taxes or for special food, clothing

Those responsible for this document would, no doubt, be shocked at the suggestion that it might have some relevance for women's child-related labor. Forced labor seems to be a well-defined notion, and the authors are quick to exclude women from its demands altogether. Presumably it would never have occurred to them that, from an egalitarian perspective, much of what women experience might fall squarely under its purview.[20] Perhaps they would, if pressed, include women's child-related work under the exclusions cited in note 18, either as "the work or service which forms part of the normal civil obligations of the citizens of a fully self-governing country," or "minor communal services of a kind which, being performed by the members of the community in the direct interest of the community, can therefore be considered as normal obligations incumbent upon the members of the community."[21]

The authors of the ILO Convention on Forced Labor would no doubt be inclined to compare women's child-related labor to military service expected of men or perhaps even men's productive labor. But these comparisons are not successful. It is true that most societies have expected men to be available for military service. Such service has often severely limited men's liberty and sadly, has cost many their lives.[22] However, periods of service are usually limited, well short of the twenty years or so it takes to raise a child, and participation may be voluntary for all but the poorest men. Furthermore, men often enjoy special privileges, such as free medical care or veteran's points in civil service exams, in return for their military service.[23]

_____

or accommodation supplied to a worker for the purpose of maintaining him in fit condition to carry on his work . . . or for the supply of tools" (ibid., pp. 803–4).

[20] That authors of human rights documents (most of whom are, after all, men) write from traditional rather than egalitarian perspectives is evident after even a cursory examination of the *Encyclopedia of Human Rights*. Of particular relevance here are the 1957 additions to the ILO Convention on Forced Labor, the ILO Abolition of Forced Labor Convention. The latter asserts that forced labor is prohibited "as a means of racial, social, national or religious discrimination" (p. 1334). Notice the glaring absence of sexual discrimination. Another important example is the comment of the Human Rights Committee on article 1 of the International Covenant on Civil and Political Right, which proposes that governments must represent "the whole people belonging to the territory without distinction as to race, creed, or colour" (p. 1334). Once again, the potential for lack of representation on the basis of sex either never enters the picture or is dismissed altogether. Presumably the justification for such dismissal is that women's interests are represented by those of the men to whom they are attached. For trenchant critiques of this notion, see recent feminist scholarship, most notably Susan Okin, *Justice, Gender, and the Family* (New York: Basic Books, 1989).

[21] Lawson, *Encyclopedia of Human Rights*, p. 802.

[22] As has childbearing for women.

[23] None of this is to deny that men have often been unjustly robbed by military service, or war itself, of their self-determination. But that fact does not imply that women also deserve such ill-treatment. The right response is to attempt to eradicate militarism.

Might women's child-related labor be compared with men's daily labors in the work force? Let us first notice that, with a few exceptions, women have always participated in productive labor, even if their contribution has not always been recognized. Today, studies show that women generally work more hours than men, because they do both productive and reproductive labor. So the nostalgic fiction of homemaking women and men hard at work outside it is not a realistic basis for comparison. Furthermore, men, except again for those on the bottom, have many more options about what work they will undertake and are far more often rewarded for their work with privilege, money, security, and power.[24]

Attempts to fend off uncomfortable comparisons of women's child-related work to forced labor would face additional serious difficulties. One is the caveat appended to the second that "members of the community or their direct representatives shall have the right to be consulted in regard to the need for such services."[25] It is surely doubtful that women as a group or their representatives agree to compulsory pregnancy and its attendant childbearing duties.[26] Nor would they agree that this unequal division of labor would be in the interest of the community as a whole. Polls show that a majority of women want abortions available, and it would, in any case, be implausible to base any national policy on the claim that women are adequately represented when such a small proportion of legislators are themselves women. So even though reproductive service may very well be viewed as part of "the normal civic obligations of the citizens of a fully self-governing country," the burning question is whether the assumption is morally tenable, especially where overpopulation is more of a problem than underpopulation.

It is instructive to compare the conditions under which forced labor is considered acceptable by the 1930 convention with those under which most women rear children. First, forced labor is prohibited where it is used as a means of discrimination. It is true that sexual discrimination is not included in the list of unacceptable discriminations, but that just demonstrates how widely accepted is women's second-class status. If sexual discrimination were included, compulsory childbearing and rearing would have to be illegal, given their consequences.[27]

---

[24] Once again, the fact that many men are deprived of significant choices about their work and enjoy few rewards does not justify the same conditions for women. The right response is greater egalitarianism with respect to these matters.

[25] Lawson, *Encyclopedia of Human Rights*, p. 802.

[26] By "compulsory pregnancy," I refer to the situation where a pregnant woman is refused an abortion she desires.

[27] One might want to distinguish here between intentionally discriminatory actions and those which merely have discriminatory consequences. But if discrimination is the evil, once the causal relationship is known, consequences are what count.

Second, forced labor is not supposed to benefit private parties; yet forcing women to bear and rear children against their will often benefits men who want children without taking full responsibility for them.[28] Otherwise women could choose to conceive only by men who can be trusted to share the burdens of reproduction as fully as possible.[29]

Third, compulsory pregnancy and childrearing do not meet the requirement that forced labor be of important and direct interest to the community. Although it is true that once children are born their care is of important and direct interest to the community, the same is not true of compulsory pregnancy itself unless a community is threatened with extinction and all agree that that outcome would be undesirable. Furthermore, there is little discussion about whether forced childbearing and rearing impose "too heavy" a burden on women, but consider the outcry if state-imposed mandates placed the same constraints on men in the name of community service. It should also be noted that compulsory pregnancy and childbearing violate the proviso that the relevant labor could not be obtained on the free market at fair wages.

Last, but not least, mothering, especially mothering in poverty, violates the time limitations placed on acceptable forced labor. Remember that forced labor can be required no more than sixty days a year, but women rearing children they did not want must often labor on their behalf 365 days a year. Forced labor is to be limited to normal working hours, with overtime for extra hours. But most women work, directly or indirectly, on behalf of their children for more than forty hours a week; nor do they receive pay of any kind for their direct labor, no matter how long their hours.[30] Remember, too, that there is to be a weekly day of rest, but there is no day of rest for most women raising children.[31]

---

[28] This is a particularly interesting issue, as the question of who benefits from child-related labor is as yet unresolved. Common arguments against the provision of benefits for individuals who are rearing children are predicated on the assumption that children are a private luxury. It would follow from this position that childrearing labor does indeed benefit private parties. However, it does seem clear that society as a whole does benefit from having some number of children, assuming it wants a future. But whether it now benefits from the existence of unwanted children is questionable.

[29] This raises the question of why women have sexual intercourse with men who are not likely to be reliable partners. Sometimes they have little choice in the matter. The rest of the time such behavior is no doubt voluntary, even if often uninformed. In any case, it is hard to see why women must be held responsible for the full consequences of unwise sexual attraction when men so often go scot-free.

[30] Some years ago economists began to compile statistics on market rates for the kinds of work undertaken by typical housewives.

[31] Examining the international conventions on slavery with this same purpose would be no less interesting.

This kind of comparison suggests that despite many social changes, the situation for many women today is not so different from the one that prompted John Stuart Mill to comment:

> The general opinion of men is supposed to be, that the natural vocation of a woman is that of a wife and mother. I say, is supposed to be, because, judging from acts—from the whole of the present constitution of society—one might infer that their opinion was the direct contrary. They might be supposed to think that the alleged natural vocation of women was of all things the most repugnant to their nature; insomuch that if they are free to do anything else—if any other means of living, or occupation of their time and faculties, is open, which has any chance of appearing desirable to them—there will not be enough of them who will be willing to accept the conditions said to be natural to them.

He goes on to assert: "I should like to hear somebody openly enunciating the doctrine . . . 'It is necessary to society that women should marry and produce children. They will not do so unless they are compelled. Therefore it is necessary to compel them.' The merits of the case would then be clearly defined." He compares this case with the argument for slavery, which ran thus: "It is necessary that cotton and sugar should be grown. White men cannot produce them. Negroes will not, for any wages which we choose to give. *Ergo* they must be compelled." The same kind of argument used to be made for the impressment of sailors. It is, as Mill pointed out, open to the reply "First pay the sailors the honest value of their labour. When you have made it as worth their while to serve you, as to work for other employers, you will have no more difficulty than others have in obtaining their services. To this there is no logical answer except 'I will not.' "[32] But Mill argues that as people are now both ashamed of and no longer desire to rob workers in this way, such logic is no longer respectable.

Although conditions for women have, for the most part, improved dramatically, the core of what Mill has to say here is still relevant. Of course despotic husbands may now be divorced, but the existence of children often leads women to stay with abusive men. Single parenthood, whether it came about as a result of divorce or unwedded motherhood, places enormous burdens on most women and is likely to be comfortable only for the wealthiest women. But few women are wealthy. The application of Mill's moral here is that if having children were properly respected and

[32] Mill, "The Subjection of Women"; all quotations from p. 155.

remunerated, then many women would undoubtedly choose to have them even if they were free not to do so. Forcing pregnant women to choose between life-threatening illegal abortions or childrearing suggests that people are well aware that if women had other choices they would be much less likely to choose motherhood under the current circumstances.

Revolutionary theory, just war theory, or even international law recognize certain threats to life as a defense of violence. One common defense of abortion draws on this appeal to self-defense by arguing that women have a right to kill fetuses that threaten their lives. But it is erroneously assumed that the defense of violence is limited to threats to life, whereas a variety of different threats are widely recognized as such a defense.

Take the Declaration of Independence, for instance, which contains a fascinating list of grievances against the British. A few involve unjust loss of life, but the others are for the most part rooted in loss of individual or group self-determination.[33] Just war theories envisage similarly broad grounds for war. For instance, Francisco de Vitoria, a pivotal figure in the history of just war theory, asserted numerous justifications for war. Although the religious reasons now sound a little quaint, it doesn't take much imagination to see their relevance for contemporary philosophical disagreements. And the secular ones still form the core of rhetoric about international conflict.[34]

Self-determination plays a central role in international law. In 1984, the Human Rights Committee adopted a special comment on article 1 of the International Covenant on Civil and Political Rights, declaring that "the right of self-determination is of particular importance because its realization is an essential condition for the effective guarantee and observance of individual human rights and for the promotion and strengthening of those

[33]See the Declaration of Independence, in Lawson, *Encyclopedia of Human Rights*, pp. 1633–34.

[34]I say "rhetoric" because so much international conflict seems to arise from perceived self-interest rather than moral principle. Vitoria was a sixteenth-century Spanish theologian whose thinking on the concept of just war was provoked by the Spanish conquest of America. Although he is skeptical of the defenses claimed by the Spanish for their war against the Indians, he goes on to consider what would constitute reasonable grounds for making war against them. Among the religious reasons are (1) if the Indians refused to let the Spanish preach Christianity to them; or (2) if their ruler threatened or punished converts or potential converts or permitted them to be threatened by others. Among the secular reasons are if the Indians (1) refused to allow visitors or settlers in their land; (2) refused the Spanish the right to trade with them; (3) treated the Spanish worse than other foreigners; or (4) refused citizenship to those born in Indian lands. Vitoria also argues that (5) it is permissible to come to the aid of wronged friends or allies, and (6) that one may fight to prevent tyranny, especially where it is causing the death of innocents. He also entertains the idea of improving leadership of incompetent peoples. (See my unpublished dissertation, *An Analysis of Francisco de Vitoria's Law of Peace*.)

rights."[35] Furthermore, the same document emphasizes that a people's right to self-determination is compatible with, indeed, presupposes, a right to individual self-determination: "the self-determination of citizens, individually, on the basis of the recognition of their political rights, is a prerequisite of the effective realization of self-determination as the people's collective right."[36] The document recognizes this right only for peoples who are under "colonial and alien" domination, not those already organized in the form of a free state, because it does not wish to promote the disruption of countries. It comments, however, that such a government must represent "the whole people belonging to the territory without distinction as to race, creed or colour," a standard that is, of course, conspicuous for the absence of sex, suggesting a traditional view of sex roles unbefitting those who would be deemed sensitive to the multifarious forms of oppression.

Other states are not only required to "refrain from opposing and impeding the exercise of the right to self-determination, but also are under a positive obligation to help in securing its realization."[37] They are to do so by helping countries to achieve their independence and to support them in gaining complete sovereignty.

In 1979, the United Nations issued a further study of self-determination, entitled *The Right to Self-Determination: Implementation of United Nations Resolutions*.[38] This document elaborates on the notions of political, economic, social, and cultural factors inherent in the concept of self-determination. It holds that peoples have a right to determine their economic system and that they enjoy permanent sovereignty over their natural resources. It also holds that "the social aspects of the right of peoples to self-determination are related, in particular, to the promotion of social justice, to which every people is entitled and which, in its broadest sense, implies the right to the effective enjoyment by all the individual members of a particular people of their economic and social rights without any discrimination whatsoever." Cultural self-determination implies in its turn, "a right to determine and establish the cultural regime or system under which it is to live."[39] The precise content of cultural rights are left rather vague, but even this outline would suggest the wrongness of a system that systematically drafts half the population for childrearing service at the expense of their full participation in every facet of society.

---

[35] Lawson, *Encyclopedia of Human Rights*, p. 1332. The document is U.N. Doc. A/39/40, Annex VI, para. 1–8.

[36] Ibid., p. 1334.

[37] Ibid.

[38] This report was prepared by Mr. Hector Gros Espiell, special rapporteur of the U.N. Sub-Commission on Prevention of Discrimination and Protection of Minorities. U.N. Publication, Sales No. r/79.XIV.5.

[39] Lawson, *Encyclopedia of Human Rights*, p. 1335.

If self-determination is so highly valued, what role does it play in contemporary thinking about war? Michael Walzer writes that the defense of rights is the only reason for fighting and that "the wrong the aggressor commits is to force men and women to risk their lives for the sake of their rights."[40] The central rights he emphasizes are territorial integrity and political sovereignty.[41] Using what he calls the "legalist paradigm" that sees the realm of states as a society of individuals writ large, these threats can reasonably be translated as bodily control and some degree of control over one's resources.[42]

Those who find my comparison of women's and men's rights to self-determination perverse will no doubt be distressed by my attempt to conflate individual rights and those of nations. They will attempt to distinguish them by laying out morally relevant distinctions between the situation of women and that of wronged nations. The central political problem for women, as I see it, is that for various reasons, women are likely to remain spread among national groups rather than gathering together in such a way that their special interests could be protected. But the moral—as opposed to the political—significance of this state of affairs is questionable. What matters morally, and what ought to matter politically, is that the rights at issue for them are those for which men are often ready to die.

Compulsory pregnancy would violate women's self-determination even if they had no qualms about adopting out their infants. But women are

---

[40] Michael Walzer, *Just and Unjust Wars* (New York: Basic Books, 1977), p. 51. Of course, rights violations do not, by themselves, justify war. First, war must be fought according to certain rules, for example, those that protect civilians. Second, to be just, the decision to go to war must be made by the right authority, with the right intention, and only as a last resort. The war must also be likely to result in peace, and the total evil of the acts done under its name must be proportionate to the good achieved. See Duane L. Cady, *From Warism to Pacifism: A Moral Continuum* (Philadelphia: Temple University Press, 1989), p. 24. These criteria could quite well be applied to decisions about abortion. Notice that abortions are, overall, much less destructive than the average war.

[41] Walzer, *Just and Unjust Wars*, p. 52.

[42] Ibid., chap. 4. It is true that he sees these threats as more serious on the international level than he does at the individual level, because there they cannot be countered without risking loss of life. But if the rights in question are considered sufficiently important to warrant killing for at the international level, it is hard to see why they shouldn't be defended with equal vigor at the personal level. After all, Walzer believes that the rights involved in territorial integrity and political sovereignty are based on the rights of individuals, "and from them they take their force" (p. 53). He goes on to assert that "when states are attacked, it is their members who are challenged, not only in their lives, but also in the sum of things they value most, including the political association they have made. If they were not morally entitled to choose their form of government and shape the policies that shape their lives, external coercion would not be a crime; nor could it so easily be said that they had been forced to resist in self-defense. Individual rights (to life and liberty) underlie the most important judgments that we make about war. . . . States rights are simply their collective form" (pp. 53–54).

rarely willing to do that. On the one hand, most women appear to be deeply shocked at the notion of giving up a baby, and that is hardly surprising, given the relentless socialization girls undergo toward motherhood. On the other hand, although such pronatalism and sex-based socialization should be abolished, it would be harmful, under anything like our present circumstances, to stop emphasizing responsibility toward our offspring. Although it seems clear that we need to rethink the importance of biological relationships, children would be even worse off than they are now if more individuals rejected responsibility for the welfare of their children.

The upshot is that few women seriously entertain the notion of giving up a child. Unwanted pregnancy therefore drafts women into motherhood. But even if such motherhood does not threaten a woman's life or health, her choices become much more limited, as most of her resources must now be committed to those children. This state of affairs usually excludes full participation in the social, cultural, and political life of society and, under current arrangements, often leads to impoverishment and lack of respect for her as a person. In short, motherhood, especially responsible motherhood, forecloses many worthwhile options.

The options in question are ones men take for granted. Although class and race make a big difference in the goods a person enjoys, men generally have—and expect to have—a great deal more freedom to determine the conditions under which they will live than similarly situated women. Men are willing to go to great lengths to protect these same values. They would be shocked if it were suggested that the goods in question were insubstantial, mere matter of convenience, rather than centrally important liberties to determine how they will live. Only a worldview that sees women as less than Kantian persons could acquiesce in the same judgment on their behalf. Calling abortions desired to preserve these same goods for women a matter of "convenience" therefore constitutes an untenable double standard.

Where does all this leave us? On the one hand, it seems clear that society is prepared to accept many deaths to enhance convenience, even as it tries to avert its eyes from the implications of its choices. So even if, as so many opponents of abortion assert, abortions truly were a matter of convenience, it would not follow that they should be prohibited. Consistency requires that the same contextual decision-making procedures be applied to abortion as to those other death-producing situations.

On the other hand, a careful look at the values protected by access to abortion reveals that describing them as mere matters of convenience constitutes a double standard. Men are often ready and willing to kill to protect themselves from similar demands.

Are those values worth bloodshed? If they are, then how can women be denied abortions? Many innocents are killed in war to preserve such values, and fetuses are only questionably granted that status of innocent persons. If these values are not worth bloodshed, then society might demonstrate its good faith by abolishing war before it calls for an end to abortions.[43]

---

[43] If chivalry is not reason enough, perhaps men will be moved by the fact that most of those killed in the war are self-conscious persons with an irrefutable right to life, persons whose loss will be felt by those who love them for themselves, not for what they might become.

CHAPTER 9

Abortion and the Husband's Rights: A Reply to Teo

In "Abortion: The Husband's Constitutional Rights," Wesley Teo attempts to defend the view that husbands have constitutionally recognized rights with respect to their wives' abortions.[1] He argues that although *Roe v. Wade* prohibited state interference in first-trimester abortions, it did not address the question of fathers' rights, leaving the decision to a woman and her physician. Yet Teo believes that if women are free to go ahead in this way, their husbands are (1) denied their right to procreate; (2) discriminated against on the basis of sex; and (3) denied equal protection of the laws.

To support his claim that men are denied their right to procreate, Teo cites *Skinner v. Oklahoma,* where the Supreme Court threw out an Oklahoma statute providing for the sterilization of habitual criminals because it failed to meet the test of "rational classification" required by the Fourteenth Amendment. To support his claim that depriving men of their say about their wives' abortions discriminates against them on the basis of sex, Teo asserts that because the fetus is their joint creation, a husband's interest in it is as important and legitimate as a wife's. Basing a woman's right to decide about whether to have an abortion on the contingent fact that she is the one who carries the fetus is sex-based discrimination. And to support his claim that a woman's right to choose abortion violates the Equal Protection clause of the Fourteenth Amendment, Teo argues that the law favors the wife, even though husband and wife are similarly situated.

[1] Wesley D. H. Teo, "Abortion: The Husband's Constitutional Rights," *Ethics* 85, no. 4 (July 1975): 337–42.

Teo concludes: "In the preceding I have not argued, nor do my arguments imply, that the husband be given veto power in the matter of abortion. My arguments cut both ways. Neither spouse may be accorded an exclusive right. The constitutionally sound position is that an abortion decision, as far as a married couple is concerned, must be made jointly." This is an unexceptionable position. Surely any couple having difficulties with a pregnancy should discuss the matter and decide on a course of action suitable to both parties, for each has a right to participate in decisions affecting them. This right would be violated if the wife had an abortion without consulting her husband, or if he simply denied her that option. But why did Teo write the main body of his article if this reasonable conclusion is all that he intends?

For in it he envisages circumstances in which the partners cannot agree: a woman wants an abortion and her husband does not. He gives constitutional arguments that *do* imply that a husband could go to court and that a judge could uphold his legal right to require her to bear their child regardless of her wishes. If a judge were to use the arguments developed in Teo's paper to support a finding against the wife, he would be using his authority on the husband's behalf to override her wishes. It is true that this does not, strictly speaking, create a veto for the husband because it is the court, not the husband himself, who is judging that the husband's right has priority. Nevertheless, such a legal procedure is undesirable. For a court decision of this kind does not constitute the "joint" decision Teo recommends—it is an imposition of the husband's will on his wife. But Teo has failed to show that such an imposition is ever justifiable.

Let us examine his arguments in more detail. As we have seen, Teo claims that to deny a husband an equal right in decisions whether to obtain a first-trimester abortion infringes three rights guaranteed by the Constitution. These rights are (1) the right to procreate; (2) the right not to be discriminated against on the basis of sex; and (3) the right to equal protection under the laws. His arguments are legal, not moral. But I will assume that his position is a moral as well as legal one and argue that these principles do not entail the moral or legal conclusion that a court may deny a wife an abortion.

I will center my criticisms of his claim about two major issues: the "right to procreate" and the consequences of sexual differences for moral reasoning.

Teo's first claim is that a husband has a basic right to procreate. He derives this conclusion from an analysis of *Skinner v. Oklahoma,* in which the Supreme Court held that habitual criminals may not be sterilized. Teo quotes the Court's remark that it is dealing with "legislation which involves one of the basic rights of man. Marriage and procreation are fundamental to the very existence and survival of the race" (p. 340). How does the Skinner case apply to the abortion issue? According to Teo, if an abortion decision may be made by a wife alone, then it ceases "to be meaningful to speak of procreation as a basic *human* right. It has become an individual right, belonging solely to the woman" (p. 340). He goes on to say that this "constructively sterilizes" men (p. 340).

But surely Teo is reading a good deal more into *Skinner* than is really there. The Court made two points. The first is that it is unjust to sterilize certain criminals because cases relevantly similar are treated dissimilarly. The second is a rather ill-defined sense of procreation. But what was at issue was the *capacity* to procreate, not an unlimited right to *use* such capacity. The Court did not, after all, conclude that one may not prevent prisoners from procreating: it concluded that it is unjust to take away their capacity to procreate.

Assuming this claim has moral force, how ought we to view Teo's conclusion that a wife "constructively sterilizes" her husband by aborting a fetus against his will? The claim is obviously untrue. To be sterilized is to be permanently deprived of the capacity to father a child. A man whose wife aborts a pregnancy or refuses to get pregnant[2] is not in this position. If after discussion with his wife a husband concludes that his desire for a child is greater than his respect for his wife's deeply felt wishes, then the conflict should be handled like any other irreconcilable difference in marriage. The wife can be confronted with the choice between bearing a child and divorce. If she chooses to dissolve the already badly damaged marriage, the husband can try to find another woman willing to have a child. It would, of course, be preferable to attempt to avoid such unhappy endings by discussing the matter prior to marriage.

Indeed, guidelines for childbearing should perhaps be included in a marriage contract. Teo thinks that the husband's interest in the fetus derives from the fact that he contributes the sperm setting its development in motion. This, for reasons too complicated to explain at length here, is an unacceptable position: it would, for example, establish a father's interest in a child conceived by rape or artificial insemination. A more satisfactory claim would be that a woman's obligation to continue a pregnancy stems instead from an agreement between the spouses. What establishes such an agreement? Neither marriage nor consent to sexual relations implies an

---

2 For Teo's purposes, the two acts appear to be equivalent. If one is "sterilized" by having one's wife's fetus aborted, because one cannot have a child when one wants it, then one must be "sterilized," too, if one is not permitted to attempt to impregnate one's wife. Therefore, on his view, a husband must have the right to require his wife to attempt to become pregnant by him. Given the conclusion of his article, he must think that this right could be upheld in court. In other words, a court could require a wife to attempt to become pregnant by her husband.

agreement to have children. An explicit agreement about the matter is unlikely to specify any particular pregnancy and should not be considered unconditionally binding. Only if the husband knows that his wife has no strong objection to a child, and if, in addition, she agrees to have one, should she be bound. But then she will not change her mind without a good reason. Women do not choose abortion capriciously: the procedure is unpleasant, costly, and risky, and fetus killing is at best distasteful.

It should be emphasized that none of these objections to Teo's claim should be taken to deny a husband's interest in his child. The soundness of Teo's argument for this interest is denied, as is his contention that it includes a husband's right to ask a court to intercede.

Why would it in general be unjust for a court to deny a woman a first-trimester abortion at her husband's behest? One reason is that, contrary to Teo's claim, some sexual differences do make a moral difference.

Teo argues that, if a man is denied a voice in his wife's decision to abort, he is being discriminated against purely on account of his sex. (Notice that Teo's formulation is misleading: he is claiming that there is discrimination if a court will not sometimes uphold a husband's wish. This claim is much stronger than the one that there is discrimination if a wife is unwilling to discuss the matter at all.) He says that to "argue that a wife has the exclusive right to do whatever she pleases with a fetus simply because it is in her body is obviously to base an argument arbitrarily on one function of the human body which is unique to one sex" (p. 341). He adds: "That she happens to be the one who must carry the fetus in her womb is what nature ordains. However, to employ this biological fact as a basis for asserting a legal right is obviously to engage in sex-based discrimination" (p. 340). And such discrimination, whether on the basis of sex, color, religion, or national origin, is illegal (p. 341). It is illegal because it does not meet the test of rationality: "A classification 'must be reasonable, not arbitrary, and must rest upon some ground of difference having a fair and substantial relation to the object of the legislation, so that all persons similarly circumstanced shall be treated alike' " (p. 341). He then cites a case in which the Court declared unconstitutional a statute giving preference to males in employment, and he maintains that should the abortion case come before the Court, "the result would be similar" (p. 341).

What is he saying here? He is saying that no difference in sex, color, religion, or national origin makes any legal (or moral) difference. But this is false. Moral rights and duties regarding activities such as screening programs for genetically and sex-linked diseases differ vastly. It would be foolish to require blacks to be screened for Tay-Sachs disease, but not at all so for Jews, and the same mutatis mutandis for sickle-cell anemia. It is quite possible that future legal rights and duties will be found to reflect those moral ones.

Now it has been conceded that a husband ought to be consulted about an abortion decision by virtue of his being affected by it. But this sex-discrimination argument cannot do the job Teo wants it to do, namely, to justify a possible injunction against a wife's abortion. For, in fact, the biological differences between men and women do make a moral difference, and hence ought to make a legal one, too. This difference is clear to anyone who has seriously contemplated the situation: the fact that the fetus is in the woman's body and is carried, nourished, and given birth to by the woman means that the considerable burdens and risks of childbearing fall almost exclusively on her. In addition, there are social burdens: the responsibility for rearing a child falls mainly on the mother. If there is a divorce, an increasingly common possibility, the usual arrangement (although this is slowly changing) is for the child to live with its mother, with the father providing some financial support. It is the mother whose life is affected by the presence of the child, and it is the mother who must somehow meet the child's needs if the father falls behind in his payments.[3]

Given these facts, and in the absence of some compelling counterclaim, it is unreasonable to argue that a husband has a right to ask a court to deny his wife an abortion. Teo has provided no such counterclaim: on his theory, a wife has at least as much interest in the fetus as a husband. Because, in addition, biological and social burdens fall on her rather than him, it is hard to see why his claim ought to override hers in court when they cannot agree. If the burdens fell on him instead, the law would have reason to recognize his ultimate right to abort.

The situation is not one where compromise is possible: even an arbitrator can only impose one party's will. Therefore, the fairest procedure would be to recognize the right of the partner not desiring a child to prevail. This is not discriminatory, because it may entail a wife's moral duty to abort if her husband does not want a child. The lines along which such a proposal might be defended can only be indicated here. It could, I think, be derived from considerations of the just distribution of burdens, together with the probable impaired welfare of children born into disharmonious marriages, and social and ecological concerns.

It has been suggested that the social burden on the mother could be removed if the father were to undertake sole custody of the child as soon as

---

[3] Teo would probably regard the social argument as irrelevant. If sexual differences are irrelevant to moral concerns, they why should social differences caused by sexual differences be morally relevant? Both claims seem equally dubious.

it was born, the marriage having previously been dissolved. The woman's biological burden would, however, be undiminished, and divorce for a woman at this time would create an added strain. Finally one need not be a Kantian to recognize the immorality of forcing a woman to be used as an incubator. This is a paradigm case of treating another person as a mere means, an object, rather than a person. Hence any solution other than the one I propose brings back the days when a wife was a chattel and the end of marriage was to produce heirs or workers for the husband.

The peculiarity of Teo's argument is illustrated by his last claim, that if a husband cannot sometimes obtain a court decision requiring his wife to continue her pregnancy, he is denied equal protection under the Fourteenth Amendment. Teo says that, unless a husband can do this, a wife can determine whether she will become a mother, where he cannot determine whether he will become a father, although both are in the same position.

If a woman is granted the right to abort in the face of her husband's objection, it is true that she can deny him a child. However, as we saw, a husband is not completely without remedy. But Teo tries to show that the husband's situation is still more unenviable: a wife can make her husband a father even if he does not want a child.

This is a red herring: women have always had the power to force fatherhood on their sexual partners. Denying a woman the right to abort her pregnancy in no way changes the situation: she will have the power to *continue* the pregnancy, whether she is granted the right to *terminate* it or not. Therefore, no sound reason exists for denying women abortions on this ground.

Thus it seems to me that none of Teo's arguments entails his conclusion that a man has the right to ask the courts to deny his wife a first-trimester abortion. Even were his arguments convincing, however, such a right would introduce many problems. One is that there is little probability of getting a hearing before the first-trimester of pregnancy has elapsed. Another is the difficulty of any outsider ascertaining the merits of such a case: it will surely involve a tangled skein of personal values. What morally acceptable legal principle could be used or created to help sort them out and come to a "fair" decision? In addition, the intrusion of a court in this capacity could well be found to infringe upon the right to privacy which is now in the process of being defined by the Supreme Court, and to which *Roe v. Wade* was an important contributor. A third point is that if spouses disagree about so fundamental an issue, their marriage is almost certainly doomed. If it did survive a compulsory pregnancy, it would not provide the desirable climate for childraising, which Teo recognizes all children deserve. He admits that many states now require a joint decision in adoption cases: "After all, a child must be wanted and loved by both parents in order to have a suitable home environment" (p. 342). If a couple should act jointly to adopt a child, how much more ought they to do so if they deliberately create one? Yet to suggest that a judge should sometimes uphold a husband's desire for a child over his wife's objections is to permit a child to be born to a hostile mother. And last, how would a ruling against a wife be enforced and, if disobeyed, punished?

In sum, there are many reasons why Teo's position is unacceptable. Not the least of those is that it contradicts his claim that decisions about childbearing ought to be jointly made. Teo's legal arguments, together with his recommendation that the matter be decided in court on its merits, seem clearly meant to show that a husband may sometimes obtain an injunction denying his wife an abortion. This is no joint decision.

PART III

NEW WORLDS:

COLLABORATIVE

REPRODUCTION

Scientific advances no doubt provided one of the major stimuli for the new interest in applied ethics in the late 1960s. Some of the most astounding advances came in biology, especially in the area of reproduction, and have provided increasingly exotic fare for bioethics. At the same time, some members of the rising generation were testing long-held assumptions about important social conventions, including traditional sexual arrangements and social roles. The conjunction of these two developments is leading to ever-bolder reproductive possibilities.

A considerable amount of work on what might best be dubbed "collaborative" reproduction continues to be done by those with conservative assumptions about sex and sex roles. Chapter 10, "The Morality of New Reproductive Technologies," was written in the mid-1970s when it was even more common than it is today. My intention was to uncover the sexist assumptions embedded in such work and to point out how the new developments might empower women. At the same time, other feminists were focusing on the exploitive potential of the new collaborative arrangements and technologies. Their voices underlined the sexism that permeates thinking about these matters and the dangers posed by new kinds of reproduction.

Despite the value of this feminist work, I often find myself disagreeing with it. As almost everybody is by now aware, feminism is no monolithic philosophy, but rather a chorus of voices that rarely sings in unison. In my view, one of the most agonizing sources of discord arises from the fact that we must try to decide what will make life better overall for women *now* and in the near future, in very imperfect societies. That goal often leads me to disagree with other feminists who are thinking more about the long term and about the transition between the two. Both activities are necessary and worthwhile, and minding the distinction between the two would probably reduce our sense that internecine warfare is sometimes occupying more time than constructive work.

It is this concern about the near term, as well as the feeling that some of these feminist arguments were going seriously astray, that led me to write Chapter 11, "Surrogate Mothering: Exploitation or Empowerment?," and Chapter 12, "Another Look at Contract Pregnancy." In these pieces, I try to take a careful look at the competing interests that show up in this approach to reproduction, shying away from the wholesale condemnations that seem so attractive. As with the right to reproduce and the right not to reproduce, it is clear that my approach has significant dangers: unqualified, general principles can sometimes prevail politically where a more complex one confuses or fails to convince. Yet this path has its dangers, too, as I have argued elsewhere.

The distance between even a relatively moderate feminist stance and the bioethics establishment becomes obvious, however, in Chapter 13, "*Children of Choice:* Whose Children? At What Cost?". John Robertson's work is clear and well argued. Much of what he has to say is thoughtful, and he is often more sensitive to women's needs and interests than his peers. Quite often, I find myself in agreement with him on specific issues. Yet even so, a feminist critique of his new book on reproduction reveals deep differences, especially about the new reproductive technologies. These differences usually show up more in the reasoning that supports his conclusions than in the conclusions themselves. But consonant with his enthusiasm for procreative liberty, he sees a far more prominent role for assisted reproduction than seems sensible to me. As we have seen, unlike many other feminists, I believe that a cautious and carefully regulated use of some such techniques can empower women. But I see greater promise for women's welfare in more broadly conceived social measures, such as alleviating poverty, eradicating discrimination, and cleaning up the environment. Again, it is difficult to chart a middle path that tries to set collaborative reproduction in the larger context, neither rejecting it out of hand nor embracing it wholeheartedly. This kind of work endears one to neither camp, but it seems to me that an optimal future depends on it.

The Morality of New

Reproductive Technologies

Science is revolutionizing human reproduction. New techniques are already with us, such as artificial insemination, the freezing of sperm, in vitro fertilization, and the use of surrogate mothers. Artificial wombs are clearly on the horizon.

These developments are the subject of much debate, debate that cannot be expected to diminish as ever more radical possibilities open up before us. The central issue is whether these new techniques are moral and ought to be used.

Moral debate can be about the intrinsic quality of new technologies or about their consequences. I concentrate on the latter because I do not believe that actions have intrinsic moral qualities. Two questions are therefore paramount: What are the consequences of using such new technologies? and Are these consequences desirable? Specifically, we need to know whether new methods harm babies or affect family relationships or society adversely and whether people benefit from them.

I am not be concerned here with the question of harm to babies: this is, after all, a relatively straightforward empirical issue, to be answered by biological research.[1] Rather, I assume that the consequences for babies are

From the *Journal of Social Philosophy* 18, no. 1 (Winter 1987). Reprinted by permission of the *Journal of Social Philosophy*.
[1] See the chapter on human reproduction in my unpublished manuscript, *Freedom to Live and Die: Biomedical Predicaments.*

no worse than if they were born the usual way, and I go on to consider the other questions.[2]

Let us therefore look at the family. There are two areas of concern: the relationship between child and parent and the general institution and well-being of the family.

Some fear that parents will not take proper care of their children unless they are created the usual way: "Is there perhaps some wisdom in that mystery of nature which joins the pleasure of sex, the communication of love, and the desire for children in the very activity by which we continue the chain of human existence? Is not biological parenthood a built-in 'mechanism,' selected because it fosters and supports in parents an adequate concern for and commitment to their children?"[3]

This question raises important issues, ones that are never far below the surface of any discussion of these matters. It suggests, wrongly, I suspect, that parenting has been and is now generally adequate.[4] It seems further to suggest that inadequate parenting occurs because children are not born of pleasurable sex, loving communication, or a desire for children. If so, then the remedy is obvious, if difficult: if we care about good parenting, we must ensure that children are born only in such conditions. There are, however, more plausible explanations. Children have specific needs, needs that can only be met when those bringing them up have certain material resources at hand, understand how to meet the needs, and are emotionally mature enough to do so. Having a good sexual relationship, a loving spouse, and the desire for a baby are not sufficient conditions for being able to meet children's needs; indeed, there seems to be no particular reason for believing that they are even necessary conditions.[5] If so, then new reproductive technologies would have no bearing on parent–child relationships unless they affect the way children's needs are met. It is worth pointing out in this context that there is no evidence that adopted children get worse parenting, despite the lack of direct biological connection.

---

[2] If these techniques should turn out physically to harm babies, the question about whether they should be used will have to be assessed carefully in terms of benefits and burdens to all involved parties.

[3] Leon Kass, "The New Biology: What Price Relieving Man's Estate?," *Science* 174 (November 19, 1971): 784. This objection to artificial reproductive technologies and others raised in my article are, I believe, representative of deeply felt, although not always articulated, beliefs held by educated members of American society.

[4] This is a question that philosophers and others seem loath to examine. If Lloyd deMause can be relied on, the treatment of children during much of history has been inadequate; see *The History of Childhood* (New York: The Psychohistory Press, 1974). There is also much evidence to suggest that contemporary parents do not always do a good job of childrearing.

[5] This raises many interesting issues that I hope to pursue elsewhere, such as single parenting, gay parenting, and so forth.

In the same vein, Vance Packard asks: "Can married women develop the love and sacrifice and dedication required to rear a child successfully if they deliberately abstain from bearing it?"[6] Questions about the assumptions underlying this question are legion. Above all, what has the method of getting a child to do with one's "love and sacrifice and dedication" to it? Considering that fathers often do as well by their children as mothers and women manage to love and cherish adopted children, stepchildren, lovers, friends, and pets, it is hard to see what motivates Packard's concern. We seem to be faced with the reincarnation of Freud's belief in feminine masochism, with its implication that women will not love their children unless they suffer for them. Effective criticism has been aimed at this theory by Millett, Horney, and others,[7] and there is, to my knowledge, no empirical evidence that could support it.[8] But let us suppose for a moment that Packard's assumption is true—that women who do not bear their children the usual way are less inclined to devote their lives to them. It is no longer radical to suggest that spreading responsibility. for childrearing more evenly among members of society might benefit both women and children. Hence, even were there any basis for this worry, it would not necessarily constitute a reason for rejecting new technologies.

So much for women's attitudes toward their children. What about children's attitudes toward their mothers? Some people have speculated about "the possible psychological complications if a cow-gestated child knew he had spent nine months in a pasture while his human genetic mother was busy giving parties."[9] Others are concerned about children's attitudes about women who carried them for others, "deliberately but without loving them."[10]

In view of the extraordinary ease with which children adjust to new situations if presented to them as "normal," fears that such knowledge would cause psychological harm to children seem unrealistic. However, the context in which this concern is raised also reveals a disturbing conception of the moral order, one where preventing the slightest harm to children has priority over any concern about women. Women should receive consideration at least equal to that accorded children, and when their interests

---

[6] Vance Packard, *The People Shapers* (Boston: Little, Brown, 1977), p. 212.

[7] See Kate Millett, *Sexual Politics* (New York: Doubleday, 1970); and *Psychoanalysis and Women*, ed. Jean Baker Miller (Middlesex, Eng.: Penguin, 1973), pp. 21–38.

[8] For instance, do women who have hard labors love their children more than women who had easy ones?

[9] Packard, *People Shapers*, p. 212.

[10] Gerald Leach, *The Biocrats* (Middlesex, Eng.: Penguin, 1972), p. 103. One wonders where such speculations are when the matter of abortion arises: how, after all, must it feel to know that you were conceived by accident and were born and raised only because abortion was not available?

conflict, we should evaluate harms and benefits affecting the two by means of the same rules we would use for deciding between conflicting interests of other moral equals. Thus, if certain technologies can prevent great harm to women (by saving their lives or health, for instance) at the cost of some possible emotional upset to their children, women have a right to have their interests prevail. Moral philosophy has for too long treated women as appendages with no interests of their own that might legitimately override the interests of others.

Consequently, none of the foregoing has provided any reason to deny use of reproductive technologies because of harm to parent–child relationships. Let us now therefore consider whether anyone has so far provided reason for believing that their use would harm marriage or the family.

Vance Packard muses: "The wedding vow is based on an assumption of exclusivity in all matters relating to planting seed and bearing children. We would have to change our concepts of what a family is and broaden the definitions of such words as *father, mother, parent,* and *motherhood.*"[11] Kass holds that great changes have already occurred: in fact, the family has lost all but childbearing functions: "Sex is now comfortably at home outside of marriage; childrearing is progressively being given over to the state, the schools, the mass media, and the child-care centers. Some have argued that the family, long the nursery of humanity, has outlived its usefulness."[12] He concludes: "Transfer of procreation to the laboratory will no doubt weaken what is presently for many people the best remaining justification and support for the existence of marriage and the family."[13]

Kass's depressingly utilitarian view of the family is revealed by the gap in his list: where is satisfaction of the desire for intimacy generated by intense, long-lasting love? He also fails to provide evidence for the claim that families do not play a significant role in childbearing. In any case, childbearing and childrearing are independent of each other. Children born with the aid of artificial reproductive technologies can be raised in a traditional family and children born the usual way can be raised in nontraditional

---

[11] Packard, *People Shapers,* p. 202.

[12] Kass, "The New Biology," p. 784.

[13] Kass's belief that the family is important is based on the following considerations: the only institution in an increasingly impersonal world where each person is loved not for what he does or makes, but simply because he is. The family is also the institution where most of us, both as children and as parents, acquire a sense of continuity with the past and a sense of commitment to the future. Without the family we would have little incentive to take an interest in anything after our own deaths. These observations suggest that the elimination of the family would weaken ties to past and future, and would throw us, even more than we are now, to the mercy of an impersonal, lonely present. (Ibid., p. 784.)

ways. As long as substantial numbers of children continue to be raised in the family, however, it has plenty of work.

Both Packard and Kass view change with alarm. This suggests the dubious assumptions that current arrangements are optimal. We clearly need to compare the advantages and disadvantages of alternative approaches to problems. But such speculation laden with unfocused moral foreboding as current writers on the subject provide is no basis for rational decision making. As of yet, we have no reason to fear the expansion of artificial reproductive technologies.

Let us therefore go on to consider the third major concern voiced by opponents of these technologies: it is that society will be harmed by reliance on them.[14]

Some reject technology altogether and wish us back in preindustrial days. Although it is true that we have misused technology, such misuse has most often had political origins. Because technology also brings great benefits, it would seem that the best solution would be to fight for improvements in harmful political arrangements. In any case, we are not likely to be rid of technology now unless we bring some great worldwide catastrophe on ourselves.

Others hold that certain uses of technology change us in undesirable ways: they cause "dehumanization" or "depersonalization." For instance, Kass asserts that

the price to be paid for the "optimum baby" is the transfer of procreation from the home to the laboratory and its coincident transformation into manufacture. Increasing control over the product is purchased by the increasing depersonalization of the process. The complete depersonalization of procreation (possible with the development of the artificial placenta) shall be, in itself, seriously dehumanizing, no matter how optimum the product. It should not be forgotten that human procreation not only issues new human beings, but is itself a human activity.[15]

The main problem with such charges is that they are vague. We are never furnished with a clear, precise meaning for "dehumanizing" or "depersonalizing," and no rule for recognizing instances of them is provided. The implication that using technology is not a human activity is clearly false.

It seems reasonable to infer from the context of this quote that Kass links these concepts with "distinctively human" acts and morality, in such a way

---

[14] One set of objections focuses on the practical legal problems we would face as a result of introducing new technologies. None seems insurmountable.

[15] Kass, *The New Biology*, p. 784.

that morality consists in doing what is "distinctively human." "Dehuman-ization" and "depersonalization," then, are ways of describing the bad con-sequences of departing from "distinctively human"—in short, moral, practices.

But what are "distinctively human" acts? For Kass, they appear to be tra-ditional practices, such as those involved in "natural" procreation and maintenance of the family. This appears to be the only plausible interpreta-tion of his position, despite the fact that we have such practices in common with some animals. However, it could be argued that what is "distinctively human" is manipulating our environment to suit our needs and desires.[16]

Despite the prevalence of this kind of position, it is beside the point: hu-man interests ought to figure largely in moral thinking, regardless of whether they are interests we have in common with animals. We cannot as-sume that tradition offers us the best way of satisfying those interests, as Kass seems to recognize when he urges on us a "reinvestigation of the an-cient and enduring questions of what is a proper life for a human being, what is a good community, and how they are achieved."[17] His condemna-tion of departures from tradition are incompatible with his skepticism about having the right answers.

We must also consider the effect of the new technologies on women, who constitute an important segment of society. Some feminists are very nega-tive about their potential.[18] They see the world polarized into two armed camps. The male camp has most of the power and would, if possible, erad-icate females if reproduction could be ensured.[19] Such writers ask why there is so much interest in artificial reproduction, if not to control women? The standard answer, that it is to help infertile women have babies, has, I con-cur, a hollow ring, given the general uninterest in other pressing aspects of women's welfare. However, although it is obvious that there is widespread discrimination against women in most societies, based on self-serving false ideas about their nature and needs, I am reluctant to attribute such sinister attitudes to men in general. The track record of the medical profession is not reassuring.[20] But it is compatible, I believe, with the view that although

[16] Arno G. Motulsky, "Brave New World?," in *Human Genetics*, ed. Thomas Mertens (New York: Wiley, 1975), p. 303.

[17] Kass, *The New Biology*, p. 786.

[18] See, for example, *The Custom-Made Child? Women-Centered Perspectives*, ed. Helen B. Holmes, Betty B. Hoskins, and Michael Gross (Clifton, N.J.: Humana Press, 1981); also *Test-Tube Women: What Future for Motherhood?*, ed. Rita Arditti, Renate Duelli Klein, and Shelly Minden (London: Pandora Press, 1984); and "Conference Reports," in *Women's Studies In-ternational Forum* 7, no. 6 (1984): i–xii.

[19] See, for example, Gena Corea, "Egg Snatchers," in *Test-Tube Women*, pp. 37–51.

[20] See, for example, Barbara Seaman and Gideon Seaman, *Women and the Crisis in Sex Hor-mones* (New York: Rawson Associates Publishers, 1977); Gena Corea, *The Hidden Malpractice*

some powerful men have hostile and punishing attitudes toward women as a sex, much of the harm that has come to them is a result of misguided concern, uninterest, and/or simple irresponsibility. The current interest in artificial reproductive technologies might be understood as yet another instance of society's fascination with technically interesting questions. Whether it can be so construed remains to be shown. The important point to be garnered from the radical feminist stance is that women must make sure they have a large say in the development and use of new technologies to ensure that they are used to satisfy women's legitimate interests, not to control them.[21]

In general, then, we must beware of potentially harmful applications of technology and exercise constant vigilance in discovering and evaluating its effects on us and our environment.

At present there seem to be no grounds for judging the use of artificial reproductive technologies wrong; but is there any good reason for using them? The use of such technologies would be justified (other things being equal) if they helped people to achieve legitimate goals they could not otherwise attain. Thus, for example, some technologies allow persons who could not otherwise have them to have babies. The legitimacy of this goal is frequently questioned by those worried about the population problem. It seems to me, however, that their condemnation of the use of resources for this purpose is based on faulty reasoning. The population problem arises not because there are too many people, but because there is an imbalance between people and resources. On this view, anything that increases the imbalance exacerbates the problem. Thus, using resources foolishly is just as harmful as producing more people. Many individuals have a strong desire for children, and society, in general, holds the satisfaction of this desire to be good. To deny its validity for those requiring special help in achieving that goal is unnecessarily cruel because the imbalance between people and resources could be improved by other methods that cause less suffering. For instance, much land is given over to the production of grains for alcoholic beverages and tobacco; some of it could be used for food instead. Not only would this help balance population and resources, but also it could help reduce consumption of alcohol and tobacco, which is desirable on other grounds. Other things being equal, then, helping people have children

---

(New York: Jove Publications, 1977); and Barbara Ehrenreich and Deirdre English, *For Her Own Good* (New York: Anchor Books, 1979).

[21] Thus, for instance, we must fight for fair practices in surrogate parenting, using organizations such as the National Women's Health Network. For a thought-provoking discussion of some of the issues, see Susan Ince, "Inside the Surrogate Industry," in *Test-Tube Women*, pp. 99–116.

can be counted as a good reason to perfect and use artificial reproductive technologies.

Are there any others? Most of the controversy centers about the use of surrogate and artificial wombs. Probably typical is Packard's attitude: "And it is all so unnecessary! The only social gain of any significance would be to free the workingwoman from having to interrupt her job in order to produce her baby. But for most workingwomen pregnancy is no problem at all for the first seven months. . . . I have known successful career women who stayed right on the job until labor started, with no ill effects."[22] Let us consider why their use might be desirable, even if not "necessary."

One reason for having alternative modes of childbearing available is that pregnancy can be both uncomfortable and risky. Women with already existing diseases can be harmed. For example, kidney disease can be aggravated, and cardiac patients can die from congestive heart failure. Diabetics die at twice the normal rate.[23] It would therefore be good if surrogate mothers or artificial wombs were available for such women.

Moreover, even normal women could benefit from their use, for the risk of death and disease, and pain from pregnancy is more significant than many people seem to realize. The death rate from pregnancy is 17 per 100,000 for women aged 15 to 45.[24] Mortality from all other causes in this group is 80 per 100,000.[25] Thus 18 percent, or about one of every five deaths among these women results from childbearing. These figures can be placed in perspective by examining the death rates from all causes in the general population. These deaths constitute 2 percent of all deaths—about the same number as diabetes, the sixth leading cause of death in the general popula-

---

[22] Packard, *People Shapers*, p. 216.

[23] These statistics are from *The Merck Manual*, 14th ed., ed. Robert Berkow (Rawhay, N.J.: Merck, Sharp and Dohme Research Laboratories, 1982), pp. 1735–40.

[24] *Our Bodies, Ourselves*, The Boston Women's Health Book Collective, rev. ed. (New York: Simon & Schuster, 1976), p. 189. These statistics have changed substantially in the last twenty years, in part because of AIDS and better maternal care. Nonetheless, pregnancy still has its risks. Consider also the claim that maternal mortality statistics do not accurately reflect the true number of deaths resulting from pregnancy:

Undoubtedly there are many patients who die each year of conditions resulting from pregnancy whose deaths are not so classified. This is due to failure to make mention of pregnancy or delivery on the death certificate. . . .

Another important factor in producing inaccurate maternal mortality rates is diversity of the definition of maternal death. . . . When pregnancy is associated with conditions such as organic heart disease, tuberculosis, or chronic hypertensive vascular disease, resulting fatalities are often not considered maternal deaths. (Schuyler G. Kohl and John Whitridge, Jr., "Maternal Health Services," in *Maxcy-Rosenau: Preventive Medicine and Public Health*, ed. Philip E. Sartwell (New York: Appleton-Century-Crofts, 1973), p. 777.)

[25] *Our Bodies, Ourselves*, p. 189.

tion.[26] No doubt women with special problems account for a disproportionate share of these deaths, and so is poor prenatal care, which could be
remedied by social measures.[27] However, I suspect that there is an irreducible fraction of deaths that is not significant. Artificial wombs could
eliminate them.[28] Risk of death is not the only possible drawback of pregnancy in normal women. Nausea and vomiting are common. Toward the
end of pregnancy, many women are uncomfortable because of their swollen
condition. Persistent tiredness may also occur. Other possibilities of "minor" discomfort are constipation, leg cramps, indigestion, heartburn, hem-
orrhoids, varicose veins, and nosebleeds. Pain may also be caused by the
fetus's pressure on the bladder or on the nerves at the top of the leg.[29] More
serious illness during pregnancy is also possible. Toxemias of pregnancy,
for instance, pose significant maternal risk. Symptoms may include
headaches, epigastric pain, nausea and vomiting, bleeding, urinary tract
problems, convulsions, and coma. They can cause still more serious problems such as liver or kidney damage, heart failure, and cerebral hemor-
rhage.[30] Labor and childbirth can be both painful and dangerous. The
occurrence of pain is well documented and needs no comment here. A condition known as placenta previa may result in death for the woman, as can
premature separation of the placenta. The latter may necessitate a hys-
terectomy.[31] Iatrogenic disease may follow interventions during labor.[32]

[26] *Facts of Life and Death*, U.S. Dept. of Health, Education, and Welfare (Washington, D.C.:
U.S. Government Printing Office, 1978), p. 31.

[27] Kohl and Whitridge suggest that approximately two-thirds of maternal deaths are considered preventable (p. 777). It is not clear from the context whether this refers to reported
maternal deaths or to the true figure.

[28] Until artificial wombs are available, the risk associated with childbearing raises the
specter of well-to-do women paying poor women to take the burden, much as men used to
pay others to perform military service. In general, all such cases are undesirable and should
be eradicated. However, in the context of current American society, it is important to notice
that this situation is routine, and the arguments against this particular instance of it are not
obviously stronger than those against the others. So unless one is willing to argue for a radical restructuring of society, one has no special case against the use of surrogates. It should
also be borne in mind that we pay others to bear risks in all sorts of ways that we take for
granted, not just the obvious ones. The most obviously risky occupations are rarely chosen
by middle-class individuals. And we tend to be unaware of the risks involved in such common occupations as hair dresser, gas station attendant, and dry cleaner. For more information, see sources such as Nicholas A. Ashford, *Crisis in the Workplace: Occupational Disease
and Injury* (Cambridge: MIT Press, 1976), or *Cancer and the Worker* (New York: The New York
Academy of Sciences, 1977). Working as a surrogate might pose less risk to poor women
than many of their usual occupations.

[29] *The Merck Manual*, p. 845.

[30] *Our Bodies, Ourselves*, pp. 257–65.

[31] *The Merck Manual*, pp. 850–51.

[32] *Our Bodies, Ourselves*, pp. 278–82.

Caesarean sections, increasingly popular of late, have a considerably higher risk of maternal death than vaginal delivery.[33] Women may also develop puerperal infection, which can cause severe pain, peritonitis, and/or pelvic thrombophlebitis; it may be followed by toxic shock, kidney disease, or death.[34] Eliminating these risks would be sufficient reason to use artificial reproductive technologies for high-risk patients.

In addition to reducing risk and pain, using alternative modes of child-bearing could help women to live more satisfying lives. Not everyone would agree, however, that such use is legitimate: "the application of embryo transfer should be subservient to therapeutic considerations: any other motivation—coquetry, ambition, or pursuit of a career where asthetics are essential—should exclude such action. The publicity roused by these latter applications is enough to remind us that solutions which are therapeutically acceptable can become scandalous when there is no medical justification for them."[35] But why is ambition, presumably admirable in a man, not equally admirable and worthy of support in a woman? Clearly, the quoted writer thinks the only appropriate life for a woman to be the traditional one of self-sacrifice, in the home, for husband and children.

He implies that ambition or pursuit of a career where esthetics are essential is somehow frivolous. But who is he to say that a career in dance, gymnastics, or modeling is not desirable? And who is he to judge the activities of any bureaucrat or politician more socially useful or important than those of a gifted ballerina? He belittles the ambition, hard work, and talent necessary to succeed in many professions; he also ignores the fact that relatively few such interesting occupations have been open to women until recently. Only thus could he dismiss so easily the possible loss of such a career due to missed opportunities or physical problems resulting from pregnancy. Naturally, these can harm women pursing other interests, too, as well as those staying at home with children.

Most people seem to be unaware of the foregoing issues or to discount them; however, they constitute reason enough for attempting to develop alternatives to normal childbearing. In our society, we devote vast resources to social projects. Convenience, prestige, or profit are thought adequate grounds for the expenditure of large sums and/or tolerating great side effects: consider the automobile-based transportation system or the space program. Are the needs they are supposed to meet more pressing than the ones we are discussing?

---

[33] Ibid., p. 289.
[34] *The Merck Manual*, p. 863.
[35] M. Revillard, quoted in Philip Reilly, *Genetics, Law, and Social Policy* (Cambridge: Harvard University Press, 1977), p. 218.

Women's needs would be pressing even if they only wanted to spend their time giving parties. We do not ask other potential recipients of expensive medical technologies to devote themselves to good works: relieving their pain and repairing their handicaps is deemed reason enough to proceed. Why then demand this of women? Most women, in any case, do play an important role in society. Few while their lives away playing bridge. A majority of women now work outside the home, in most cases as much to maintain an adequate standard of living for themselves or their families as for their own satisfaction, and most of the rest work at home with young children. Many, in addition, volunteer to do for free the essential jobs capitalism leaves to the private sector. This contribution to society might be enlarged still more if appropriate artificial reproductive technologies were available, to the benefit of both women and society.

I began this paper by asking whether there is a case for using artificial reproductive technologies. First, I considered possible risks. Those affecting the fetus were not discussed, because the matter is a technical one, although evidence suggests that there are few special risks associated with existing technologies. I also concluded that no one has convincingly argued that such technologies harm families or society as a whole. They do have potential for controlling women in undesirable ways, and we must fight to prevent such harm.

Next, I considered the possible advantages of artificial reproductive technologies. One major benefit is that they can help women to have babies safely. Another is that they can help women to live satisfying lives. Not only would this be advantageous for society, but also it is crucial for women's well-being. Women have traditionally been expected to forego either interesting work or childbearing. But women are human beings with the same need as men for financial security, independence, achievement, interesting work, and respect; many also want children. Society has tried to help men to satisfy all these desires: now it ought to do the same for women. If artificial reproductive technologies can contribute to this end, we ought to use them.

CHAPTER 11

Surrogate Mothering:

Exploitation or Empowerment?

"Pregnancy is barbaric," proclaimed Shulamith Firestone in the first heady days of the new women's movement; she looked forward to the time when technology would free women from the oppression of biological reproduction. Yet as reproductive options multiply, some feminists are making common cause with conservatives for a ban on innovations. What is going on? Firestone argued that nature oppresses women by leaving them holding the reproductive bag, whereas men are free of such burden; so long as this biological inequality holds, women will never be free.[1] It is now commonplace to point out the naivety of her claim: it is not the biological difference per se that oppresses women, but its social significance. So we need not change biology, only attitudes and institutions.

This insight has helped us to see how to achieve a better life for women, but I wonder if it is the whole story. Has Firestone's brave claim no lesson at all for us?

Her point was that being with child is uncomfortable and dangerous and that it can limit women's lives. We have become more sensitive to the ways in which social arrangements can determine how much these diffi-

From *Bioethics* 3, no. 1 (January 1989): 18-34. Reprinted by permission of Blackwell Publishers.
[1] Shulamith Firestone, *The Dialectic of Sex: The Case for Feminist Revolution* (New York: Bantam, 1970), pp. 198–200. A version of this article was given at the Eastern Society for Women in Philosophy meeting, March 26, 1988. I would like to thank especially Helen B. Holmes and Sara Ann Ketchum for their useful comments on this article; they are, of course, in no way responsible for its perverse position! Thanks also to the editors and referees of *Bioethics* for their helpful criticisms.

culties affect us. However, even in feminist utopias, where sex or gender are considered morally irrelevant except where they may entail special needs, a few difficulties would remain. Infertility, for instance, would exist, as would the desire for a child in circumstances where pregnancy is impossible or undesirable.

At present, the problem of infertility is generating a whole series of responses and solutions. Among them are high-tech procedures, such as in vitro fertilization, and social arrangements, such as surrogate motherhood. Both these techniques are also provoking a storm of concern and protest. As each raises a distinctive set of issues, they need to be dealt with separately. Here I consider only surrogate motherhood.

One might argue that no feminist paradise would need any practice such as this. As Susan Sherwin argues, it could not countenance "the capitalism, racism, sexism, and elitism of our culture [that] have combined to create a set of attitudes which views children as commodities whose value is derived from their possession of parental chromosomes."[2] Nor will society define women's fulfillment only in terms of their relationship to genetically related children. No longer will children be needed as men's heirs or women's livelihood.

We will, on the contrary, desire relationships with children for the right reasons: the urge to nurture, teach, and be close to them. No longer will we be driven by narcissistic wishes for clones or immortality to seek genetic offspring no matter what the cost. Indeed, we will have recognized that children are the promise and responsibility of the whole human community. And childrearing practices will reflect these facts, including at least a more diffuse family life that allows children to have significant relationships with others. Perhaps childbearing will be communal.

This radically different world is hard to picture realistically, even by those like myself who, I think, most ardently wish for it. The doubts I feel are fanned by the visions of so-called cultural feminists who glorify traditionally feminine values. Family life can be suffocating, distorting, even deadly.[3] Yet there is a special closeness that arises from being a child's primary caretaker, just as there can be a special thrill in witnessing the unfolding of biologically driven traits in that child. These pleasures justify risking the health of neither the child[4] nor of the mother; nobody's general

---

[2] Susan Sherwin, "Feminist Ethics and in Vitro Fertilization," *Science, Morality, and Feminist Theory*, ed. Marsha Hanen and Kai Nielson, *Canadian Journal of Philosophy* 13 (supp.) (1987): 277.

[3] Consider the many accounts of the devastating things parents have done to children, in particular.

[4] See Laura M. Purdy, "Genetic Diseases: Can Having Children be Immoral?," in *Genetics Now: Ethical Issues in Genetic Research*, ed. John L. Buckley, Jr. (Washington, D.C.: University Press of America, 1978).

well-being should be sacrificed to them or warrant huge social investments. However, they are things that, other things being equal, it would be desirable to preserve so long as people continue to have anything like their current values. If this is so, then evaluating the morality of practices that open up new ways of creating children is worthwhile.[5]

MORAL OR IMMORAL?

What exactly is surrogate mothering? Physically, its essential features are as follows: a woman in inseminated with the sperm of a man to whom she is not married. When the baby is born she relinquishes her claim to it in favor of another, usually the man from whom the sperm was obtained. She provides the egg, so her biological input is at least equal to that of the man. Surrogate mothering may not therefore be the best term for what she is doing.[6]

By doing these things she also acts socially—to take on the burden and risk of pregnancy for another and to separate sex and reproduction, reproduction and childrearing, and reproduction and marriage. If she takes money for the transaction (apart from payment of medical bills), she may even be considered to be selling a baby.

The bare physical facts would not warrant the welter of accusation and counteraccusation that surrounds the practice.[7] It is the social aspects that have engendered the acrimony about exploitation, destruction of the family, and baby selling. So far we have reached no consensus about the practice's effect on women or its overall morality.

I believe that the appropriate moral framework for addressing questions about the social aspects of contracted pregnancy is consequentialist.[8] This

---

[5] Another critical issue is that no feminist utopia will have a supply of "problem" children whom no one wants. Thus the proposal often heard nowadays that people should just adopt all those handicapped, non-white kids will not do. (Nor does it "do" now.)

[6] I share with Sara Ann Ketchum the sense that this term is not adequate, although I am not altogether happy with her suggestion that we call it "contracted motherhood" ("New Reproductive Technologies and the Definition of Parenthood: A Feminist Perspective," paper given at the 1987 Feminism and Legal Theory Conference, University of Wisconsin at Madison, summer 1987, pp. 44ff). It would be better, I think, to reserve terms such as "mother" for the social act of nurturing. I shall therefore substitute the terms "contracted pregnancy" and "surrogacy".

[7] This is not to say that no one would take the same view as I: the Catholic Church, for instance, objects to the masturbatory act required for surrogacy to proceed.

[8] The difficulty in choosing the "right" moral theory to back up judgments in applied ethics, given that none are fully satisfactory, continues to be vexing. I would like to reassure those who lose interest at the mere sight of consequentialist—let alone utilitarian—judgment, that there are good reasons for considering justice an integral part of moral reasoning, as it quite obviously has utility.

A different issue is raised by the burgeoning literature on feminist ethics. I strongly suspect that utilitarianism could serve feminists well, if properly applied. (For a defense of this framework requires us to attempt to separate those consequences that invariably accompany a given act from those that accompany it only in particular circumstances. Doing this compels us to consider whether a practice's necessary features lead to unavoidable overridingly bad consequences. It also demands that we look at how different circumstances are likely to affect the outcome. Thus a practice that is moral in a feminist society may well be immoral in a sexist one. This distinction allows us to tailor morality to different conditions for optimum results without thereby incurring the charge of malignant relativism.

Before examining the arguments against the practice of contracted pregnancy, let us take note of why people might favor it. First, as noted, alleviating infertility can create much happiness. Second, there are often good reasons to consider transferring burden and risk from one individual to another. Pregnancy may be a serious burden or risk for one woman, whereas it is much less so for another. Some women love being pregnant, others hate it; pregnancy interferes with work for some, not for others; pregnancy also poses much higher levels of risk to health (or even life) for some than for others. Reducing burden and risk is a benefit not only for the woman involved, but also for the resulting child. High-risk pregnancies create, among other things, serious risk of prematurity, one of the major sources of handicap in babies. Furthermore, we could prevent serious genetic diseases by allowing carriers to avoid pregnancy. A third benefit of surrogate mothering is that it makes possible the creation of nontraditional families. This can be a significant source of happiness to single women and gay couples.

All of these aspects presuppose that there is some advantage in making possible at least partially genetically based relationships between parents and offspring. Although, as I have argued, we might be better off without this desire, I doubt that we will soon be free of it. Therefore, if we can satisfy it at little cost, we should try to do so.

IS SURROGATE MOTHERING ALWAYS WRONG?

Despite the foregoing advantages, some feminists argue that the practice is *necessarily* wrong: it is wrong because it must betray women's and society's basic interests.[9]

---

position, see the last part of the Introduction of this volume, which was originally given as a paper, "Do Feminists Need a New Moral Theory?" at the University of Minnesota, Duluth, at the conference "Explorations in Feminist Ethics: Theory and Practice," October 8-9, 1988.)

[9] See, for example, Gena Corea, *The Mother Machine* (New York: Harper & Row, 1985), and Christine Overall, *Ethics and Human Reproduction* (Winchester, Mass.: Allen & Unwin, 1987).

What, if anything, is wrong with the practice? Let us consider the first three acts I described: transferring burden and risk, separating sex and reproduction, and separating reproduction and childrearing. Separation of reproduction and marriage will not be dealt with here.

Is it wrong to take on the burden of pregnancy for another? Doing this certainly makes sense, for pregnancy can threaten comfort, health, even life. One might argue that women should not be allowed to take these risks, but that would be paternalistic. We do not forbid mountain climbing or riding a motorcycle on these grounds. How could we then forbid a woman to undertake this particular risk?

Perhaps the central issue is the transfer of burden from one woman to another. However, we frequently do just that—much more often than we recognize. Anyone who has her house cleaned, her hair done, or her clothes dry-cleaned is engaging in this procedure;[10] so is anyone who depends on agriculture or public works such as bridges.[11] To the objection that in this case the bargain includes the risk to life and limb, as well as use of time and skills, the answer is that the other activities just cited entail surprisingly elevated risk rates from exposure to toxic chemicals or dangerous machinery.[12]

Furthermore, it is not even true that contracted pregnancy merely shifts the health burden and risks associated with pregnancy from one woman to another. In some cases (infertility, for example), it makes the impossible possible; in others (for women with potentially high-risk pregnancies), the net risk is lowered.[13] As we saw, babies benefit, too, from better health and fewer handicaps. Better health and fewer handicaps in both babies and women also mean that scarce resources can be made available for other needs, thus benefiting society in general.

I do think that there is, in addition, something suspect about all this new emphasis on risk. Awareness of risks inherent in even normal pregnancy constitutes progress: women have always been expected to forge ahead with childbearing oblivious to risk. Furthermore, childbearing has been thought to be something women owed to men or to society at large, regardless of their own feelings about a given, or any, pregnancy. When women had little say about these matters, we never heard about risk.[14] Why

---

[10] These are just a couple of examples in the sort of risky service that we tend to take for granted.

[11] Modern agricultural products are brought to us at some risk by farm workers. Any large construction project will also result in some morbidity and mortality.

[12] Even something so mundane as postal service involves serious risk on the part of workers.

[13] The benefit to both high-risk women and society is clear. Women need not risk serious deterioration of health or abnormally high death rates.

[14] See my Chapter 10, "The Morality of New Reproductive Technologies."

are we hearing about risk only now, now that women finally have some choices, some prospect of remuneration?[15] For that matter, why is our attention not drawn to the fact that surrogacy is one of the least risky approaches to nontraditional reproduction?[16]

Perhaps what is wrong about this kind of transfer is that it necessarily involves exploitation. Such exploitation may take the form of exploitation of women by men and exploitation of the rich by the poor. This possibility deserves serious consideration and will be dealt with shortly.

Is there anything wrong with the proposed separation of sex and reproduction? Historically, this separation, in the form of contraception, has been beneficial to women and to society as a whole. Although there are those who judge the practice immoral. I do not think we need to belabor the issue here.

It may be argued that not all types of separation are morally on a par. Contraception is permissible, because it spares women's health, promotes autonomy, strengthens family life, and helps make population growth manageable. But separation of sex and reproduction apart from contraception is quite another kettle of fish: it exploits women, weakens family life, and may increase population. Are these claims true and relevant?

Starting with the last first, if we face a population problem, it would make sense to rethink overall population policy, not exploit the problems of the infertile.[17] If family strengthening is a major justification for contraception, we might point out that contracted pregnancy will in some cases do the same. Whether or not having children can save a failing marriage, it will certainly prevent a man who wants children from leaving a woman incapable of providing them. We may bewail his priorities, but if his wife in sufficiently eager for the relationship to continue it would again be paternalistic for us to forbid surrogacy in such circumstances. That surrogacy reduces rather than promotes women's autonomy may be true under some circumstances, but there are good grounds for thinking that it can also enhance autonomy. It also remains to be shown that the practice systematically burdens women, or one class of women. In principle, the availability of new choices can be expected to nourish rather than stunt women's lives, so long as they retain control over their bodies and lives. The claim

---

[15] For an elaboration of this view, consider Jane Ollenburger and John Hamlin, "'All Birthing Should Be Paid Labor'—A Marxist Analysis of the Commodification of Motherhood," in *On the Problem of Surrogate Parenthood: Analyzing the Baby M Case*, ed. Herbert Richardson (Lewiston, N.Y.: The Edwin Mellen Press, 1987).

[16] Compare the physical risk with that of certain contraceptive technologies, and high-tech fertility treatments such as in vitro fertilization.

[17] Infertility is often a result of social arrangements. This process would therefore be especially unfair to those who already have been exposed to more than their share of toxic chemicals or other harmful conditions.

that contracted pregnancy destroys women's individuality and constitutes alienated labor, as Christine Overall argues, depends not only on a problematic Marxist analysis, but also on the assumption that other jobs available to women are seriously less alienating.[18]

Perhaps what is wrong here is that contracted pregnancy seems to be the other side of the coin of prostitution. Prostitution is sex without reproduction; surrogacy is reproduction without sex. But it is difficult to form a persuasive argument that goes beyond mere guilt by association. Strictly speaking, contracted pregnancy is not prostitution; a broad-based Marxist definition would include it, but also traditional marriage. I think that in the absence of further argument, the force of this accusation is primarily emotional.

Perhaps the dread feature contracted pregnancy shares with prostitution is that it is a lazy person's way of exploiting their own "natural resources." But I suspect that this idea reveals a touchingly naive view of what it takes to be a successful prostitute, not to mention the effort involved in running an optimum pregnancy. Overall takes up this point by asserting that it

> is not and cannot be merely one career choice among others. It is not a real alternative. It is implausible to suppose that fond parents would want it for their daughters. We are unlikely to set up training courses for surrogate mothers. Schools holding "career days" for their future graduates will surely not invite surrogate mothers to address the class on the advantages of their "vocation." And surrogate motherhood does not seem to be the kind of thing one would put on one's curriculum vitae. (p. 126)

But this seems to me to be a blatant ad populum argument.

Such an objection ought, in any case, to entail general condemnation of apparently effortless ways of life that involved any utilization of our distinctive characteristics.

We surely exploit our personal "natural resources" whenever we work. Ditchdiggers use their bodies, professors use their minds. Overall seems particularly to object to some types of "work": contracted pregnancy "is no more a real job option than selling one's blood or one's gametes or one's bodily organs can be real job options" (p. 126). But her discussion makes clear that her denial that such enterprises are "real" jobs is not based on any social arrangements that preclude earning a living wage doing these things, but rather on the moral judgment that they are wrong. They are wrong because they constitute serious "personal and bodily alienation." Yet her ar-

---

[18] Overall, *Ethics and Human Reproduction*, chap. 6. Particularly problematic are her comments about women's loss of individuality, as I will be arguing shortly.

guments for such alienation are weak. She contends that women who work as "surrogates" are deprived of any expression of individuality (p. 126), are interchangeable (p. 127), and have no choice about whose sperm to harbor (p. 128). It is true that, given a reasonable environment (party provided by the woman herself), bodies create babies without conscious effort. This fact, it seems to me, has no particular moral significance: many tasks can be accomplished in similar ways yet are not thought valueless.[19]

It is also usually true that women involved in contracted pregnancy are, in some sense, interchangeable. But the same is true, quite possibly necessarily so, of most jobs. No one who has graded mounds of logic exams or introductory ethics essays could reasonably withhold their assent to this claim, even though college teaching is one of the most autonomous careers available. Even those of us lucky enough to teach upper level courses that involve more expression of individual expertise and choice can be slotted into standardized job descriptions. Finally, it is just false that a woman can have no say about whose sperm she accepts: this could be guaranteed by proper regulation.

I wonder whether there is not some subtle devaluing of the physical by Overall. If so, then we are falling into the trap set by years of elitist equations of women, nature, and inferiority.

What I think is really at issue here is the disposition of the fruit of contracted pregnancy: babies. However, it seems to be generally permissible to dispose of or barter what we produce with both our minds and our bodies—except for that which is created by our reproductive organs. So the position we are considering may just be a version of the claim that it is wrong to separate reproduction and childrearing.

Why? It is true that women normally expect to become especially attached to the product of this particular kind of labor, and we generally regard such attachment as desirable. It seems to be essential for successfully rearing babies the usual way. But if they are to be reared by others who are able to form the appropriate attachment, then what is wrong if a surrogate mother fails to form it? It seems to me that the central question here is whether this "maternal instinct" really exists and, if it does, whether suppressing it is always harmful.

Underlying these questions is the assumption that bonding with babies is "natural" and therefore "good." Perhaps so: the evolutionary advantage of such a tendency would be clear. It would be simple-minded, however, to assume that our habits are biologically determined: our culture is

---

[19] Men have been getting handsome pay for sperm donation for years; by comparison with childbearing, such donation is a lark. Yet there has been no outcry about its immorality. Another double standard?

permeated with pronatalist bias.[20] "Natural" or not, whether a tendency to such attachment is desirable could reasonably be judged to depend on circumstance. When infant mortality is high[21] or responsibility for childrearing is shared by the community, it could do more harm than good. Beware the naturalistic fallacy![22]

But surely there is something special about gestating a baby. That is, after all, the assumption behind the judgment that Mary Beth Whitehead, not William Stern, had a stronger claim to Baby M. The moral scoreboard seems clear: they both had the same genetic input, but she gestated the baby, and therefore has a better case for social parenthood.[23]

We need to be very careful here. Special rights have a way of being accompanied by special responsibilities: women's unique gestational relationship with babies may be taken as reason to confine them once more to the nursery. Furthermore, positing special rights entailed directly by biology flirts again with the naturalistic fallacy and undermines our capacity to adapt to changing situations and forge our destiny.[24]

Furthermore, we already expect many varieties of such separation. We routinely engage in sending children to boarding school, foster parenting, daycare, and so forth; in the appropriate circumstances, these practices are clearly beneficial. Hence, any blanket condemnation of separating reproduction and childrearing will not wash; additional argument is needed for particular classes of cases.

John Robertson points out that the arguments against separating reproduction and childrearing used against contracted pregnancy are equally valid, but unused, with respect to adoption. Others, such as Herbert Krimmel, reject this view by arguing that there is a big moral difference be-

---

[20] See Ellen Peck and Judith Senderowitz, *Pronatalism: The Myth of Mom & Apple Pie* (New York: Crowell, 1974).

[21] As it has been at some periods in the past. See, for example, information about family relationships in Philippe Ariès, *Centuries of Childhood: A Social History of Family Life,* trans. Robert Baldick (New York Knopf, 1982), and Lloyd DeMause, ed., *The History of Children* (New York: Psychohistory Press, 1974).

[22] Consider the arguments in chap. 8 of *Woman's Work: The Household Past and Present,* by Ann Oakley (New York: Vintage, 1974).

[23] One of the interesting things about the practice of contracted pregnancy is that it can be argued to both strengthen and weaken the social recognition of biological relationships. One the one hand, the pregnant woman's biological relationship is judged irrelevant beyond a certain point; on the other, the reason for not valuing it is to enhance that of the sperm donor. This might be interpreted as yet another case where men's interests are allowed to overrule women's. But it might also be interpreted as a salutory step toward awareness that biological ties can and sometimes should be subordinated to social ones. Deciding which interpretation is correct will depend on the facts of particular cases, and the arguments taken to justify the practice in the first place.

[24] Science fiction, most notably John Wyndham's *The Midwich Cuckoos,* provides us with thought-provoking material.

tween giving away an already existing baby and deliberately creating one to give away.[25] This remains to be shown, I think. It is also argued that as adoption outcomes are rather negative, we should be wary of extending any practice that shares its essential features. In fact, there seems to be amazingly little hard information about adoption outcomes. I wonder if the idea that they are bad results from media reports of offspring seeking their biological forebears. There is, in any case, reason to think there are differences between the two practices such that the latter is likely to be more successful than the former.[26]

None of the social descriptions of surrogacy thus seem clearly to justify the outcry against the practice. I suspect that the remaining central issue is the crucial one: surrogacy is baby selling and participating in this practice exploits and taints women.

IS SURROGACY BABY SELLING?

In the foregoing, I deliberately left vague the question of payment in contracted pregnancy. It is clear that there is a recognizable form of the practice that does not include payment; however, it also seems clear that controversy is focusing on the commercial form. The charge is that it is baby selling and that this is wrong.

Is paid surrogacy baby selling? Proponents deny that it is, arguing that women are merely making available their biological services. Opponents retort that as women are paid little or nothing if they fail to hand over a live, healthy child, they are indeed selling a baby. If they are merely selling their services, they would get full pay, even if the child were born dead.

It is true that women who agree to contracts relieving clients of responsibility in this case are being exploited. They, after all, have done their part, risked their risks, and should be paid, just like the physicians involved.

---

[25] John Robertson, "Surrogate Mothers: Not So Novel After All," *Hastings Center Report* 13, no. 5 (October 1983): 28–34; Herbert T. Krimmel, "The Case against Surrogate Parenting," in *Bioethics*, ed. Rem B. Edwards and Glenn Graber (San Diego: Harcourt, Brace, Jovanovich, 1988).

[26] One major difference between adoption and contracted pregnancy is that the baby is handed over virtually at birth, thus ensuring that the trauma sometimes experienced by older adoptees is not experienced. Although children of contracted pregnancy might well be curious to know about their biological mother, I do not see this as a serious obstacle to the practice, because we could adopt an open-file policy for them. There is also reason to believe that carefully screened women undertaking a properly regulated contracted pregnancy are less likely to experience lingering pain of separation. First, they have deliberately chosen to go through pregnancy, knowing that they will give the baby up. The resulting sense of control is probably critical to both their short- and long-term well-being. Second, their pregnancy is not the result of trauma. See also Monica B. Morris, "Reproductive Technology and Restraints," *Transaction/SOCIETY* (March–April 1988): 16–21, esp. 18.

Normal childbearing provides no guarantee of a live, healthy child—why should contracted pregnancy?

There are further reasons for believing that women are selling their services, not babies. First, we do not consider children property. Therefore, as we cannot sell what we do not own, we cannot be selling babies. What creates confusion here is that we do think we own sperm and ova. (Otherwise, how could men sell their sperm?) Yet we do not own what they become, persons. At what point, then, does the relationship cease to be describable as "ownership"?

Resolving this question is not necessary for the current discussion. If we can own babies, there seems to be nothing problematic about selling them. If ownership ceases at some time before birth (and could thus be argued to be unconnected with personhood), then it is not selling of babies that is going on.

Although this response deals with the letter of the objection about baby selling, it fails to heed its spirit, which is that we are trafficking in persons and that such trafficking is wrong. Even if we are not "selling," something nasty is happening.

The most common analogy, with slavery, is weak. Slavery is wrong according to any decent moral theory: the institution allows people to be treated badly. Their desires and interests, whose satisfaction is held to be essential for a good life, are held in contempt. Particularly egregious is the callous disregard of emotional ties to family and self-determination in general. But the institution of surrogate mothering deprives babies of neither. In short, as Robertson contends, "the purchasers do not buy the right to treat the child . . . as a commodity or property. Child abuse and neglect laws still apply."[27]

If "selling babies" is not the right description of what is occurring, then how are we to explain what happens when the birth mother hands the child over to others? One plausible suggestion is that she is giving up her parental right to have a relationship with the child.[28] That it is wrong to do this for pay remains to be shown. Although it would be egoistic and immoral to "sell" an ongoing, friendly relationship (doing so would raise questions about whether it was friendship at all), the immorality of selling a relationship with an organism your body has created

[27] There may be a problem for the woman who gives birth, as the Baby M case has demonstrated. There is probably a case for a waiting period after the birth during which the woman can change her mind. Robertson, "Surrogate Mothers," p. 33.

[28] Heidi Malm argues for this position in "Commodification or Compensation: A Reply to Ketchum," in *Feminist Perspectives in Medical Ethics,* ed. Helen B. Holmes and Laura M. Purdy (Bloomington: Indiana University Press, 1992).

but with which you do not yet have a unique social bond is a great deal less clear.[29]

People seem to feel much less strongly about the wrongness of such acts when motivated by altruism; refusing compensation is the only acceptable proof of such altruism. The act is, in any case, socially valuable. Why then must it be motivated by altruistic considerations? We do not frown on those who provide other socially valuable services even when they do not have the "right" motive. Nor do we require them to be unpaid. For instance, no one expects physicians, no matter what their motivation, to work for beans. They provide an important service; their motivation is important only to the extent that it affects quality.

In general, workers are required to have appropriate skills, not particular motivations.[30] Once again, it seems that there is a different standard for women and for men.

One worry is that women cannot be involved in contracted pregnancy without harming themselves, as it is difficult to let go of a child without lingering concern. So far, despite the heavily publicized Baby M case, this appears not to be necessarily true.[31]

Another worry is that the practice will harm children. Children's welfare is, of course, important. Children deserve the same consideration as other persons, and no society that fails to meet their basic needs is morally satisfactory. Yet I am suspicious of the objections raised on their behalf in these discussions: recourse to children's alleged well-being is once again being used as a trump card against women's autonomy.

First, we hear only about possible risks, never possible benefits, which, as I have been arguing, could be substantial.[32] Second, the main objection raised is the worry about how children will take the knowledge that their genetic mother conceived on behalf of another. We do not know how children will feel about having had such surrogate mothers. But as it is not a completely new phenomenon we might start our inquiry about this topic

[29] Mary Anne Warren suggests, alternatively, that this objection could be obviated by women and children retaining some rights and responsibilities toward each other in contracted pregnancy. Maintaining a relationship of sorts might also, she suggests, help to forestall and alleviate whatever negative feelings children might have about such transfers. I agree that such openness is probably a good idea in any case.

[30] Perhaps lurking behind the objections to surrogacy is some feeling that it is wrong to earn money by letting your body work, without active effort on your part. But this would rule out sperm selling, as well as using women's beauty to sell products and services.

[31] See, for example, James Rachels, "A Report from America: Baby M," *Bioethics* 1, no. 4 (October 1987): 365. He reports that there have been over six hundred successful cases; see also note 26 above.

[32] Among them the one mentioned of being born healthier.

with historical evidence, not pessimistic speculation. In any case, if the practice is dealt with in an honest and commonsense way, particularly if it becomes quite common (and therefore "normal"), there is likely to be no problem. We are also hearing about the worries of existing children of women who are involved in the practice: there are reports that they fear their mother will give them away, too. But surely we can make clear to children the kinds of distinctions that distinguish the practice from slavery or baby selling in the first place.

Although we must try to foresee what might harm children, I cannot help but wonder about the double standards implied by this speculation. The first double standard occurs when those who oppose surrogacy (and reproductive technologies generally) also oppose attempts to reduce the number of handicapped babies born.[33] In the latter context, it is argued that despite their problems handicapped persons are often glad to be alive. Hence it would be paternalistic to attempt to prevent their birth.

Why then do we not hear the same argument here? Instead, the possible disturbance of children born of surrogacy is taken as a reason to prevent their birth. Yet this potential problem is both more remote and most likely involves less suffering than such ailments as spina bifida, Huntington's disease, or cystic fibrosis, which some do not take to be reasons to refrain from childbearing.[34]

Considering the sorts of reasons why parents have children, it is hard to see why the idea that one was conceived in order to provide a desperately wanted child to another is thought to be problematic. One might well prefer that to the idea that one was an "accident," adopted or born because contraception or abortion were not available, conceived to cement a failing marriage, to continue a family line, to qualify for welfare aid, to sex-balance a family, or as an experiment in childrearing. Surely what matters for a child's well-being in the end is whether it is being raised in a loving, intelligent environment.

The second double standard involves a disparity between the interests of women and children. Arguing that surrogacy is wrong because it may upset children suggests a disturbing conception of the moral order. Women should receive consideration at least equal to that accorded children. Conflicts of interest between the two should be resolved according to the same rules we use for any other moral subjects. Those rules should never pre-

[33] To avoid difficulties about abortion added by the assumption that we are talking about existing fetuses, let us consider here only the issue of whether certain couples should risk pregnancy.
[34] There is an interesting link here between these two aspects of reproduction, as the promise of healthier children is, I think, one of the strongest arguments for contracted pregnancy.

scribe sacrificing one individual's basic interest at the mere hint of harm to another.

In sum, there seems to be no reason to think that there is anything necessarily wrong with surrogate mothering, even the paid variety. Furthermore, some objections to it depend on values and assumptions that have been the chief building blocks of women's inequality. Why are some feminists asserting them? Is it because surrogacy as currently practiced often exploits women?

IS SURROGATE MOTHERING WRONG IN CERTAIN SITUATIONS?

Even if surrogate mothering is not necessarily immoral, circumstances can render it so. For instance, it is obviously wrong to coerce women to engage in the practice. Also, certain conditions are unacceptable. Among them are clauses in a contract that subordinate a woman's reasonable desires and judgments to the will of another contracting party,[35] clauses legitimating inadequate pay for the risks and discomforts involved, and clauses that penalize her for the birth of a handicapped or dead baby through no fault of her own. Such contracts are now common.[36]

One popular solution to the problem of such immoral contracts is a law forbidding all surrogacy agreements; their terms would then be unenforceable. But I believe that women will continue to engage in surrogate mothering, even if it is unregulated, and this approach leaves them vulnerable to those who change their mind or will not pay. Fair and reasonable regulations are essential to prevent exploitation of women. Although surrogate mothering may seem risky and uncomfortable to middle-class persons safely ensconced in healthy, interesting, relatively well-paid jobs, with adequate regulation it becomes an attractive option for some women. That these women are more likely than not to be poor is no reason to prohibit the activity.

As I suggested, poor women now face substantial risks in the workplace. Even a superficial survey of hazards in occupations available to poor women would give pause to those who would prohibit surrogacy on the grounds of risk.[37]

Particularly shocking is the list of harmful substances and conditions to which working women are routinely exposed. For instance, cosmeticians and hairdressers, dry cleaners, and dental technicians are all exposed to

---

[35] What this may consist of naturally requires much additional elucidation.

[36] See Susan Ince, "Inside the Surrogate Industry," in *Test-Tube Women*, ed. Rita Arditti, Renate Duelli Klein, and Shelley Minden (London: Pandora, 1984).

[37] See, for example, Jeanne Mager Stellman, *Women's Work, Women's Health: Myths and Realities* (New York: Pantheon, 1977).

carcinogens in their daily work. Most low-level jobs also have high rates of exposure to toxic chemicals and dangerous machinery, and women take such jobs in disproportionate numbers. It is therefore unsurprising that poor women sicken and die more often than other members of society.[38]

This is not an argument in favor of adding yet another dangerous option to those already facing such women. Nor does it follow that the burdens they already bear justify the new ones. On the contrary, it is imperative to clean up dangerous workplaces. However, it would be utopian to think that this will occur in the near future. We must therefore attempt to improve women's lot under existing conditions. Under these circumstances it would be irrational to prohibit surrogacy on the grounds of risk when women would instead have to engage in still riskier pursuits.

Overall's emphatic assertion that contracted pregnancy is not a "real choice" for women in unconvincing. Her major argument, as I have suggested, is that it is an immoral, alienating option. But she also believes that such apparently expanded choices simply mask an underlying contraction of choice. She also fears that by "endorsing an uncritical freedom of reproductive choice, we may also be implicitly endorsing all conceivable alternatives that an individual might adopt; we thereby abandon the responsibility for evaluating substantive actions in favour of advocating merely formal freedom of choice." Both worries are, as they stand, unpersuasive.[39]

As I argued before, there is something troubling here about the new and one-sided emphasis on risk. If nothing else, we need to remember that contracted pregnancy constitutes a low-tech approach to a social problem, one that would slow the impetus toward expensive and dangerous high-tech solutions.[40]

A desire for children on the part of those who normally could not have them is not likely to disappear anytime soon. We could discount it, as many participants in debate about new reproductive technologies do. After all, nobody promised a rose garden to infertile couples, much less to homosexuals or to single women. Nor is it desirable to propagate the idea that having children is essential for human fulfilment.

But appealing to the sacrosancity of traditional marriage or of blood ties to prohibit otherwise acceptable practices that would satisfy people's de-

---

[38] Ibid., app. 1 and 2. See also George L. Waldbott, *Health Effects of Environmental Pollutants* (St. Louis: Mosby, 1973); Nicholas Ashford, *Crisis in the Workplace: Occupational Disease and Injury* (Cambridge: MIT Press, 1976); Phyllis Lehman, *Cancer and the Worker* (New York: The New York Academy of Science, 1977); William D. McKee, ed., *Environmental Problems in Medicine* (Springfield, Ill.: Charles C. Thomas, 1974).

[39] Overall, *Ethics and Human Reproduction*, pp. 24, 25.

[40] These are the ones most likely to put women in the clutches of the paternalistic medical establishment. Exploitation by commercial operations such as that of Noel Keane could be avoided by tight regulation or prohibition altogether of for-profit enterprises.

sires hardly makes sense, especially when those practices may provide other benefits. Not only might contracted pregnancy be less risky and more enjoyable than other jobs women are forced to take, but there are other advantages as well. Because being pregnant is not usually a full-time occupation, surrogate mothering could buy time for women to improve their lot significantly: students, aspiring writers, and social activists could make real progress toward their goals.

Women have until now done this reproductive labor for free.[41] Paying women to bear children should force us all to recognize this process as the socially useful enterprise that it is and children as socially valuable creatures whose upbringing and welfare are critically important.

In short, surrogate mothering has the potential to empower women and increase their status in society. The darker side of the story is that it also has frightening potential for deepening their exploitation. The outcome of the current warfare over control of new reproductive possibilities will determine which of these alternatives comes to pass.

[41] The implications of this fact remain to be fully understood; I suspect that they are detrimental to women and children, but this is a topic for another article.

CHAPTER 12

Another Look at

Contract Pregnancy

It is not surprising that the practice now widely known as "surrogate motherhood" has excited so much interest, so many articles, even books.[1] The practice—even though it need involve nothing more high-tech than a turkey baster—invites us to reconsider some of the most fundamental human relationships and raises a host of issues and problems. What, if any, are the necessary and sufficient conditions of motherhood? Who should have the right to rear a child when biological mother and father do not live together? What are the grounds for claims to children, anyway? Is it wrong for women deliberately to bear a child for others to raise? And if not, should they be paid? The questions go on and on, and new twists, such as egg donation and contracted embryo gestation, simply add more dimensions for moral philosophers and lawyers to ponder.

I have already argued in Chapter 11 (and will not recapitulate the details here) that if stringently regulated with an eye toward women's welfare—a big "if"—contract pregnancy could offer significant benefits for women and perhaps also for the babies.[2] Nevertheless, many objections to contract pregnancy have been raised. The transfer of risk and burden from one woman to another has been characterized as either contingently or neces-

From *Issues in Reproductive Technology I*, edited by Helen B. Holmes (New York: Garland, 1992). Reprinted by permission of the editor. The essay also appears in *Issues in Reproductive Technology*, edited by Helen B. Holmes (New York: New York University Press, 1994).
[1] See Helen B. Holmes, "Contract Pregnancy: An Annotated Bibliography," in *Issues in Reproductive Technology I: An Anthology* (New York: Garland, 1992).
[2] See Chapter 11, "Surrogate Mothering: Exploitation or Empowerment?," and "A Response to Dodds and Jones," *Bioethics* 3, no. 1: 40–44.

sarily involving class- or race-based exploitation. Another argument is that the practice degrades women because it reinforces the view of them as "brood-mares" and harms them by violating their maternal instincts. Furthermore, the practice is held to constitute morally undesirable baby selling and to harm children by disrupting their sense of family. I believe that these objections are less well founded than is generally recognized and have argued against them elsewhere.[3] However, it also seems clear that there is more to be said about some of these issues. In particular, it would be helpful to look in more detail at ideals of motherhood, the moral status of infertility, and what I label "utilitarian worries."

MOTHERHOOD: SURROGATE OR OTHERWISE

One problematic aspect of the practice of women's bearing babies for others to rear, one that is indicative of the moral tangles lurking here, is what to call it. "Surrogate motherhood" seems inappropriate, both because it looks peculiar to call a woman pregnant with her own fertilized egg a surrogate and because it calls up undesirable associations with respect to motherhood. Sara Ann Ketchum attempted to resolve this problem by referring to the practice as "contracted motherhood" or "baby contracts."[4] But the former creates similar assumptions about motherhood, and the latter seems to focus on the baby, leaving the woman invisible. Previously, I used "contracted pregnancy" which still seems to me the most accurate term; for simplicity's sake, I will shorten it to "contract pregnancy".[5]

This is not just a semantic issue. Contract pregnancy (along with new conceptive technologies generally) raises pressing new questions about the whole notion of motherhood. Because language both expresses underlying assumptions and contributes to future ones, the implications of our linguistic choices are not always trivial.

My concern about calling pregnant women "mothers" is that it suggests without argument that they have at least the same obligations toward their fetuses that they do toward their children. That conclusion, however, should not be accepted without further argument, given its bearing both on the morality of abortion and on women's legal duties toward fetuses they plan to carry to term.[6] A related problem, as Mary Mahowald notes, is that

[3] See Chapter 11, "Surrogate Mothering: Exploitation or Empowerment?," and "A Response to Dodds and Jones."
[4] See Sara Ann Ketchum, "Selling Babies and Selling Bodies," in *Feminist Perspectives in Medical Ethics*, ed. Helen B. Holmes and Laura M. Purdy (Bloomington: Indiana University Press, 1992).
[5] See Chapter 11, "Surrogate Mothering: Exploitation or Empowerment?"
[6] See Chapter 4, "Are Pregnant Women Fetal Containers?"

"mother" suggest that fetuses are separate individuals, with all the moral baggage implied by that claim.[7] It would therefore seem preferable to reserve the term "mother" for women who nurture a child.

This move seems perfectly plausible until we ask whose child she is nurturing. Does the child in question have to be biologically hers? If so, that leaves out many women who are doing all the same things mothers do. If not, then what is the status of the woman who bore the child? As the furor over the Baby M case shows, these issues should not be decided by manipulating definitions or by tradition—but by solid argument. In the meantime, neutral terms are needed that do not prejudice the matter one way or the other. It follows that Patricia Spallone's assertion that "the woman who goes through pregnancy and gives birth is the mother" is also to be regarded as problematic.[8]

Until recently such a claim would have been considered simply bizarre, for mothering just *was* the natural progression of pregnancy, labor, delivery, and nurturing. Of course, some unfortunate women and children did not fit this mold. Some women adopted children because they were unable to have their own; others married widowers or divorced men with children; still others got pregnant in inconvenient circumstances and gave up their babies for adoption. Likewise, some children lost their mothers and acquired "new" ones by dint of their fathers' remarriage or by being adopted. But these were peripheral cases, if not statistically, then psychologically. However, contemporary social conditions and scientific knowledge are, as Michelle Stanworth puts it, "deconstructing" motherhood: "motherhood as a unified biological process will be effectively deconstructed: in place of 'mother,' there will be ovarian mothers who supply eggs, uterine mothers who give birth to children and, presumably, social mothers who raise them."[9]

What are we to make of this development? First, it constitutes explicit recognition of the split between biological and social relationships already existing in human lives. And, it should be noted that splitting the two has often enhanced welfare: it has, among other things, permitted women un-

[7] Mary Mahowald, "Fetal Tissue Transplantation and Women," paper presented at the meeting of the Eastern Division, American Philosophical Association, December 27–30, 1990, Boston. I believe that the usual assumptions about the implications of describing fetuses as part of their mothers do not necessarily hold, however. See Chapter 4, "Are Pregnant Women Fetal Containers?"

[8] Patrica Spallone, *Beyond Conception* (Granby, Mass.: Bergin & Garvey, 1989), p. 176.

[9] Michelle Stanworth, "Reproductive Technologies and the Deconstruction of Motherhood," in *Reproductive Technologies: Gender, Motherhood, and Medicine*, ed. Michelle Stanworth (Minneapolis: University of Minnesota Press, 1987), p. 16. Christine Pierce beautifully describes the difficulties in any such claim. See "Natural Law Language and Women," in *Sex Equality*, ed. Jane English (Englewood Cliffs, N.J.: Prentice-Hall, 1977).

able to rear their children to give them over to others more able to do so, a practice that has often benefited all. Of course, too, the outcome has often been less satisfactory, as where adoptive parents have been insensitive to the special problems faced by their children, or where prejudice based on race, class, or sexual orientation has led the state to appropriate children unjustifiably. Second, by now distinguishing genetic and gestational components of biological motherhood, deconstructed motherhood also constitutes a new dimension of that split.

This fragmentation of the concept of "mother" is deeply disturbing to some critics of the new conceptive technologies, including many feminists. "Motherhood," is, after all, an enormously complicated term because of its emotional associations. They fear its loss and see it as a way of reducing women's power as mothers, just as the power inherent in skilled labor is undermined when complicated industrial processes are broken up into smaller sections, each of which can be done by more easily exploitable unskilled workers. In reproduction, the threat inherent in this process is reinforced by the fact that such a division of labor entails relying on technology controlled mainly by men: it takes technology to get eggs out of women, as well as to fertilize them and put them back in. Thus the division of labor and reliance on technology render the new conceptive technologies dangerous terrain for women.

The worries about these technologies do not constitute sufficient grounds for rejecting them, although they do suggest a need for extreme caution. I am more troubled at present by something else. I am grateful to the radical feminist critics of the new conceptive practices for their vigorous attention to new developments, even though I often disagree with their conclusions, for they bring to light dimensions of the issues that might otherwise remain hidden. But their positions, too, sometimes rest on inadequately articulated presuppositions that need to be brought out into the open. In particular, I have been increasingly concerned about the images of womanhood and motherhood on which many of their criticisms of the conceptive technologies rest, images that draw much of their strength from a disconcerting appeal to nature that, as Michelle Stanworth argues, "ignores . . . the strenuous and partly successful efforts of the women's movement to transcend the identification of women with nature."[10] The image I question is that of ideal motherhood, constituted by a natural progression of pregnancy, labor, and childrearing.

Before going any further, note the invisibility of sex here. Mercifully, it is absent from this progression, although it is hard to see on what theoretical

---

[10] Michelle Stanworth, "Birth Pangs: Conceptive Technologies and the Threat to Motherhood," in *Conflicts in Feminism*, ed. Marianne Hirsch and Evelyn Fox Keller (New York: Routledge, 1990), p. 299.

basis it has been excluded. Why do I say this? On the one hand, pregnancy must be preceded by sex, given radical feminist doubts about new conceptive technologies, as there is no other safe way to initiate pregnancy. On the other, surprisingly, pregnancy might have to follow sex.

First, consider Stanworth's perceptive rebuttal to the radical criticism of infertile women's dependence on male-controlled technology: "is it only infertile women whose attendance at medical clinics validates medical power, or is this an unintended side-effect of the use of many contraceptive or abortion or birthing technologies as well as of conceptive ones?[11] In other words, it may be inconsistent to regard contraception and abortion as innocuous but conceptive technologies as dangerous! Feminists have rightly been quite outspoken about the defects of contemporary contraceptive technologies and about medical control of abortion, but rejecting them wholesale would leave us still worse off. Furthermore, the same point could be extended to any technology on which we come to depend, such as clothes washers or optometry. Thus, if we are not to be reduced to some fairly primitive state, we must surely focus on bending technology to our needs rather than becoming Luddites.

Second, some radical ecofeminist critiques reject the whole notion of controlling nature. They see our desire to do so as the source of most of our woes; a few have not flinched at extending that rejection to women's control over their bodies. The logical extension of concern about women's dependence on technology as well as ecofeminist attempts to locate in obsession with controlling nature the root of many of our problems obviously have disturbing implications for those of us who take it as given that the advantages of separating sex from reproduction are overwhelming, not only for heterosexual women, but also for lesbians.

Now the appeal to nature here arises from far different motivations than the transparently controlling versions promoted by such institutions as the Catholic Church.[12] It seems to me to be compounded of a number of perfectly defensible motivations. First, although I do not subscribe to the extreme gender-polarized picture of human society that motivates the radical feminist rejection of the new conceptive technologies, women obviously do need to be on their guard toward a medical establishment whose track record on their behalf leaves a great deal to be desired. Second, celebrating the female bodily functions and activities that have been so devalued by most human societies is a good thing. However, it is essential to do this in

---

[11] Ibid., p. 293.
[12] Janice G. Raymond, "Fetalists and Feminists: They Are Not the Same," in *Made to Order: The Myth of Reproductive and Genetic Progress*, ed. Patricia Spallone and Deborah Lynn Steinberg (Oxford: Pergamon, 1987).

ways that ensure that it does not become as constricting as more traditional views of the good life for women. This task is part of the more general enterprise of feminist ethics, which must find ways to validate connections and relationships without devaluing some of the choices that liberal theory rightly aims to protect.[13]

Such constriction can arise from surprising corners. Thus, for instance, consider the apparently progressive view that the primary obstacles to happy motherhood are social arrangements created by patriarchy and capitalism. The assumption is that if pregnant women had access to good prenatal care and guarantees of economic and social support for rearing their children, they would not have abortions or adopt out their children. Although women clearly need much more help than they are getting, and they do sometimes abort or give up their babies for such reasons, the way these claims are often asserted holds up a standard that could make it quite difficult for a pregnant woman who is *not* economically oppressed to refuse motherhood.

Even an unimaginably supportive society—especially one of the sort argued for by some radical feminists where abortion for genetic defect is frowned upon—will not take all the burden of motherhood from women. There will always be women whose other projects are incompatible with those demands, and it is surely best for both woman and child if such a reluctantly pregnant woman either aborts or lets others do the rearing. The perfect contraceptive may considerably reduce this problem, but it will not, given human imperfection, make it go away altogether. In any case, we do not want a society in which women cannot change their minds about a given pregnancy.

Surely, abortion should always remain a legal option, and it would be surprising were feminists to disagree about this. However, is it far-fetched to worry about the possibility of an "ethic" that could, for all practical purposes, foreclose it as a real choice? To judge by statistics and new reports, such an ethic is already influential among poor women of color. Furthermore, similar attitudes are already apparent in many of my students who believe that although abortion ought to be available, they personally would never have one. Whether or not they do go on to have abortions, their attitude is significant and derives from a number of factors that will continue to be a factor in women's thinking. It reflects in part the intellectual strategy chosen by the national women's institutions leading the pro-choice movement that has emphasized the moral difficulty of abortion decisions,

[13] I am not talking about promoting the purely contractual view of human relationships that leads to so much misery, but about the kind of freedom from certain kinds of social pressure discussed by John Stuart Mill in *On Liberty*.

while affirming our right to make them. This strategy was chosen, I suspect, because of the philosophically demanding nature of the arguments in favor of abortion, arguments ill-suited for the emotionally charged political environment in which the abortion debate has had to be carried out. Worse yet, even absent that emotional element, few people in our philosophically unsophisticated society—whether inclined toward the pro-choice position or not—have the background or patience to work through the arguments in search of a sound position on abortion. Therefore, the potential for a negative view of abortion becoming widespread is real and, combined with the assumptions underlying the radical feminist critique, could be more coercive than even current pro-life rhetoric, because the latter does at least promote adoption as a moral alternative for unwanted babies.

Conversely, there will probably always be women who love being pregnant but who do not particularly enjoy child rearing. Surely, it would be regrettable is social pressure to live up to the idealized version of motherhood described earlier prevented them from providing infertile women with babies they could not otherwise have.

INFERTILITY AND ITS REMEDIES

The natural image of motherhood implicit in the comments of some feminist critics of the new technologies is integral to their conception of a new and better society. Yet this image seems to leave out in the cold women who cannot conceive when they want to. Nor does it leave any remedy for single individuals or homosexual couples. What about them? One thing seems clear: in that better society there will not be many, if any, babies available for adoption. Nor should there be any of the pitiful older children now desperate for good homes, the handicapped, the racially mixed, the emotionally disturbed; they will all be cared for already.

The radical feminist answer is, in part, as Patricia Spallone rightly points out, that infertility will be much reduced because of better "primary health care for women, screening for pelvic inflammatory disease and cervical cancer, by securing a higher standard of hygiene and nutrition for poor women, by cleaning up the workplace from environmental hazards that cause infertility in women and men, and congenital health problems in infants."[14] One might also add that infertility could quite likely be reduced still further by social policies that permit women to have babies at a time in their life that is now "too soon" for many professions.

What about those women who remain infertile despite all these improvements? Apparently, according to many radical feminists, they will

[14] Spallone, *Beyond Conception*, p. 27.

have to grin and bear it: women do not really need babies to be fulfilled and their conviction that they do is just a consequence of socially promoted pronatalism. Yet this answer would not really be consistent with the more humane attitudes we all hope for in a better society, as that pronatalism would be gone, along with other patriarchal pressures. However, not only will there undoubtedly be a transitional period where the legacy of such pressures persist, but also, more generally, the ease with which the desire for children is dismissed is troubling: I do not believe that the strong desire for children is merely an artifact of patriarchy. As a voluntarily childless woman myself, I am as aware as anybody that life can be fulfilling without a child of your own. However, as one who has also participated in parenting, I also know that—for better or worse—there is nothing else quite like it. It just will not do to tell people that they should adopt a Girl Scout troop instead. A special closeness arises from being a child's primary caretaker and a special thrill in witnessing the child's development into a human person. In addition, for some people, their ties to children are the strongest and most enduring human connections they will ever make. So long as we think human survival desirable, these interests are likely to unite into a wish to be involved in childrearing.

Now it is true that wanted X does not necessarily justify your having it; after all, going after it may be harmful to others so that their interests override yours. But rejecting women's desires as unreasonable or immoral without adequate consideration of possible compromises is a hallmark of traditional sexist attitudes toward women; it pains me to see it reproduced in some feminist thinking.

A cavalier attitude toward the infertile, despite ritual expressions of concern for them, seems to me implicit in the answers currently promoted for infertile women who want children. They are told that their desire for a healthy, genetically related baby is not "authentic" and that if they truly want to be parents they should be ready to adopt an older child, even if he or she is handicapped, emotionally disturbed, or of a different ethnic background.[15] It is also suggested that any attempt to create a new, genetically related child via conceptive technologies is so immoral as to override any standing the desire for such a child might have. These uncompromising and unsympathetic stands strike me as likely to obscure the important issues raised by radical feminist critiques.

Consider first that adoption is not necessarily the panacea it might seem. As Stanworth points out, "The description of infertility as a social condition of involuntary childlessness doesn't hold for all women. For some, preg-

---

[15] Comments such as these about adoption come with utter predictability from most of those who consider themselves socially progressive. See Stanworth, "Birth Pangs," p. 291.

nancy and childbirth are not only a route to a child, but a desired end in itself (p. 293). This desire must surely count for something with those who want to validate women's experiences of gestation and labor.

She notes two other difficulties with adoption. First, "adoption and fostering are often subject to strict surveillance and regulation . . . not necessarily benign to women" (p. 293). She defends her claim by describing some of the standards used to judge whether women should be granted a child:

> Their policies and criteria of assessment are framed against a conventional notion of parenting—and particularly, of motherhood—which will deter many would-be mothers. Adoption agencies in Britain may (and often do) refuse single women or those aged over thirty; may (and usually do) refuse those who are not heterosexual, whether married or not; may (and sometimes do) refuse women who have jobs, women who have had psychiatric referrals, women with disabilities, women whose unconventional lifestyles cast doubt—for the social workers at least—on their suitability as mothers. (p. 294)

Second, adoption may well mean taking a child from another woman: "The pressures that lead some women to surrender their babies for adoption are very like those condemned in the case of surrogate mothers, right down to the possibility of exploitation of women from subordinate ethnic communities or from poorer nations" (p. 294). According to Stanworth, white parents in Britain can no longer easily adopt black children because of worry about the potential for exploitation of this sort. Such realism about the conditions and consequences of different remedies for problems such as infertility is essential; all too often, the disadvantages of a disfavored solution are contrasted with the advantages of the favored one, where a more thorough assessment would suggest quite a different picture.

Even if a woman morally can adopt, reluctance to do so is often brushed off as prejudice by radical feminist critics of the new conceptive technologies. Thus, for instance, the desire for a young baby is, despite ample evidence of the importance of the early years for later development, discounted: infertile women should be ready to take on whatever painful legacy is left by inadequate care, just as they should be ready to take on the physical or emotional problems that might afflict a "hard-to-adopt" child.

As I have argued elsewhere, there are two points that need to be made about this position.[16] On the one hand, raising difficult children is not a task to be undertaken lightly, for it can be so demanding as to require virtual abandonment of all other significant plans. It is easy for those who do not

---

[16] Purdy, "A Response to Dodds and Jones," p. 44.

have to face such daily realities as high-priced, inaccessible medical care, incontinence, special equipment, full-time surveillance, lack of mobility, violent antisocial behavior, and the like to recommend that others should take them on. Nor should critics ignore the fact that, as society is currently organized, most of those left to cope with these problems will be women, not men. Is this the price radical feminists want to extract from their sisters who want to mother a child? "Normal" reproduction, too, is a kind of lottery, of course: fertile couples are not guaranteed normal children, although most get them. That some people are willing to devote their lives to difficult children in admirable and to be encouraged; asking those who might be excellent parents of a normal child to parent an especially demanding one may be, as things now stand, a recipe for misery and perhaps even child abuse. We, as a society, are not doing much to relieve such parents of the special burden they bear; providing this kind of help as a matter of course would undoubtedly also reduce the number of children given out for adoption as well as encourage adoption of those who are now given up. Our collective failure to render such help is unconscionable.

On the other hand, given our collective irresponsibility here, who are we to hold only the infertile responsible for difficult children? Why do we expect such supererogatory behavior of them without seeing that the same arguments apply to the fertile? Why, indeed, do radical feminists not argue that so long as there are homeless children, it is wrong for the *fertile* to have their own babies? As Stanworth rightly suggests, "Our critique of pronatalism and of reproductive technologies will be all the more persuasive when it ceases to distinguish so categorically between fertile women and infertile."[17]

Some of the same points could be made about accusations of racism. Undoubtedly, there are racist whites who look down on people of color and would not have such a baby in the house. Bigotry of this kind is obviously deplorable and ought to be eradicated as quickly as possible, but forcing black or Chicano children on such individuals is hardly in anyone's best interest. Furthermore, it is inaccurate to attribute all reluctance at interracial adoption to such base motives. As noted, some situations might entail exploitation of poor women of color. In others, individuals might quite rightly fear serious difficulty for the children in question. For example, in a white rural area such a child would stand out in a very uncomfortable way. Although it could be argued that forging ahead despite that possibility is the only way to change racist attitudes, once again this position underestimates the probable cost to these pioneers and discounts other less traumatic ways of making social progress. Another problem with such adoptions is the

[17] Stanworth, "Birth Pangs," p. 293.

identity issue the children would face as they grow up in what is still a racially polarized world, one where they may face discrimination from whites because of their color but where members of their own ethnic group might see them as "oreos."

UTILITARIAN WORRIES

The preceding points should make it clear that some objections to unorthodox reproduction are more problematic than they might at first seem. The ideal of motherhood against which practices such as contract pregnancy are measured contains its own Achilles heel, and the most obvious traditional approaches to infertility may often be unsatisfactory. Contract pregnancy and other conceptive technologies might still not be justifiable, however, if radical feminists' conception of reality were accurate.

Some such feminists argue that men, as a class, and for a variety of reasons, want to control women. Women, despite a long history of restriction, still largely control reproduction, and much of their power and perceived value are predicated on this control. The new reproductive practices show promise, however, of finally putting reproduction in men's hands, partly because it is men who control technology and partly because technology has a logic of its own that promotes hierarchy. Hence, even if certain conceptive technologies benefit particular women, they harm women as a class.

The most extreme versions of this picture suggest that what men really want is to eliminate the need for women altogether. Now this aim would clearly be short-sighted, for we generally still do more than our share of such tasks as childrearing for which men in general show little enthusiasm. Furthermore, unless we are also to believe that all men are latent homosexuals, we would be missed in other ways as well.

But do men want to control (as opposed to eliminate) women? It is undeniable that some men do want to control us; it is also undeniable that many men unconsciously act in ways compatible with such a desire. If nothing else, the widespread violence against women shows that men's attitudes toward women are less than egalitarian. Women's inferior social position is obvious from the statistics on work, income, and wealth; that most positions of power are occupied by men also supports this conclusion.

Now this is obviously not the place for a detailed examination of the radical feminist view of society, but deciding about contract pregnancy cannot wait until the issue is resolved. How, in the meantime, is it possible to proceed?

First, it seems to me that the situation is a good deal more complicated than the foregoing would suggest. On the one hand, individual men do not necessarily hold these negative attitudes. On the other, factors such as class and race interact with gender in ways that would complicate this picture considerably, even if it were accurate. Some writers, like Maria Mies, implicitly recognize this fact when they reject the claim that if and when more women become technical experts we would have less to fear from technology. For instance, she asserts that "we can no longer pursue the biologistic fallacy that social conditions would change if as many women as possible were sitting at the control panels of power, in the privileged positions in politics, economics, culture, and in the ever more elitist and centralist world of the new technology." She goes on to say that "we must ask what policies, what aims these women represent. The existing technology is still an instrument of domination if women control it. If they do no want to fight patriarchy and capital at the same time, they will turn it against women, too."[18]

It will be no easy matter, given the ongoing and sometimes violent disagreement among feminists, to decide where this pessimistic view of human society intersects with reality. Despite the obvious hostility of substantial numbers of men, I am still unconvinced that the battle lines are so irrevocably drawn as the radical feminist picture would suggest. Furthermore, like Stanworth, I am convinced that even were it accurate, negativism about conceptive technologies is not necessarily the best coping strategy.[19] She asks, for example, whether wholesale rejection of them

is really the best way to protect women who have sought (and will continue to seek) their use. An implacable opposition to conceptive technologies could mean that any chance of exerting pressure on those who organize infertility services—for example, pressure for better research and for disclosure of information; for more stringent conditions of consent; for means of access for poorer women, who are likely to be the majority of those with infertility problems—would be lost. Would it be wise to abandon infertile women to the untender mercies of infertility specialists, when a campaign, say, to limit the number of embryos that may be implanted (and thereby to reduce multiple pregnancies, pressures for selective reduction, and so forth), or to regulate the use of hormonal stimulation, might do a great deal to reduce the possible risks to women and to their infants?[20]

Her general point, though well taken, still leaves unanswered the objection that it is not maltreatment of the infertile that is most worrisome, but

[18] Maria Mies, "Why Do We Need All This? A Call Against Genetic Engineering and Reproductive Technology," in *Made to Order*, p. 41.
[19] Stanworth, "Birth Pangs," p. 295.
[20] Ibid., pp. 295–96.

the consequences for women as a group if the infertile, seeking to advance what they see as their own interest, make the overall situation worse. Among the objections of this type are that recourse to such practices as contract pregnancy, especially when money changes hands, promotes the view of women as breeders, exploits poor women, and is potentially racist in new and horrifying ways.

What evidence is there that letting women engage in contract pregnancies for money will cause deterioration in men's attitudes toward women? I believe that reasonable men who do not already have unfounded negative attitudes toward women will not be precipitated by the existence of paid contract pregnancy to the view that women are primarily breeders. However, we have little evidence one way or the other on this empirical issue; what *can* be said is that there is nothing about the practice itself that would justify any such judgment.[21]

Is the assertion that contract pregnancy exploits poor women better founded? I have shown elsewhere that arguments so far given for this claim are unsuccessful. Neither Christine Overall's Marxist argument that it constitutes an especially degrading kind of alienated labor nor the standard liberal argument about appropriate protection from risk are persuasive.[22] The latter, in particular, depends on ignorance of the kinds of risks working-class people routinely face; it also depends on a refusal to take seriously the fact that circumstances ought to make a difference in whether a given act is judged prudent or moral.

What needs to be shown here is that contract pregnancy is more exploitive than other services the rich now buy from the poor. The rich, by definition, have more money than the poor; that is why the rich dine in expensive restaurants that employ poor waiters, hire help to clean their houses, and procure for themselves a variety of other services the poor cannot afford. Of course, the gap between rich and poor ought to be smaller so that the poor can have greater access to some of these luxuries. That way, for example, more poor women at risk for health problems in pregnancy could avoid them just as their richer sisters can now do via contract pregnancy.[23] A more economically just society would not, by itself, necessarily provide women with appropriate protection from exploitation, although the pool of women who would submit to any indignity for money would be greatly reduced.

[21] See Christine Overall, *Ethics and Human Reproduction: A Feminist Analysis* (Boston: Allen & Unwin, 1987), chap. 6, and my Chapter 11, "Surrogate Mothering: Exploitation or Empowerment?"

[22] Overall, *Ethics and Human Reproduction,* and my Chapter 11, "Surrogate Mothering: Exploitation or Empowerment?"

[23] I am well aware that many, but not all, health problems endured by the poor are a result of poverty itself.

It is undeniable that the potential for exploitation in our own inegalitarian society is substantial, for poor women are much less able to protect their own interests than they would be in a better society. However, it does not follow from this that potentially exploitable but otherwise morally permissible practices should be banned altogether. One way to protect otherwise vulnerable individuals is to regulate them. With respect to contract pregnancy no one has yet shown either that it is not morally permissible or that such regulation is impossible.

Here, for example, the state could set a minimum wage for contract pregnancy and lay out a model contract prohibiting some of the conditions now routinely required of women. The now standard $10,000 for U.S. women *does* constitute exploitation, given the risk, discomfort, and responsibility that go with pregnancy: $20,000 would be a much fairer fee. Certainly, paying the woman and broker both the same wages as is now common degrades women and continues the unacceptable and insulting tradition of devaluing women's work. It would, in any case, be necessary to outlaw private brokers because their interests would too often conflict with those of the other participants.

Some would argue that upping the compensation for engaging in contract pregnancy is precisely the wrong response to the problem of exploitation. They suggest that, on the contrary, women should only be allowed to do it for free; otherwise they are selling babies or commodifying themselves. I have argued elsewhere against the accusation of baby selling and will not recapitulate those claims here. The commodification argument also seems to me naive, as it fails to show that there is any morally relevant difference between engaging in contract pregnancy and many other occupations. Furthermore, this argument seems to accept and promote the view that women can be respected for altruistic and socially useful actions only when they receive no monetary compensation, whereas men—physicians, scientists, politicians—can be both honored and well paid. Finally, women have until now been expected to do such reproductive labor for free. Seeing them paid for some of it might just remind us that it is socially valuable.[24]

What about the accusation of racism? The last word here cannot come from members of the dominant group because we may be racist in ways that we, despite the best intentions, are unaware of. However, this fact does not relieve us of responsibility for attempting to evaluate such claims as best we can.

So against this backdrop, what can be said here? The case that surrogacy watchers have been waiting for happened in summer 1990. Anna Johnson, a black woman, bore a boy from the fertilized egg of Crispina and Mark

---

[24] See Chapter 11, "Surrogate Mothering: Exploitation or Empowerment?"

Calvert; finding herself attached to him, she sued for (and was denied) visitation rights.[25] Egg donation of this kind also raises the possibility of Third World women of color being used as even cheaper incubators for white couples.[26]

Now, is the practice of white couples hiring a women of color to gestate their babies racist?[27] In the Calvert case, Katha Pollitt suspects that the Calverts deliberately chose Johnson to gestate the baby because they knew that no judge would find for a black woman who wanted to keep a white baby.[28] If that were true, their behavior would indeed have been racist, although an interesting wrinkle here is provided by the fact that Crispina Calvert is herself Asian, not "white." The most despicable racism, however, would be on the part of a society that rewards racist individuals with judgeships, making the couple's parasitical racism possible.

The more interesting question here is whether the fact of using women of color in this way, whether in the United States or in the Third World, is, other things being equal, racist. Racism would be implicit in the judgment that they are "good enough" to gestate a child, but that their own "colored" eggs would not be acceptable. This position is clearly racist, and hiring women of color on that basis would also be clearly racist, although if the women benefited anyway, the practice would not necessarily be wrong. However, whites hiring a woman of color need not be racist. After all, the main point here is to create a genetically related child; if one cares about this sort of thing, then having a child who is genetically related to both woman and man is better than having one related only to the latter. This point is reinforced by the fact that in traditional contract pregnancy, as critics point out, the wives of male clients have no genetic link to the children, and hence, according to the trend in recent court decisions, no claim on them.[29] So one could easily imagine that were the positions reversed, a black couple would also prefer to use their own egg. That they might not *would* be a symptom of the society's racism: the social rewards for light skin might lead them to prefer, after all, the white woman's egg.

---

[25] Katha Pollitt, "When Is a Mother Not a Mother?" *The Nation*, December 31, 1990, p. 842.
[26] Gena Corea, *The Mother Machine: Reproductive Technologies from Artificial Insemination to Artificial Wombs* (New York: Harper & Row, 1985), p. 215.
[27] The whole notion of race is problematic as biologists now speak of genetic pools and breeding populations instead. Furthermore, the categories we routinely apply to the U.S. population are especially questionable, given the large amount of mixing that has occurred and the extent to which "blacks" and "whites" share a gene pool. Nonetheless, "race" is a socially constructed category that will continue to have some usefulness as long as distinctions in treatment are based on it.
[28] Pollitt, "When Is a Mother Not a Mother?," p. 842.
[29] Ibid., p. 842, and Katha Pollitt, "The Strange Case of Baby M," *The Nation*, May 23, 1987, p. 683.

But it does not follow from this that it would always be racist for a white couple to use their own egg.

One might argue, too, that an attempt to avoid racist instances of the practice by banning interracial transactions could have racist consequences, just as legislation "protecting" the class of women from certain occupational choices turned out in many cases to be sexist: it might bar women of color from jobs they want and could, on balance, benefit from. A better solution would be to include in the regulation of contract pregnancy clauses that would take into account the special vulnerability of women of color.

Do the same sorts of considerations apply to foreign women of color? One major complication here is the fact that they would be paid less, although if they were paid wages comparable in buying power to what U.S. women ought to be getting, then they would not, other things being equal, be economically exploited. The danger here is that other things may be far from equal. There may be, for instance, far different cultural attitudes toward family, such that contract pregnancy "costs" them more emotionally; more concretely, factors such as bad nutrition and health care due to extreme poverty pose special danger to women's welfare. Should this kind of contract pregnancy therefore be banned? Again, it is by no means easy to make the right decision in that context of a world saturated with class hierarchy, racism, and sexism. This background could lead women to accept conditions seriously detrimental to their own interest. Yet, if regulated to avoid these worst cases, contract pregnancy might help women to better their circumstances within that context. Regulation would be still more problematic than in the United States, however, as it would require cooperation on the part of both our government and others that have still worse records of protecting their citizens. Hence, the prospect of a morally tenable practice of contract pregnancy abroad is substantially more dubious than at home. A truly well-informed decision here, nevertheless, would require the views of a spectrum of potentially affected Third World women.

A TENABLE STRATEGY

I have been proposing a series of solutions that attempts to maximize contract pregnancy's possible benefit and to minimize its possible harm. These ideas will no doubt infuriate both those who see the limits I propose as unreasonable fetters on freedom and those who disagree with my premise that there is substantial good to be derived from a carefully formulated reproductive policy that includes contract pregnancy. On the one hand, to have a tolerable society, individual freedom must quite often be limited in the name of the greater good, despite libertarians' belief to the contrary. On the other, because the burden of proof is on those who would limit freedom,

such proposed limits require more searing scrutiny than contract pregnancy has so far received.

One of the most troublesome issues here is the extent to which we try to
tailor our positions to what we perceive as contemporary reality, as opposed to some better future state. According to Maria Mies, "It is a historical fact that technological innovations within exploitative relationships of
domination only lead to an intensification of the exploitation of the groups
being oppressed."[30] However, I am unconvinced that fighting for morally
desirable technologies is such an all-or-nothing prospect: I agree with Stanworth that it is both desirable and worth doing.

Consider one harmful potential of contract pregnancy: a major objection
to it, argues Katha Pollitt, is that it could limit women's physical freedom.
She adds:

> Right now a man cannot legally control the conduct of a woman pregnant
> by him. He cannot force her to have an abortion or not have one, to manage
> her pregnancy and delivery as he thinks best, or to submit to fetal surgery
> or a Caesarean. Nor can he sue her if, through what he considers to be neg-
> ligence, she miscarries or produces a defective baby. A maternity contract
> could give a man all those powers, except, possibly, the power to compel
> abortion.[31]

Pollitt is certainly right that no contract containing such clauses should be
written or enforced. This could be done either by banning contract pregnancy altogether or by fighting for model regulation that rules these sorts
of things out. Given the foregoing, I think the latter should be first on our
agenda. Not only would that go far toward making contract pregnancy a
fair practice, but it would also help establish legal precedents for women's
more general right to control their bodies in pregnancy. If, on the other
hand, we concentrate on getting rid of the practice of contract pregnancy,
we will not necessarily have made any progress at all on this latter important issue. The realities of class-, gender-, and race-based discrimination in
this world mean that we cannot seek only to eradicate their symptoms, but
that we must rather seek to win the most broadly based victories we can.
Otherwise, as with the Hydra, two frightening new heads may sprout for
every one we chop off.

In conclusion, I think that the arguments against contract pregnancy do
not show that it should be prohibited; they do show that it must be strin-

---

[30] Mies, "Why Do We Need All This?," p. 42.
[31] Pollitt, "When Is a Mother Not a Mother?," p. 684.

gently regulated so as to protect the interests of the women who participate. This would include standardized contracts guaranteeing the kind of conditions I have suggested here, such as better pay, physical autonomy, and so forth. Such a model contract would also have to contain clauses on other issues I have not argued for here, such as full pay for stillborn babies and perhaps provision for women (whether they provided their own egg or not) to change their mind about keeping the baby or having visitation rights. In the absence of such protections, women will be exploited and abused, and the practice should be discouraged or banned.

In general, I think that in a better society, the call for contract pregnancy would be less, but so would the risks. In our own society the practice could have, as I have argued, substantial benefits to all parties. It is tempting to reject such technological and social innovations out of hand, partly, perhaps, to counterbalance the uncritical enthusiasm with which every dream-child of science seems to be received in many quarters. It is also all too easy to evaluate them solely from our own privileged perspective, forgetting that it may blind us to the kinds of choices daily faced by some of those about whom we are arguing.

CHAPTER 13

Children of Choice:

Whose Children? At What Cost?

In *Children of Choice*,[1] John Robertson argues for the primacy of procreative liberty in decision making about reproduction. Procreative liberty is the freedom to decide whether or not to have offspring. The primacy of procreative liberty means that debates about reproduction must be resolved in favor of enhancing reproductive choice unless there is excellent reason for believing that serious harm will result from the decision.

Robertson considers four categories of human activity that fall under the rubric of reproductive choice: (1) avoiding reproduction (contraception and abortion); (2) treating infertility; (3) controlling the quality of offspring; and (4) using reproductive capacity for nonreproductive ends.[2] In each of these categories, Robertson points out six possible ethical problems: (1) interference with nature; (2) respect for prenatal life; (3) welfare of offspring; (4) impact on family; (5) effect on women; and (6) costs, access, and consumer protection.[3]

Given the scope of Robertson's work, this chapter must necessarily be selective. Although there may be feminist concerns about his approach to the

From *Washington and Lee Law Review* 52, no. 1 (1995), the Bioethics Symposium issue.

[1] John A. Robertson, *Children of Choice: Freedom and the New Reproductive Technologies* (Princeton: Princeton University Press, 1994). A shorter version of this chapter was originally presented at "A Brave New World? *Children of Choice* in the Age of Reproduction Technology," a symposium at the Frances Lewis Law Center of the Washington and Lee University School of Law, September 1994. This is a revised version of the longer essay in the *Washington and Lee Law Review* 52, no. 1 (1995), 197–24.

[2] Robertson, *Children of Choice*, p. 6.

[3] There is, of course, overlap in these categories; see ibid., pp. 6, 12–15.

right to avoid reproduction, what he says about it is relatively unproblematic, so I will concentrate on other areas. Likewise, although feminists may worry about Robertson's positions on interfering with nature, respect for prenatal life, possible impact on families, and costs, access, and consumer protection, I will, for the most part, focus here on the welfare of offspring and effect on women.

Generally speaking, Robertson concedes that procreative liberty should be limited by the harm principle; however, in practice his stringent criteria for harm rules out most restrictions.[4] Robertson's worldview seems quite individualistic in the sense that procreative liberty is chiefly negative and focuses on noninterference, even if some enabling legislation is assumed. Robertson recognizes that unequal access to costly services is a problem, but he does not press for welfare rights to them.

Feminists will find a good deal to applaud in *Children of Choice,* but many will also disagree with both his fundamental assumptions and his treatment of specific issues. Although they will approve of Robertson's firm convictions about some aspects of choice, they will question his narrow conception of harm. Most will also be critical of the individualistic streak that runs through his work, as it favors those with more power and disadvantages those who, such as white women and people of color, tend to have less. Other more radical writers, such as Gena Corea, Helen Holmes, Ruth Hubbard, Abby Lippman, and Christine Overall, are highly critical of new reproductive arrangements and technologies and, unlike Robertson, believe that the burden of proof about their use should rest on the shoulders of those who recommend them, not those who would limit their use.[5] Thus they will deny the priority of procreative liberty.

Feminism is not a monolithic position, and I have considerable sympathy for what Robertson has to say. From my somewhat rough-hewn utilitarian perspective, the high value he places on freedom makes sense, at least when coupled with a more broadly conceived harm principle. Although utilitarianism differs in many respects from the classical liberalism in which his view seems rooted, I believe that any plausible version of utilitarianism must recognize how important freedom is for human happiness.

---

[4] The harm principle says that the only reason for prohibiting acts is the risk of harm to others.
[5] See Gena Corea, *The Mother Machine: Reproductive Technologies from Artificial Insemination to Artificial Wombs* (New York: Harper & Row, 1985); Helen B. Holmes, Betty B. Hoskins, and Michael Gross, eds., *The Custom-Made Child? Women-Centered Perspectives* (Clifton, N.J.: Humana Press, 1981); Ruth Hubbard, *The Politics of Women's Biology* (New Brunswick, N.J.: Rutgers University Press, 1990); Gwynne Basen, Margrit Eichler, and Abby Lippman, eds., *Misconceptions: The Social Construction of Choice and the New Reproductive Technologies,* vol. 1 (Hull, Quebec: Voyageur Publishing, 1993); Christine Overall, *Ethics and Human Reproduction* (Boston: Allen & Unwin, 1987).

None of this means that Robertson is completely "off the feminist hook," however. My criticisms would alter both the course of his arguments and some of his conclusions. They are offered here as friendly amendments that, I believe, would strengthen his already powerful work. I will focus primarily on assisted reproduction.

PROCREATION AND THE SELF

My most general question about Robertson's views centers on his moral theory. He presents procreative liberty as a freestanding principle, limited only by the harm principle. However, a clearer conception of how procreative liberty is situated within the larger theoretical context would be helpful in evaluating the picture he draws for us. Only such context could help us to understand more fully from whence the many subsidiary principles, rules, and values necessary for fleshing out procreative liberty arise, including his conception of what is to count as serious harm. These matters are pivotal for an account of reproductive rights that is properly sensitive to gender and other markers of disadvantage.

Robertson's defense of procreative liberty also raises questions. He maintains that "control over whether one reproduces or not is central to personal identity, to dignity, and to the meaning of one's life."[6] Women, he rightly emphasizes, are especially burdened if society fails to recognize their right not to reproduce. And, "being deprived of the ability to reproduce prevents one from an experience that is central to individual identity and meaning in life."[7]

I agree that preventing the conception of children you don't want and having the children you do want are central to human happiness and that denying people the power to carry through on their choices about these matters adds significantly to human misery. But is it really such a good idea to conceptualize the relationship between childbearing status and one's core self the way that Robertson does?

As things now stand, women are defined largely by their reproductive status. Women who fail to bear children, or who bear them but fail to rear them, are often seen as barren and inadequate. Anything they achieve is seen as mere compensation for their reproductive failure, and their failure as women is defined as a failure to be fully human. Men are not defined by their relationship to children in this way. Men can be successful even if they don't have children, although if they do, they may be applauded for being "good family men." Their fatherly status is not seen as crucial, and nobody thinks the less of great men if they don't have children.

---

[6] Robertson, *Children of Choice*, p. 24.
[7] Ibid.

Robertson's emphasis on the relationship of childbearing to identity seems to assimilate (or recommend assimilating) men's experience to that of women. One might want to argue that it is a good thing. After all, men often feel less responsibility toward their children—even to the point of abandoning them altogether far more often than do women. If men's parental status were more tightly woven into their core selves, perhaps they would be more responsible fathers.

Is such identification necessary or sufficient for responsible parenthood? On the one hand, some people who make much of their parental status are not particularly responsible parents. On the other, some for whom the status is a relatively unimportant part of their lives (or not socially recognized, like step-parents) can be excellent parents. More broadly, having a cat by no means defines who I am, yet the distinctness between me and my cat diminishes neither my responsibility for her nor my sense of responsibility for her. So there seems to be no reason for believing that responsibility is tied to identity or that it ought to be.

Furthermore, there are good reasons for rejecting this model of the self. First, it encourages people to care too much about their ability to have children. Although men and women in the more privileged classes in developed countries are now generally able to ensure that they will not have children if they don't want them, there is no way to guarantee that a particular individual *will* have children. If a person's whole self-concept depends on having them, they are set up for devastating disappointment.

The impact of such a model of the self is also differentiated by gender, since women, because of their socialization—as well as continuing sexist and pronatalist pressure—will more likely adopt this understanding of the meaning of life without seriously questioning it. And women, because of their biologically more extensive role in reproduction, are also more likely to bear the risks entailed by the assisted reproduction that might be necessary to fulfill this conception of the self.

Second, this model of the self encourages people to see the decision to have children primarily as a personal decision about themselves, *not* as a moral decision affecting others. This moral dimension of childbearing is obscured by the emphasis on self-creation, making it almost impossible to discuss, let alone construct, moral standards. Thus, it is hardly possible to talk about such matters as wrongful life or overpopulation without seeming to violate individuals' most intimate self.[8]

---

[8] A still more sinister implication of this identification of child and self is evident in Erin Conn's appeal for veto power over his wife's abortion. He pleads: "after that child is born, half of that child—part of that child is me. And I'm part of that child. And I feel like by her having the right to abort that child is her having the right to destroy a part of me without me

Feminists have been as guilty as anybody else here, in part because of their quite reasonable fear that emphasizing the moral dimension of reproduction will constitute yet another excuse for the imposition of control over women. Robertson himself avoids many potential difficulties by relying on something like Derek Parfit's widely accepted conclusion that we do not harm future people by bearing them unless their lives would be so miserable that they would prefer to be dead.[9] This standard seems to impose few limits on what we can do since bearing a child who cannot be expected to have a satisfying life is still assumed to be in the child's best interest.

I believe that this reasoning is flawed. Robertson might have noticed that Parfit does not conclude that because we fail to harm individuals by bringing them into adverse circumstances, we are thereby freed of responsibility. Instead, Parfit explores the feasibility of adopting a different standard.[10] In addition, embracing the moral minimalism implied by Parfit's initial argument would lead to a great deal of unnecessary misery. It would be far better to adopt a demanding moral standard the required more of us, but from which we could also expect more care and benefit. Many theorists, including feminists, have pointed out the inconsistency of the pervasive minimalist approach, based as it is on an unrealistically individualistic conception of human relationships.[11] Because society does not—and cannot—really function according to the minimalist approach, the illusion of a libertarian public life is maintained by an officially invisible (and therefore unrewarded) base of work, mainly offered up by or, when necessary, extracted from women.[12]

Given the high priority that he accords to the right to procreate, Robertson's tight linking of the self with that right creates additional problems. This constellation of values leads Robertson to view procreative liberty as a justification for a variety of subsidiary rights of questionable wisdom—rights to anything individuals could want before attempting to reproduce.[13]

---

me having any say-so." Susan Bordo, *Unbearable Weight* (Berkeley: University of California Press, 1993), p. 91, quoting *Nightline: Abortion Rights* (ABC television broadcast, July 22, 1988).

[9] See Derek Parfit, *Reasons and Persons* (Oxford: Clarendon, 1984).

[10] Ibid., p. 443.

[11] See, for example, Alison Jaggar, *Feminist Politics and Human Nature* (Totowa, N.J.: Rowman & Allenheld, 1983), pp. 40–41.

[12] For somewhat more discussion of the Parfit problem and the morality of bringing impaired persons into the world, see Chapter 2, "Loving Future People."

[13] I use the word "individual" here, but Robertson's leaning seems to be toward couples, as he argues at one point that single rearers might have less exclusive rights with respect to children because of children's need for at least two rearers (p. 134).

Robertson's conception of procreative liberty repeatedly leads him to endorse extensive and far-reaching technologies intended to produce healthy offspring. However, his professed principles seem insufficient to defend such broad-ranging powers. He argues that "for many couples the decision whether to procreate depends on the ability to have healthy children. Without some guarantee or protection against the risk of handicapped children, they might not reproduce at all. Thus viewed, quality control devices become part of the liberty interest in procreating or in avoiding procreation, and arguably should receive the same degree of protection."[14] I have argued at length that we owe it to our potential children not to conceive them if they can be expected to have too low a quality of life; I also believe that it is beneficial if people can be reassured that their fetuses do not suffer from any known problems.[15] There are reasons for seeing these rights as much more limited than the ones that Robertson endorses.[16] One reason is that to avoid potential harm, a much more fine-grained analysis of the components of any right to healthy children is necessary. Another is that new reproductive technologies and arrangements may not be the best way to ensure healthy children.

Robertson's rejection of most such challenges to the right to reproduce, together with his endorsement of subsidiary enabling rights, opens the door to extensive genetic engineering. If couples have a right to healthy offspring (otherwise they would not undertake the project at all), then how can they be denied offspring of a desired sex, level of intelligence, or even hair color? Although Robertson considers this question, I do not think that his treatment of it is adequate.[17]

Many people think that it is possible to distinguish between morally acceptable negative genetic engineering that eradicates defects and morally dubious positive genetic engineering that enhances desirable traits. I believe that it is by no means obvious how to justify that distinction, but also that it has less moral weight than is often supposed.

---

[14] Robertson, *Children of Choice*, p. 33.

[15] See Chapter 1, "Genetics and Reproductive Risk: Can Having Children Be Immoral?," and Chapter 2, "Loving Future People."

[16] This same constellation of principles leads Robertson to take a still more dubious position with respect to surrogacy. See, for example, p. 131, where he argues that persons who pay women to carry a baby for them would be deterred from procreating if they could not be guaranteed that the baby would be turned over to them at the end of the pregnancy. But it's not clear to me that this is really true, or that it would even be sufficient reason in all circumstances for requiring a woman to give up a baby. Furthermore, this same reasoning could be used to justify a variety of morally repellent restrictions on the woman undertaking the pregnancy.

[17] Robertson, *Children of Choice*, pp. 165–67.

A great deal of resistance to positive engineering is probably rooted in the assumption that any genetic tinkering is Nazi eugenics and, thus, unthinkable. The rest probably comes from a variety of worries about interference with nature, responsibility for acts of commission (but not acts of omission), and the like. Some of these worries are speculative, as Robertson suggests,[18] and could not be assuaged by any proposed safeguards, no matter how carefully thought out. Some, however, seem to me to be quite realistic. They are based on justifiable caution about rushing ahead in the face of obvious and significantly incomplete knowledge and on the awareness of past disasters caused by enthusiasm for technological fixes, sometimes pursued in the hopes of grandiose profits. These pedestrian, but nonetheless crucial, worries should be taken seriously, and they do provide an additional stopper that should save us from the prospect of monkeying with delicate biological mechanisms to achieve either trivial benefits (curly hair) or characteristics of doubtful benefit to the child (super tall). Once again, although genetic and biological engineering is not intrinsically wicked and could potentially—if pursued with all due caution—provide substantial benefits, it seems doubtful that the overall welfare is served by emphasizing genetic approaches at the expense of preventive social programs.

Of course, we need to recognize that certain limits or costs will discourage people from reproducing. But it would be a mistake to dismiss those limits too quickly or to raise the burden of proof against them so high that they automatically become indefensible. Surely, if the discouraging factors arise from other serious moral considerations, then their effect on procreation must be analyzed in the knowledge that carefully crafted trade-offs may be necessary. Otherwise procreative liberty and its entourage become a moral bulldozer that crushes all competing interests. It is difficult to see why procreative liberty should be granted such priority.

One should also note the selectivity of Robertson's application of the principle that there is a prima facie right to anything individuals regard as necessary for procreation, such as the promise of a healthy baby. First, he fails to take seriously the fact that the limits he is prepared to put on the behavior of pregnant women that he discusses would be sufficient to deter many women from going ahead with a pregnancy.[19] Second, the principle that one has a right to anything one regards as a prerequisite for procreation plays havoc with the strict line he draws between the negative liberty to procreate and welfare rights that would create more equal access to that liberty. After all, lack of such welfare rights prevents many people from taking advantage of expensive methods of assisted reproduction. Still more

---

[18] Ibid., p. 162.
[19] Ibid., chap. 8.

notably, the absence of welfare rights prevents people from having the number of children they want (by the usual methods) because they cannot afford them. Yet the services that would alleviate this problem are routine in other developed Western nations. Why should the right to healthy children be limited to reproductive technologies when such goods as universal access to health care and a clean environment would protect fertility and improve children's health?

In short, Robertson's justification of procreative liberty and what he takes to be its implications needs further work. As it stands, it will likely intensify the gender-based differential impact on women of new reproductive possibilities. It is also likely to undermine the notion that childbearing is a moral activity, especially if paired with an almost no-fault view of when it is permissible to conceive children.

CHOICE

Robertson chooses procreative liberty as the fundamental principle governing reproductive conflicts, but there are good reasons for recognizing some form of self-determination as the more basic principle, from which procreative liberty is derived. Self-determination emphasizes control over one's body and resources in a way that fits better with what I think are plausible intuitions about the asymmetry between the right not to reproduce and the right to reproduce.

Robertson sees the right not to reproduce and the right to reproduce as two sides of the same coin. From the fact, he seems to infer that the strong right not to reproduce implies an equally strong right to reproduce and also that this strong right to reproduce provides as much support for assisted reproduction as for so-called natural reproduction. Many feminists would reject Robertson's position, arguing that because the issues raised by assisted reproduction are so different from those raised by natural reproduction, the former should be viewed with suspicion. This position is reflected, for instance, in Christine Overall's recent claim that "the right not to reproduce is distinct from the right to reproduce."[20] She further distinguishes between weak and strong versions of each right. The weak sense (liberty) of each involves noninterference; the strong sense (welfare) involves access to services. Overall argues for both liberty and welfare versions of the right not to reproduce and for the weak version of the right to reproduce, maintaining that we should be "developing a critical analysis

---

[20] Christine Overall, *Human Reproduction: Principles, Practices, Policies* (Toronto: Oxford University Press, 1993), p. 27.

of the ways in which the right to reproduce in the strong sense is now be-ing exercised."[21]

On the one hand, I think that Overall's distinction between the two dif-ferent rights is logically incoherent: as Robertson rightly sees, the right to reproduce implies the right not to reproduce, because the right to reproduce is not a duty (that leaves one with no choice but to reproduce) but a right (that one is free to exercise or not as one wishes). On the other, I agree with Overall's desire to draw a clearer line between different types of reproduc-tion than Robertson does.[22] Unlike Overall and other feminist critics of as-sisted reproduction, I do not think that it calls for a different burden of proof, but I do believe that realistic assessments of possible harm require a much broader conception of harm and greater alertness to potential harm than is evident in Robertson's work.

Overall and other feminists focus on the questionable nature of the choices assisted reproduction opens up for women. Robertson acknowl-edges their worries that men will use reproductive technologies to control and oppress women, that assisted reproduction will reinforce the problem-atic traditional identification of women with childbearing and childrearing, and that women may be encouraged to undertake further reproductive burdens to benefit men.[23] He responds to these worries by emphasizing the desirability of the new choices available to women and underlines the safe-guards for women implicit in a rights-based framework.

Robertson's comments about the rights reflect feminist qualms about rights as intrinsically individualistic and limited in scope, qualms I don't share: rights are what we make of them, and we need not rely on them to tell the whole moral story. However, Robertson fails to do full justice to fem-inist concerns. His first response is simple to point to examples, such as Norplant, that seem to offer new power and convenience to women.[24] A bit later, he concedes that "reproductive choices will not increase self-determination for all women, because some will be pressured to make choices that they previously would not have had to face, or will lack the re-sources to take advantage of the opportunities presented."[25] But he con-cludes by saying that "on balance . . . there is no reason to think that women

---

[21] Ibid., p. 32.

[22] I have some qualms about the distinction because it is first of all relative to the accepted standards of a given group and second the engine of much social misery in societies like the United States that pour most of their effort into negative rights at the expense of positive ones.

[23] Robertson, *Children of Choice*, p. 228.

[24] Ibid., p. 229. It's not clear that using Norplant as an example really furthers Robertson's case here.

[25] Ibid., p. 231.

do not end up with more rather than less reproductive freedom as a result of technological innovation."[26] Consequently, he plumps for promoting freedom, together with the safeguards necessary for limiting its burdens, rather than wholesale prohibitions of certain techniques and practices. He comments that "even in a world without technological options now available, recognition of negative procreative liberty would be an important achievement."[27] The implication here seems to be that because procreative liberty is all of a piece, the price of recognizing the right not to reproduce is that one accept an equally strong right to assisted reproduction. That conclusion does not follow, however, because careful application of the harm principle may seriously circumscribe the right to assisted reproduction while leaving the right not to reproduce untouched.

I believe that feminist concerns about assisted reproduction deserve a closer look and the controversy about choice provides a useful context for doing so. What are the serious issues here? One problem that Robertson seems not to recognize is that what start out as new options come to be accepted as the standard of care, which women are not really free to refuse. Second, women are quite likely to end up choosing options that are not necessarily in their best interest. A third is that although an option may benefit a particular woman, it may harm others or women as a class. Let us consider each of these issues in turn.

What about those new options that turn into obligations? Examples are the electronic fetal monitors and ultrasound that are now routinely accepted parts of prenatal care, despite the problems and potential risks associated with them.[28]

There are other dangers here as well. One major source of danger is society's tendency to subordinate women's interests to those attributed to the fetus, as is demonstrated by the disturbingly large number of prebirth seizures, court-ordered treatments, and postbirth sanctions that women have suffered.[29] Enormous further potential exists for compelling women to undergo allegedly therapeutic treatments on behalf of fetuses, perhaps including even in vitro fertilization (IVF) intended to establish that a given

---

[26] Ibid.

[27] Ibid.

[28] Susan Sherwin, *No Longer Patient* (Philadelphia: Temple University Press, 1992), p. 119. Fetal monitors require that women in labor be still; they also lead to far more caesareans than the equally safe human monitoring by nurses. Ultrasound now appears to be safe, but it is being applied to developing fetuses and women without any solid evidence of its long-term safety. See Chapter 4, "Are Pregnant Women Fetal Containers?" See also Elizebeth Bartholet, "In Vitro Fertilization: The Construction of Infertility and of Parenting," in *Issues in Reproductive Technology I: An Anthology,* ed. Helen B. Holmes (New York: Garland, 1992), pp. 253, 259.

[29] See Chapter 4, "Are Pregnant Women Fetal Containers?"

fetus is free of known defects. Worse still, fertile or pregnant women might be subjected to extreme lifestyle restrictions thought to benefit fetuses.[30]

There is some tension in Robertson's views about these matters. On the one hand, as we have seen, he repeatedly relies on a Parfit-like argument about harm to future persons that severely limits the ground on which such restriction of women might be based. On the other, however, he seems quite open to the notion that women should be held responsible for harm to their fetuses and critical of feminist objections to current social trends favoring fetuses at the expense of women.[31] As I have argued elsewhere, it is plausible to believe that wide-ranging preventive measures would eliminate all but a few of these conflicts between woman and fetus.[32] And, although Robertson recognizes the point that prevention should precede any recourse to stronger measures,[33] he seems uncomfortably willing to envision coercive and punitive measures even in the absence of prevention.[34] He also invests the medical establishment with more authority than it deserves on the basis of its track record.[35]

A second problem with Robertson's treatment of choice is that a woman may choose an option that is not necessarily in her interest. Nobody, of course, ever promised humans that freedom would bring with it wisdom. But long-standing social patterns significantly raise the probability that women, especially women disadvantaged by such other such characteristics as race, class, sexual orientation, or age, will find themselves making risky decisions in the absence of adequate information. Because, for example, women are often considered less intelligent, less rational, or simply less important than similarly situated men, health care providers may not take the time to make sure that their consent is informed and truly voluntary.[36] Women may also receive information biased by a provider's interest in pro-

---

[30] Consider the now-ubiquitous signs warning pregnant women against drinking—at the same time as treatment centers for substance abuse that take pregnant women are glaringly absent. On this and other perils, see Chapter 4, "Are Pregnant Women Fetal Containers?"

[31] Robertson, *Children of Choice*, pp. 173, 190–94.

[32] See Chapter 4, "Are Pregnant Women Fetal Containers?"

[33] Robertson, *Children of Choice*, p. 194.

[34] Robertson, however, does recognize the disparity between the standards for invading men's and women's bodies at present. He concludes that if we develop policies that invade women's bodies for the benefit of fetuses, then we must be equally ready to require men to undergo invasive procedures for the benefit of their children (pp. 190–94).

[35] A very recent treatment of this subject is Eileen Nechas and Denise Foley, *Unequal Treatment: What You Don't Know about How Women Are Mistreated by the Medical Community* (New York: Simon & Schuster, 1994).

[36] A glance back at the history of medicine will remind those tempted to dismiss my claims here as paranoid that the issue is pressing. See Nechas and Foley, *Unequal Treatment*, and Mary Briody Mahowald, *Women and Children in Health Care* (Oxford: Oxford University Press, 1993).

viding profitable treatment, recruiting experimental subjects, or even, as with contract pregnancy, furthering a purely commercial enterprise. Last, but certainly not least, crucial information may simply be unavailable. This latter situation is especially problematic where its absence is barely noticed, as when a new drug or technology is firmly pronounced to be safe, despite the lack of data about long-term effects. Such situations are especially dangerous because women are often socialized to be relatively passive and because those who ask questions and think for themselves tend to be categorized as difficult or demanding.

A third closely related problem is that an option may benefit a particular woman, but harm other women, or harm women as a class.[37] In these kinds of cases, one woman may benefit from the exploitation of another. Alternatively, a new option may function like a safety valve, taking the pressure off individual women but deflecting attention from serious underlying social problems; this latter situation reflects the fact that women are, on balance, in a weaker bargaining position than similarly situated men. Women may then have recourse to practices that exploit other women or perpetuate harmful stereotypes.

Why might women be in the weaker position? First, a woman's education is still less likely than that of a man to have emphasized the type of analytic thinking required for dealing with these kinds of issues.[38] Second, women are also more likely to have been socialized to be agreeable and not to stand up for their own perceived interests. Third, women may have more at stake in making sure there is an agreement at all. After all, given the social perception of women as childbearers and nurturers, a woman is likely to feel especially insecure and inadequate if it is she who is infertile. Even if it is not her fault, a couple's "barrenness" is usually more of a liability for a woman. Helping a man fulfill the desire for a genetically related child can be an important factor in keeping a marriage together, and doing so may be important to a woman for both emotional and economic reasons.[39]

[37] Sherwin, *No Longer Patient*, pp. 132–36.

[38] This assertion would have been more obviously true in the past when women were denied education altogether, or denied higher education. However, there is ample evidence that despite the apparently equal education experience of girls and boys at present, the sexism that was so overt earlier is still there in covert form. For a recent discussion of this question, see Myra and David Sadker, *Failing at Fairness* (New York: Scribner's, 1994).

[39] It is tempting to look at infertility in isolation, but this context deeply affects the lives of women at a time when men are more likely to remarry than women in case of divorce and where women are often dependent on a man to achieve a decent standard of living. (See Barbara Bergmann, *The Economic Emergence of Women* [New York: Basic Books, 1986], p. 269, and more generally, chaps. 10 and 11.) Remember that the average woman still earns only 70 percent of what a man earns and that this statistic hides much larger differences between particular women and men. See Sara E. Rix, ed., *The American Woman: A Status Report* (The Women's Research and Education Institute, 1990), p. 391.

In addition, as I have pointed out, women are less likely to be adequately informed about the choices to be made. Consequently, women may be less able to determine what they want and to hold out for it at the bargaining table. Yet, in many cases, it is they who are most at risk, especially physically, from the proposed procedures. These issues will disappear if sexism is eradicated; in the meantime, they are ignored at women's peril.[40]

Many feminists believe that in vitro fertilization (IVF) and contract pregnancy are pressure valves for particular women.[41] Women are themselves at risk from inadequate information about what IVF entails, about possible long-term consequences, and about success rates. Furthermore, they may be driven to the procedure by the social devaluation of infertile women or by the ethic that expects women always to subordinate their own interests in the pursuit of others' goals.[42] In addition, many (but not all) feminists believe that women who contract to undertake a pregnancy for another do so only because of their already weaker position as women.[43] Perhaps the $10,000 is almost irresistible, given women's inferior economic status, or perhaps the exploitation here is more subtle—based, for example, on guilty feelings about a past abortion. Those feminists point out that the wives of men who seek contract pregnancy are in a weak position and cannot resist, because it is their own inadequacy as childbearers that the contract pregnancy offsets.[44] They also maintain that contract pregnancy practice harms women as a class, because the contract reinforces the view that women are merely childbearers and nurturers, not equal participants in human affairs who may or may not engage in procreation.[45]

A central problem for both IVF and contract pregnancy is the possibility that things will go awry and that either nobody will take responsibility for genetic materials or for a baby or too many want control over them. The latter situation can arise when people seek to escape previously agreed-upon responsibility or when they want responsibility that they earlier renounced. The kinds of feminist concerns described earlier raise questions about Robertson's hard-line solution that participants in assisted and collabora-

---

[40] We have already seen what unfairness results when decisions about the terms of divorce are made as if women and men are on an equal footing in society. See Lenore J. Weitzman, *The Divorce Revolution* (New York: Free Press, 1985).

[41] See Sherwin, *No Longer Patient,* p. 134.

[42] See Judith Lorber, "Choice, Gift or Patriarchal Bargain? Women's Consent to in Vitro Fertilization in Male Infertility," in Helen B. Holmes and Laura M. Purdy, *Feminist Perspectives in Medical Ethics* (Bloomington: Indiana University Press, 1992).

[43] See, for example, Christine Overall, *Ethics and Human Reproduction: A Feminist Analysis* (Boston: Allen & Unwin, 1987), chap. 6, esp. p. 120.

[44] Ibid., p. 118.

[45] Ibid., p. 122.

tive reproduction must make binding commitments about what they will do.[46] In principle, this is an attractive solution. However, it is less appealing if the parties are not in an equal bargaining position. As I have argued, women are typically the disadvantaged parties, although a given man, of course, may be in the weaker position.

As Robertson and some feminists recognize, the rub is that using such reasons to deny women the standing to engage in decision making about reproduction seems just as bad as ignoring the obvious disparities between women and men.[47] Denying that standing undermines women's legal personhood and invites paternalistic intrusion into women's lives. In short, there are serious risks in both paths. These risks result from the relentless sexism in society, sexism that will sully any solution. The only safe course, therefore, would be to eradicate sexism before we do anything else. Although eradicating sexism is an urgent task, we cannot stop the world until this task is completed. The question becomes what to do until then.

In the case of IVF, of course, there are other reasons for doubting the wisdom of the path society is currently pursing. On the one hand, success rates are low, probably much lower than most women engaged in it fully realize.[48] On the other hand, the procedures involve some known risks, such as roller-coaster emotions, as well as yet-unknown risks for both woman and child.[49] Under these circumstances, one must ask yet again whether expanding IVF programs is a good policy. The answer here surely has to be that it is not.

The underlying problem here, it seems to me, is that our society is based on a relatively unregulated free market—a market that produces expensive, high-tech treatments for some, while others suffer from similar problems that a more equal distribution of resources could easily prevent. Although Robertson is concerned about problems of access, he does not really address this issue at the most basic level. It seems to me that the failure to do so creates serious questions about some of his solutions, as well as about his support for assisted reproduction.

If one accepts the inegalitarian status quo, it is quite reasonable to argue, as does Robertson, that it would be unjustifiable to limit how those with money can spend it. After all, no one stops them from spending it on vacation homes or yachts, so why shouldn't they use it to have a go at producing a genetically related child? How might one respond to this argument?

---

[46] Robertson, *Children of Choice*, pp. 126, 131.
[47] Ibid., p. 132; see also Christine T. Sistare, "Reproductive Freedom and Women's Freedom: Surrogacy and Autonomy," *The Philosophical Forum* 19, no. 4 (Summer 1988): 227–40.
[48] See Sherwin, *No Longer Patient*, p. 129.
[49] Ibid.

Some have argued that the emphasis on genetically related children erroneously promotes the notion that such children are especially valuable.[50] Of course, most people don't think that that notion is erroneous—and they seem to want their "own" children very much. So even if the desire for genetically related children is morally questionable, it is important to recognize that unless education persuades people otherwise, there will continue to be much demand for them.

It would be easier to resolve this issue if the resources allocated to IVF could easily be channeled to the prevention of infertility or some other equally good cause, but resource allocation is, of course, more complicated than that. Worse still, relatively few people seem troubled by the knowledge that a more egalitarian system of resource allocation would prevent a good deal of misery; therefore, arguing for more equal allocation of resources does not make much difference politically.

Is there, nonetheless, a moral argument to be made here that the United States ought to de-emphasize high-tech approaches to infertility such as IVF and instead ought to promote basic social improvements? Given a free market economy, that change would not happen without a lot of political support, yet democratic decision making can exert some control over how and even *whether* some technologies will be developed—consider the Super Sonic Transport (SST) and the supercollider.

In vitro fertilization tends to be offered in freestanding clinics on a fee-for-service basis. Does the existence of these clinics threaten more basic services? At first blush, the answer appears to be "no." However, a look at the broader context suggests that the answer may not be quite so clear. Medical resources, after all, are limited, and educational programs, personnel, buildings, and other resources allocated to IVF cannot be used in other ways. Thus, unless other pressing health care needs are already being met (and we know that they are not), devoting resources to IVF does change the services available. In that case, training people do to IVF and setting up clinics are not just a matter of letting the wealthy decide how to use their disposable income.

Even among feminists, there is an active debate about IVF; some claim that reducing its use is to abandon the infertile unfairly,[51] and others claim that women's strong desire for babies is at least in part a noxious social construction.[52] This way of framing the debate, however, isolates it from

[50] See Overall, *Ethics and Human Reproduction*, p. 131.
[51] See Michelle Stanworth, "Birth Pangs: Conceptive Technologies and the Threat to Motherhood," in *Conflicts in Feminism*, ed. Marianne Hirsch and Evelyn Fox Keller (New York: Routledge, 1990), pp. 293–96.
[52] See Gena Corea, *The Mother Machine* (New York: Harper & Row, 1985), p. 220, and see more generally, *Pronatalism: The Myth of Mom & Apple Pie*, Ellen Peck and Judith Senderowitz, eds. (New York: Crowell, 1974).

the larger social context. There seems to be good reason to suspect that remediable social factors are implicated in rates of infertility. Addressing the social factors directly would likely prevent many cases of infertility. De-emphasizing IVF to concentrate instead on those social factors is therefore not to abandon infertile women but rather to take a different approach to the problem. Already infertile women may lose out, but those who would have become infertile because of social factors would benefit. The current approach allows infertility to develop in many women but promises the mixed blessing of IVF only to those few who can pay for it. Furthermore, judicious use of other methods, such as education, child-sharing of various kinds, adoption, or contract pregnancy, could help satisfy the already infertile.

Contract pregnancy is itself a seriously contested issue, both in the feminist community and outside it, although for different reasons. Many feminists argue that it is just the sort of debilitating choice that should not be available.[53] I have argued against this position at length elsewhere,[54] where I maintained that a carefully regulated version of the practice potentially empowers white, heterosexual women and members of other disadvantaged groups such as lesbian and gay couples.[55]

I believe that these kinds of cases demonstrate that neither a sweeping principle of procreative liberty nor a fearful elimination of worrisome options should determine what liberties are justifiable. Instead, we need an issue-by-issue discussion that keeps in mind the value of individual freedom, but that is also constantly mindful of potential harms created by the sexist context in which decisions are being made.

HARM

Freedom is an important value, and it cannot be exercised unless those who would limit freedom in the name of harm are pressed to name clear,

[53] See Overall, *Ethics and Human Reproduction*.

[54] See Chapter 11, "Surrogate Mothering: Exploitation or Empowerment?," and Chapter 12, "Another Look at Contract Pregnancy."

[55] Further details are beyond the scope of this essay, but I do have some qualms about Robertson's hardnosed approach to binding commitments in such matters, as I suggested earlier. Like many others, I cringe at the idea of a baby torn from its mother's arms, even though that is an appeal to emotion rather than moral principle. I must say I find it difficult to adjudicate between the forceful feminist arguments in favor of an escape clause for women undertaking contract pregnancy and the similarly forceful arguments offered by Robertson on this issue (Robertson, *Children of Choice*, pp. 125–27). My inclination at present is to think that this is one of the areas where it is necessary to pay special attention to women's experience in giving birth, because it seems to radically to change their perspective. As a woman who has never given birth, it may be impossible for me to make an informed and fair judgment. Naturally, that line of reasoning rules out men as well. It may be that the best those of us in that position can do is to sit back and let those who have argue it out, participating only to the extent of analyzing the arguments for the usual kinds of fallacies.

specific, and weighty concerns. The problem is to determine which threats meet those criteria.

There are always reasons for rejecting new social arrangements and technologies. Knee-jerk rejection leads to paralysis and a mind-set thing clings to tradition and that fails often enough to notice the harm caused by doing things the usual way. History is rife with dire warnings of vague horrors that never came to pass, or that, if they did, turned out to be benefits in disguise.[56] Unfortunately, some miraculous innovations that promised only good things have turned into major scourges—consider how the automobile strangles cities and how television can deaden minds. If people had predicted these outcomes, Robertson might well have described their warnings as remote and speculative, and yet they would have been quite accurate.

Today researchers and physicians are barrelling ahead, following grant money and promises of profit wherever they lead, devoting relatively little thought to the full context of their decisions—all in the name of choices for women.[57] However, the rhetoric of choice would be more convincing if the medical establishment had a better record on women's welfare.

My own eyes began to be opened some fifteen years ago by Gena Corea's groundbreaking *The Hidden Malpractice*.[58] Periodic reassessments of the sit-

---

[56] Consider, for instance, the allegedly disastrous consequences predicted for contraception in Pope Paul VI, *On the Regulation of Birth: Humanae Vitae* (July 29, 1968), p. 140, in Robert Baker and Frederick Elliston, eds., *Philosophy and Sex* (Buffalo: Prometheus, 1975). Or the absurd theories of nineteenth-century physician Edward Clarke about the consequences of higher education for women. Edward H. Clarke, *Sex in Education; or, A Fair Chance for Girls* (Boston: James R. Osgood and Company, 1873).

[57] Susan Bordo puts the matter nicely in the following comment on the situation:

In general, the New Reproductive Technology has been a confusingly mixed bag as far as the subjectivity of women is concerned. On the one hand, women now have a booming technology seemingly focused on fulfilling *their* desires: to conceive, to prevent miscarriage, to deliver a healthy baby at term. On the other hand, proponents and practitioners continually encourage women to treat their bodies as passive instruments of those goals, ready and willing, "if they want a child badly enough," to endure however complicated and invasive a regime of diagnostic testing, daily monitoring, injections, and operative procedures may be required. Thus, one element of women's subjectivity is indeed nurtured, while all other elements (investment in career, other emotional needs, importance of other personal relationships, etc.) are minimized, marginalized, and (when they refuse to be repressed) made an occasion for guilt and self-questioning . . . in our present cultural context, the New Reproductive Technologies *do* cater to women's desires (that is, to the desires of women who can afford them), but only when they are the *right* desires, desires that will subordinate all else (even in the face of technological success rates which continue to be very discouraging) to the project of producing a child. (Susan Bordo, *Unbearable Weight*, pp. 86–87.)

[58] Gena Corea, *The Hidden Malpractice: How American Medicine Mistreats Women* (New York: Jove, 1978).

uation suggest that the health care system has yet to face fully the devaluation of women's interests that was then so prevalent.[59] Only recently have the inadequacies in the health care system burst upon the wider political scene.

Not only do many people lack access to any decent care, but also subtler inequities exist. White women and members of other disadvantaged groups receive systematically worse treatment and care than do white, middle-class, heterosexual men.[60] Bioethics, the academic discipline that takes the health care establishment as its subject, has been remarkably slow to notice these facts. In particular, bioethics has been wary of feminist work and has mostly relegated it to the Siberian margins of the field, ignoring or dismissing its concerns as "political."[61]

In bioethics, as in the health care system itself, women's interests are routinely discounted or ignored altogether. Recent feminist work documents and analyzes this phenomenon.[62]

The biases built into medicine and bioethics mean that it is unwise to take much at face value. For instance, Robertson points to Norplant to show how technology can make women's lives better. However, feminists are much less quick to rely on assurances of safety or efficacy from an establishment that gave us the pill, diethylstilbestrol (DES), and the Dalkon Shield.

---

[59] See, for example, Joan M. Altekruse and Sue V. Rosser, "Feminism and Medicine: Co-optation or Cooperation?," in *The Knowledge Explosion*, ed. Cheris Kramarae and Dale Spender (New York: Teachers College Press, 1992); Mary Mahowald, *Women and Children in Health Care*; John M. Smith, *Women and Doctors* (New York: Dell, 1992); Gena Corea, *The Invisible Epidemic* (New York: Harper, 1992).

[60] Again, see Mahowald, *Women and Children in Health Care*; Nechas and Foley, *Unequal Treatment*; and Smith, *Women and Doctors*.

[61] For a refutation of this charge, see the Introduction to this volume. For further evidence, consult Sherwin, *No Longer Patient*; and Holmes and Purdy, eds., *Feminist Perspectives in Medical Ethics*.

[62] See Sherwin, *No Longer Patient*; and Holmes and Purdy, eds., *Feminist Perspectives in Medical Ethics*. There are also quite a few articles on specific topics written from a feminist point of view; for the most part they are still sprinkled here and there in the bioethics literature. See, for example, Caroline Whitbeck, "The Moral Implications of Regarding Women as People: New Perspectives on Pregnancy and Personhood," in *Abortion and the Status of the Fetus*, ed. William Bondeson, H. Tristram Engelhardt, Jr., Stuart Spicker, and Daniel Winship (Dordrecht: Reidel, 1983); Christine Overall, "New Reproductive Technology: Some Implications for the Abortion Issue," *The Journal of Value Inquiry* 19 (1985): 279–92; Susan Sherwin, "Feminist Ethics and in Vitro Fertilization," *Canadian Journal of Philosophy* (suppl. vol.) (Fall 1987); and so forth. *Hypatia* is the main journal for feminist philosophy, and it occasionally publishes articles in bioethics. Helen B. Holmes, *Issues in Reproductive Technology I*, is largely feminist, and two additional anthologies of feminist work will appear in 1995, Susan M. Wolf, ed., *Feminism and Bioethics: Beyond Reproduction*, (New York: Oxford University Press); and Joan Callahan ed., *Reproduction, Ethics, and the Law*, (Bloomington: Indiana University Press). For further discussion, see section 1 of the Introduction.

Despite assurances to the contrary, Norplant is still an experimental drug whose long-term effects are as yet unknown. Norplant also increases women's dependency on medical professionals. Obviously, sometimes such dependency cannot be helped, but it seems important both that no un-cessary dependency can be created and that any necessary dependency be accompanied by vivid awareness of its possible dangers. Thus, the depen-dency engendered by Norplant is doubly worrisome because it can lead to paternalistic refusals to remove it. Norplant's characteristics also lend themselves to potentially more sinister uses.[63]

Yet another issued raised by the Norplant example is the piecemeal ap-proach common in bioethics. Sexism and other discriminatory practices are harder to detect and bear in mind consistently when one sees bioethics as a set of separate issues. *Children of Choice* is a salutary new effort at placing re-productive issues in the unifying context of a basic moral and legal frame-work, but Robertson is not always successful at forging the necessary links. In the case of Norplant, he emphasizes its convenience and effective-ness. However, attention to its possible side effects and their significance for women's lives might reasonably lead one both to reevaluate Norplant's convenience[64] and to question the entire rationale for its use.

Surely one major concern about contraceptives such as Norplant that em-phasize convenience is that such contraceptives encourage women to rely on them without thinking about whether they need to take steps to protect themselves from serious sexually transmitted diseases such as acquired im-munodeficiency syndrome (AIDS). The answer is not necessarily to with-hold such methods; rather, it would make sense to downplay the pleasures

---

[63] Anita Hardon, "Norplant: Conflicting Views on Its Safety and Acceptability," in *Issues in Reproductive Technology I*, ed. Holmes, p. 15. See also Hilde and James Lindemann Nelson, "Other 'Isms' Aren't Enough: Feminism, Social Policy, and Long-Lasting Contraception," in *The Ethics of Long-Term Contraception: Guidelines for Public Policy*, ed. Ellen Moskowitz (Washington, D.C.: Georgetown University Press, forthcoming).

[64] For example, see Hardon, "Norplant: Conflicting Views on Its Safety and Acceptability," in *Issues in Reproductive Technology I*, ed. Holmes. She writes: "the researchers tend to define disorders such as headaches, depression, and weight gain as minor side effects, of which the relationship with Norplant has not been proven" (p. 22). But anybody who suffers from such problems knows they can be far from minor, especially in a society where women are expected to be cheerful and thin in order to maintain their jobs and their personal relation-ships. Still more worrisome is her comment that "with respect to Norplant, it is remarkable that so little has been written about the consequences of menstrual disturbances for the day-to-day life of the users. Anthropological research suggests that such consequences can be far-reaching. Menstruation is an important event in any women's life. The meaning that is attributed to this event or its loss varies, affecting among other things, cooking procedure, sexual interaction, and religious practices . . . menstrual blood is often perceived to be a dangerous element for men . . . [and] delay or absence of menstruation in many societies is considered unhealthy for wom[e]n" (pp. 23–24).

of convenience and to emphasize the importance—in all but the most solidly monogamous sexual relationship—of using condoms as well. That women are so much more at risk of contracting AIDS in heterosexual relationships then men simply reinforces this fundamental point.[65]

In short, taking seriously the sexist context in which assisted reproduction occurs means that the potential harm to women is much more immediate and serious than most people are willing to acknowlege. The evidence for a feminist perspective that recognizes the potential for such harm is compelling, but it is not, on the whole, part of accepted, public knowledge. Rather, the feminist perspective must be sought out, and those who incorporate it in their work must be willing to face the charge of having "politicized" the debate.[66] As I have suggested, none of this means that assisted reproduction should automatically be ruled out; rather, its methods should be examined on an issue-by-issue basis, with scrupulous attention to feminist objections.[67] Robertson is more sensitive to feminist concerns that most mainstream writers, but I believe that he would be even more effective if he took the literature more seriously.

There is a yet more fundamental criticism of the emphasis on the provision of assisted reproduction, however. Sexism is not the only dubious ethical tendency to which our society is prone. I have been guilty, like Robertson and so many others, of focusing on the novel, the exciting, and the bizarre. Naturally, it is imperative to attempt to evaluate new technologies because they are coming at us so quickly, and it is fun to think of reasons for rejecting what so often seems like silly opposition to bright new possibilities. However, it is all too easy to get drawn into this technological wonderland and to lose our grounding in the real world of limited resources and pervasive discrimination. The situation reminds me of plans to create space colonies to escape a polluted and worn-out earth; when we examine the issues realistically, it seems for more sensible to nurture the earth instead. Similar reasoning applies here. Many of the alleged benefits of assisted reproduction could be achieved more efficiently and more equitably by revamping familiar social arrangments.

So what is the attraction of high-tech proposals? I believe it feeds a kind of escapism that both arises from and helps to perpetuate a number of

---

[65] See A. Nicolosi, "Mechanismi di Trasmissione e rischia di infezione da virus dell'immunodeficienza acquista (HIV-1)," *Igiene Moderna* 96, no. 5 (1991): 556–82.

[66] Sherwin, *No Longer Patient*, provides an excellent introduction and compilation of studies. For a discussion of the "politicization," see my "Politics and the College Curriculum," in *University Neutrality and Academic Ethics*, ed. Robert L. Simon (Lanham, Md.: Rowman & Littlefield, 1994), and the Introduction to this volume.

[67] See, for example, Chapter 2, "Loving Future People," Chapter 11, "Surrogate Mothering: Exploitation or Empowerment?," and Chapter 12, "Another Look at Contract Pregnancy."

intellectual, moral, and political tendencies pervasive in our society, tendencies connected with our disinterest in what Virginia Warren calls *"housekeeping issues."*[68] Housekeeping issues involve ongoing situations, unlike crisis issues that can provide the satisfaction of being resolved once and for all. Housekeeping issues, unlike dramatic crisis issues, seem trivial, yet housekeeping issues require us to rethink big chunks of our lives: "our character traits, how we think about ourselves, and how we relate to others."[69] In addition, housekeeping issues call on a variety of intellectual and moral resources beyond those that we consider usual. Because of the appeal of tackling crisis issues, much of the applied ethics establishment has fallen into a sort of "crisis-of-the-month" mentality, leaping from one blaze to another, without stopping to think how those problems might be related or what might prevent them. As a result, we are drawn to stop-gap solutions that are often short-sighted, authoritarian, or punitive; technological fixes tend to look better than fundamental social change. But unless we face the ongoing, systematic problems in our social arrangements, new versions of old problems will arise to replace those that we think we've solved.

How might these realizations change our perception of assisted reproduction? Well, if infertility is such a problem, wouldn't it make more sense to investigate and eradicate its causes, concentrating on environmental toxins, STDs, iatrogenicity, and social patterns that require women to conceive later in life if they want both family and career? Addresing these moral and political issues not only would be likely to be far more successful and less risky to women and babies than new high-tech interventions, but also they would have positive "side effects" on all our lives. For example, everybody would benefit from a cleaner environment, better public health, and the kind of social equality that values equal consideration of the interests of all persons.

This approach would look less daunting if the true costs of high-tech solutions were factored into decisions about how to deal with the problems. For example, because of unwarranted technological optimism and the sexism or racism that fails to take seriously potential or real harms to members of disadvantaged groups, evaluations of high-tech solutions often underplay or fail to mention altogether the tenuous benefits and the high, socially skewed costs they involve. Thus the facts that IVF has extremely low success rates, is expensive, and puts women through a strenuous cycle of drugs and surgical interventions do not really count against IVF when policy decisions are being made.[70] Little attention is paid either to the risks for

---

[68] Virginia Warren, "Feminist Directions in Medical Ethics," in *Feminist Perspectives in Medical Ethics*, ed. Holmes and Purdy.

[69] Warren "Feminist Directions in Medical Ethics," p. 37.

[70] For a list of in vitro fertilization's possible dangers, see Corea, *The Mother Machine*, pp. 148–50.

women or to their distateful experiences during the therapy.[71] As Sherwin points out, "to date, only feminists have raised these issues."[72]

The same kinds of issues could be raised with respect to the health of fetuses and babies. I too have been guilty of focusing on the problem of genetic disease in isolation. However, looking at the place of genetic disease and other risk factors in the larger context has convinced me that it is unreasonable to concentrate on possible genetic approaches to health *before* addressing the social factors that so seriously affect perinatal morbidity and mortality. According to a government task force, "if we just delivered routine clinical care and social services to pregnant women, we could prevent one-quarter to one-third of infant mortality."[73] Children's health could be still further ameliorated by a variety of policies, such as guaranteed health care, clean environments, more liberal parental leaves, and better nutrition programs for the poor. The social choices now being made about improving perinatal health are especially troubling given their racist and sexist implications, for if poor black women did not have to live in such miserable conditions there would be far fewer dead, disabled, or sick babies. It is difficult to feel much enthusiasm for the Human Genome Project or spectacular new experimental therapies when the remedies for many problems now facing women and children are so close at hand.

It seems clear that we can't "have it all." We seems to be faced with a choice. Either we push ahead with high-tech solutions and thereby ignore the ongoing social problems that play a substantial part in creating them

---

[71] Sherwin, *No Longer Patient*, p. 124. Sherwin argues that
the bioethics literature has not considered the chemical similarities between clomid, an artificial hormone that is commonly used to increase women's rate of ovulation, and DES, a drug that has belatedly been implicated as carcinogenic for the offspring of women who were prescribed it decades before. The uncertainties surrounding superovulation and use of ultrasound and the dangers associated with administering a general anesthetic for egg collection and embryo transfer have not been deemed worthy of attention in the nonfeminist bioethics literature. Women who do succeed in achieving and sustaining pregnancies through this method experience a very high rate of surgical births, but those risks also are generally ignored. Furthermore, most ethical discussions do not explore the significant emotional costs for women that are associated with this therapy. (p. 125).
Paul Lauritzen provides something of the feel of those who go through the process of infertility workups and attempts at a technological fix, as well as an example of a woman who undertakes the risk of in vitro fertilization because of a man's infertility. See "What Price Parenthood?," *Hastings Center Report* 20, no. 2 (March–April 1990): 38–39; see also Judith Lorber, "Choice, Gift, or Patriarchal Bargain?," in *Feminist Perspectives in Medical Ethics*, ed. Holmes and Purdy. For an analysis of the differing views of the enterprise, see Lene Koch, "The Fairy Tale as Model for Women's Experience of in Vitro Fertilization," in *Issues in Reproductive Technology I*, ed. Holmes.

[72] Sherwin, *No Longer Patient*, p. 125.

[73] Cited in Bordo, *Unbearable Weight*, p. 84.

or we concentrate on alleviating the social problems and thereby de-emphasize possible high-tech solutions, including the enticing nonprocreative uses of reproduction, such as using fetal tissue for Parkinson's disease. Following either path means that some needs will not be met. Of course, there is no reason for approaching this issue in a completely all-or-nothing way. Indeed, I suspect that a primary emphasis on basic social problems, together with a limited and carefully thought-out program of technological innovation would be the optimum approach.

The questions that face us in this context are similar to the allocation questions common in the rest of the health care system, and, indeed, in society at large. The special twist here is the potential for harm to white women and members of other groups. The more cautious path I advocate bypasses those harms and begins to address age-old problems in inequality.

Thus, procreative liberty's emphasis on assisted reproduction is all very well: the shivers it elicits in those who worship tradition, predicate personhood of embryos, or fear the unknown may be groundless. When we look at the overall social context, however, funding some of the more exotic proposals cannot compete morally with the need for providing basic necessities, such as health care, nutritious food, decent shelter, education, jobs, and a clean environment for all. This is not an argument for banning the more exotic approaches but rather for more careful and selective encouragement or discouragement of particular options.

If we let high-tech approaches flourish, it will come at the expense of these more basic approaches to human well-being. We could thus create a society where some people enjoy a wide range of choices, even if those possibilities do not necessarily enhance their own welfare. We could instead work toward a society that attempts to achieve a far more fundamental and widespread kind of well-being. I believe that justice requires us to choose the latter course.

Selected Bibliography

Agonito, Rosemary. *A History of Ideas on Women: A Source Book.* New York: Putnam, 1977.

Annas, George J. "AIDS, Judges, and the Right to Medical Care." *Hastings Center Report* 18, no. 4 (August–September 1988): 20–22.

———. "Forced Caesareans: The Most Unkindest Cut of All." *Hastings Center Report* (June 1982): 16–17, 45.

———. "Protecting the Liberty of Pregnant Patients." *New England Journal of Medicine* 316, no. 19 (May 7, 1987): 1213–14.

Arras, John D. "AIDS and Reproductive Decisions: Having Children in Fear and Trembling." *The Millbank Quarterly* 68, no. 3 (1990): 353–82.

Asch, Adrienne. "Can Aborting 'Imperfect' Children Be Immoral?" In *Ethical Issues in Modern Medicine,* ed. John Arras and Nancy Rhoden. Mountain View, Calif.: Mayfield Press, 1989.

———. "Real Moral Dilemmas." *Christianity and Crisis* 46, no. 10 (July 14, 1986): 237–40.

———. "Reproductive Technology and Disability." In *Reproductive Laws for the 1990s,* ed. Sherrill Cohen and Nadine Taub. Clifton, N.J.: Humana Press, 1988.

———. *Women with Disabilities: Essays in Psychology, Culture, and Politics.* Philadelphia: Temple University Press, 1988.

Bale, Anthony. "Women's Toxic Experience." In *Women, Health, and Medicine in America: A Historical Handbook,* ed. Rima D. Apple. New Brunswick, N.J.: Rutgers University Press, 1992.

Ball, Terence, "Utilitarianism, Feminism, and the Franchise: James Mill and His Critics." *History of Political Thought* 1 (Spring 1980): 91–115.

Bartky, Sandra Lee. "Foucault, Femininity, and the Modernization of Patriarchal Power." In *Femininity and Domination: Studies in the Phenomenology of Oppression.* New York: Routledge, 1990.

239

Beauchamp, Tom, and James Childress. *Principles of Biomedical Ethics.* 4th ed. Oxford: Oxford University Press, 1994.

Belloc, Nedra, and Lester Breslow. "Relationship of Physical Health Status and Health Practices." *Preventive Medicine* 1 (1972): 409–21.

Boralevi, Lea Campos, "Utilitarianism and Feminism." In *Women in Western Political Philosophy: Kant to Nietzsche,* ed. Ellen Kennedy and Susan Mendus. New York: St. Martin's Press, 1987.

Bordo, Susan. *Unbearable Weight: Feminism, Western Culture, and the Body.* Berkeley: University of California Press, 1993.

Calabresi, Guido, and Philip Bobbitt. *Tragic Choices.* New York: Norton, 1978.

Callahan, Joan, ed. *Reproduction, Ethics, and the Law.* Bloomington: Indiana University Press, 1995.

Caplan, Arthur, H. Tristram Engelhardt, Jr., and James J. McCartney, eds. *Concepts of Health and Disease: Interdisciplinary Perspectives.* Reading, Mass.: Addison-Wesley, 1981.

Card, Claudia. *Feminist Ethics.* Lawrence: University Press of Kansas, 1991.

Chadwick, Ruth, ed. *Ethics, Reproduction, and Genetic Control.* New York: Croom Helm, 1987.

Claybrook, Joan, Jacqueline Gillan, and Anne Strainchamps. *Reagan on the Road: The Crash of the U.S. Auto Safety Program.* Washington, D.C.: Public Citizen, 1982.

Cole, Eve Browning, and Susan Coultrap-McQuin, eds. *Explorations in Feminist Ethics: Theory and Practice.* Bloomington: Indiana University Press, 1992.

Corea, Gena. *The Hidden Malpractice: How American Medicine Treats Women as Patients and Professionals.* New York: Morrow, 1977.

——. *The Mother Machine: Reproductive Technologies from Artificial Insemination to Artificial Wombs.* New York: Harper & Row, 1985.

Davis, Nancy (Ann). "The Abortion Debate: The Search for Common Ground, Part I." *Ethics* 103 (April 1993): 516–39.

De George, Richard T. *Business Ethics.* 3d ed. New York: Macmillan, 1990.

Dolnick, Edward. "Deafness as Culture." *The Atlantic* 272, no. 3 (September 1993): 37–51.

Donner, Wendy. *The Liberal Self: John Stuart Mill's Moral and Political Philosophy.* Ithaca: Cornell University Press, 1991.

Dworkin, Ronald. *Life's Dominion: An Argument about Abortion, Euthanasia, and Individual Freedom.* New York: Knopf, 1993.

Ehrenreich, Barbara, and Deirdre English. *For Her Own Good: 150 Years of the Experts' Advice to Women.* New York: Anchor Press, 1979.

Emanuel, Ezekiel J. *The Ends of Human Life: Medical Ethics in a Liberal Polity.* Cambridge: Harvard University Press, 1991.

Engelhardt, H. Tristram, Jr. "Applied Philosophy in the Post-Modern Age: An Augury." *Journal of Social Philosophy* 20 (Spring–Fall 1989): 42–48.

——.*The Foundations of Bioethics.* New York: Oxford University Press, 1986.

Feinberg, Joel. *Harm to Others.* Oxford: Oxford University Press, 1984.

Firestone, Shulamith. *The Dialectic of Sex.* New York: Bantam, 1970.

Gallagher, Janet. "Prenatal Invasions and Interventions: What's Wrong with Fetal Rights." *Harvard Women's Law Journal* 10 (1987): 9–58.

Gilligan, Carol. *In a Different Voice: Psychological Theory and Women's Development*. Cambridge: Harvard University Press, 1982.

Glover, Jonathan. *What Sort of People Should There Be?* Middlesex, Eng.: Penguin, 1984.

Gould, Carol C., ed. *Beyond Domination: New Perspectives on Women and Philosophy*. Totowa, N.J.: Rowman and Allanheld, 1983.

Harding, Sandra. "Is Gender a Variable in Conceptions of Rationality? A Survey of Issues." In *Beyond Domination*. ed. Gould.

Held, Virginia. *Feminist Morality: Transforming Culture, Society, and Politics*. Chicago: University of Chicago Press, 1993.

——."Non-Contractual Society." In *Science, Morality, and Feminist Theory*, ed. Marsha Hanen and Kai Nielsen. *Canadian Journal of Philosophy* (suppl. vol. 13), 1987.

Holmes, Helen B., ed. *Issues in Reproductive Technology I: An Anthology*. New York: Garland, 1992.

Holmes, Helen B., Betty B. Hoskins, and Michael Gross, eds. *The Custom-Made Child? Women-Centered Perspectives*. Clifton, N.J.: Humana Press, 1981.

Holmes, Helen B., and Laura M. Purdy, eds. *Feminist Perspectives in Medical Ethics*. Bloomington: Indiana University Press, 1992.

Hull, Richard, ed. *Ethical Issues in the New Reproductive Technologies*. Belmont, Calif.: Wadsworth, 1990.

Ince, Susan. "Inside the Surrogate Industry." In *Test Tube Women: What Future for Motherhood?*, ed. Rita Arditti, Renate Duelli Klein, and Shelley Minden. London: Pandora, 1984.

Jaggar, Alison M. "Feminist Ethics: Some Issues for the Nineties." *Journal of Social Philosophy* 20, no. 1–2 (Spring–Fall 1989): 91–107.

——. *Feminist Politics and Human Nature*. Totowa, N.J.: Rowman & Allanheld, 1983.

——. "Sex Inequality and Bias in Sex Differences Research." In *Science, Morality, and Feminist Theory*, ed. Marsha Hanen and Kai Nielsen. *Canadian Journal of Philosophy* (suppl. vol. 13), 1987.

Kahn, Jeffrey P. "Genetic Harm: Bitten by the Body That Keeps You?" *Bioethics* 5, no. 4 (October 1991): 289–308.

Kass, Leon. "Implications of Prenatal Diagnosis for the Human Right to Life." In *Ethical Issues in Human Genetics: Genetic Counseling and the Use of Genetic Knowledge*, ed. Bruce Hilton et al. New York: Plenum, 1973.

——. "The New Biology: What Price Relieving Man's Estate?" *Science* 174 (November 19, 1971): 779–88.

Ketchum, Sara Ann. "Selling Babies and Selling Bodies." In *Feminist Perspectives in Medical Ethics*, ed. Holmes and Purdy.

Kittay, Eva Feder, and Diana T. Meyers, eds. *Women and Moral Theory*. Totowa, N.J.: Rowman and Littlefield, 1987.

Kluge, Eike-Henner W. "When Caesarean Section Operations Imposed by a Court Are Justified." *Journal of Medical Ethics* 4, no. 4 (December 1988): 206–11.

Kolder, Veronika E.B., Janet Gallagher, and Michael T. Parsons. "Court-Ordered Obstetrical Interventions." *The New England Journal of Medicine* 316 (May 7, 1987): 1192–96.

Kosa, John, Aaron Antonovsky, and Irving Kenneth Zola, eds. *Poverty and Health: A Sociological Analysis.* Cambridge: Harvard University Press, 1969.

Ladd, Rosalind Ekman. "Women in Labor: Some Issues about Informed Consent." In *Feminist Perspectives in Medical Ethics,* ed. Holmes and Purdy.

Lang, Susan S. *Women without Children: The Reasons, the Rewards, the Regrets.* New York: Pharos Books, 1991.

Larrabee, Mary Jeanne, ed. *An Ethic of Care: Feminist and Interdisciplinary Perspectives.* New York: Routledge, 1993.

Lauritzen, Paul. "What Price Parenthood?" *Hastings Center Report* 20, no. 2 (March–April 1990): 38–46.

Lawson, Edward. *The Encyclopedia of Human Rights.* New York: Taylor and Francis, 1991.

Leach, Gerald. *The Biocrats.* Middlesex, Eng.: Penguin, 1972.

Levin, Michael. *Feminism and Freedom.* New Brunswick, N.J.: Transaction Books, 1987.

Lorber, Judith. "Choice, Gift, or Patriarchal Bargain? Women's Consent to *in Vitro* Fertilization." In *Feminist Perspectives in Medical Ethics,* ed. Holmes and Purdy.

Luker, Kristin. *Abortion and the Politics of Motherhood.* Berkeley: University of California Press, 1984.

Mahowald, Mary Briody. "Beyond Abortion: Refusal of Caesarean Section." *Bioethics* 32 (April 1989): 106–21.

——. "Fetal Tissue Transplantation and Women." Paper presented at the meeting of the Eastern Division, American Philosophical Association, December 27–30, 1990, Boston.

——. "To Be or Not to Be a Woman: Anorexia Nervosa, Normative Gender Roles, and Feminism." *Journal of Medicine and Philosophy* 17 (1992): 233–51.

——. *Women and Children in Health Care: An Unequal Majority.* New York: Oxford University Press, 1993.

Malm, Heidi. "Commodification or Compensation: A Reply to Ketchum." In *Feminist Perspectives in Medical Ethics,* ed. Holmes and Purdy.

Mies, Maria. "Why Do We Need All This? A Call against Genetic Engineering and Reproductive Technology." In *Made to Order: The Myth of Reproduction and Genetic Progress,* ed. Patricia Spallone and Deborah Lynn Steinberg. Oxford: Pergamon, 1987.

Miles, Steven H., and Allison August. "Courts, Gender and the Right to Die." *Law, Medicine, and Health Care* 18, nos. 1–2 (Spring–Summer 1990): 85–95.

Mill, John Stuart. *Utilitarianism* (1863). In *The Utilitarians.* New York: Dolphin, 1961.

Miller, Jean Baker, ed. *Psychoanalysis and Women.* Middlesex, Engl.: Penguin, 1973.

Millett, Kate. *Sexual Politics.* N.Y.: Doubleday, 1970.

Morgan, Kathryn Pauly. "Women and the Knife: Cosmetic Surgery and the Colonization of Women's Bodies." *Hypatia* 6, no. 3 (1991): 25–53.

Morgan, Robin, ed. *Sisterhood Is Global: The International Women's Movement Anthology.* Garden City, N.Y.: Anchor Press, 1984.

Mullett, Sheila. "Shifting Perspective: A New Approach to Ethics." In *Feminist Perspectives: Philosophical Essays on Method and Morals,* ed. Lorraine Code, Sheila Mullet, and Christine Overall. Toronto: University of Toronto Press, 1988.

Nadis, Steve, and James J. MacKenzie. *Car Trouble*. Boston: Beacon Press, 1993.

Noddings, Nel. *Caring: A Feminine Approach to Ethics and Moral Education*. Berkeley: University of California Press, 1984.

Okin, Susan Moller. *Justice, Gender, and the Family*. New York: Basic Books, 1989.

——. *Women in Western Political Thought*. Princeton: Princeton University Press, 1979.

Our Bodies, Ourselves: A Book by and for Women. The Boston Women's Health Book Collective, rev. ed. New York: Simon & Schuster, 1976.

Overall, Christine. *Ethics and Human Reproduction: A Feminist Analysis*. Boston: Allen & Unwin, 1987.

——. *Human Reproduction: Principles, Practices, Policies*. Toronto: Oxford University Press, 1993.

Packard, Vance. *The People Shapers*. Boston: Little, Brown, 1977.

Parfit, Derek, "On Doing the Best for Our Children." In *Ethics and Population*, ed. Michael D. Bayles. Cambridge, Mass.: Schenkman, 1976.

——. *Reasons and Persons*. Oxford: Clarendon, 1984.

Parness, Jeffrey. "The Abuse and Neglect of the Human Unborn." *Family Law Quarterly* 20 (1986): 197–212.

Peck, Ellen, and Judith Senderowitz. *Pronatalism: The Myth of Mom & Apple Pie*. New York: Crowell, 1974.

Petchesky, Rosalind Pollack. *Abortion and Woman's Choice: The State, Sexuality, and Reproductive Freedom*. Boston: Northeastern University Press, 1985.

Pierce, Christine. "Natural Law Language and Women." In *Sex Equality*, ed. Jane English. Engelwood Cliffs, N.J.: Prentice-Hall, 1977.

Pollitt, Katha. "The Strange Case of Baby M." *The Nation*, May 23, 1987, pp. 667, 682–86.

——. "When Is a Mother Not a Mother?" *The Nation*, December 31, 1990, pp. 825, 840–44.

Purdy, Laura M. *In Their Best Interest? The Case against Equal Rights for Children*. Ithaca: Cornell University Press, 1992.

——. "Politics and the College Curriculum." In *Neutrality and the Academic Ethic*, ed. Robert L. Simon. Lanham, Md.: Rowman & Littlefield, 1994.

Raymond, Janice. "Fetalists and Feminists: They Are Not the Same." In *Made to Order*, ed. Spallone and Steinberg.

Regush, Nicholas. "Toxic Breasts." *Mother Jones* (January–February 1992): 24–31.

Revkin, Andrew. "Hunting Down Huntington's." *Discover* (December 1993): 100–108.

Rhoden, Nancy K. "The Judge in the Delivery Room: The Emergence of Court-Ordered Caesareans." *California Law Review* 74, no. 6 (1986): 1951–2030.

Robertson, John A. *Children of Choice: Freedom and the New Reproductive Technologies*. Princeton: Princeton University Press, 1994.

Rosser, Sue. "Re-visioning Clinical Research: Gender and the Ethics of Experimental Design." In *Feminist Perspectives in Medical Ethics*, ed. Holmes and Purdy.

Rothman, Barbara Katz. *Recreating Motherhood: Ideology and Technology in a Patriarchal Society*. New York: Norton, 1989.

Ruth, Sheila, "Methodocracy, Misogyny, and Bad Faith: The Response of Philosophy." In *Men's Studies Modified: The Impact of Feminism on the Academic Disciplines*, ed. Dale Spender. Oxford: Pergamon, 1981.

Sadker, Myra, and David Sadker. *Failing at Fairness: How America's Schools Cheat Girls*. New York: Scribner's, 1994.

Saxton, Martha. "Born and Unborn: The Implications of Reproductive Technologies for People with Disabilities." In *Test-Tube Women: What Future for Motherhood?*, ed. Rita Arditti, Renate Duelli Klein, and Shelley Minden. London: Pandora, 1984.

Schott, Lee A. "The Pamela Rae Stewart Case and Fetal Harm: Prosecution or Prevention?" *Harvard Women's Law Journal* 11 (1988): 227–45.

Seaman, Barbara, and Gideon Seaman. *Women and the Crisis in Sex Hormones*. New York: Rawson Associates Publishers, 1977.

Shaw, Margery W. "Conditional Prospective Rights of the Fetus." *The Journal of Legal Medicine* 5, no. 1 (March 1984): 63–116.

Sherwin, Susan. "Feminist and Medical Ethics: Two Different Approaches to Contextual Ethics." In *Feminist Perspectives in Medical Ethics*, ed. Holmes and Purdy.

———. "A Feminist Approach to Ethics." *Dalhousie Review* 64, no. 4 (Winter 1984–85): 704–13.

———. "Feminist Ethics and in Vitro Fertilization." In *Science, Morality, and Feminist Theory*, ed. Marsha Hanen and Kai Nielsen. *Canadian Journal of Philosophy* (suppl. vol. 13), 1987.

———. *No Longer Patient: Feminist Ethics and Health Care*. Philadelphia: Temple University Press, 1992.

Smith, John M. *Women and Doctors: A Physician's Explosive Account of Women's Medical Treatment and Mistreatment in America Today and What You Can Do about It*. New York: Atlantic Monthly Press, 1992.

Snitow, Ann. "A Gender Diary." *Conflicts in Feminism*, ed. Marianne Hirsch and Evelyn Fox Keller. New York: Routledge, 1990.

Spallone, Patricia. *Beyond Conception: The New Politics of Reproduction*. Granby, Mass.: Bergin & Garvey, 1989.

Spallone, Patricia, and Deborah Lynn Steinberg. *Made to Order: The Myth of Reproductive and Genetic Progress*. Oxford: Pergamon, 1987.

Spelman, Elizabeth V. *Inessential Woman: Problems of Exclusion in Feminist Thought*. Boston: Beacon Press, 1988.

Stanworth, Michelle. "Birth Pangs: Conceptive Technologies and the Threat to Motherhood." In *Conflicts in Feminism*, ed. Marianne Hirsch and Evelyn Fox Keller. New York: Routledge, 1990.

———, ed. *Reproductive Technologies: Gender, Motherhood, and Medicine*. Minneapolis: University of Minnesota Press, 1987.

Sumner, Wayne L., and Joseph Boyle. *Philosophical Perspectives in Bioethics*. Toronto: University of Toronto Press, 1996.

Taylor, Gordon Rattray. *The Biological Time Bomb*. New York: Penguin, 1968.

Teo, Wesley D. H. "Abortion: The Husband's Constitutional Rights." *Ethics* 85, no. 4 (July 1975): 337–42.

Tong, Rosemarie. *Feminine and Feminist Ethics*. Belmont, Calif.: Wadsworth, 1993.

Tooley, Michael. "Abortion and Infanticide." *Philosophy & Public Affairs* 2, no. 1 (Fall 1972): 37–65.

Tribe, Laurence H. *Abortion: The Clash of Absolutes*. New York: Norton, 1990.

Warren, Mary Anne. "The Moral Significance of Birth." In *Feminist Perspectives in Medical Ethics,* ed. Holmes and Purdy.

Warren, Virginia. "Feminist Directions in Medical Ethics." In *Feminist Perspectives in Medical Ethics,* ed. Holmes and Purdy.

Whitbeck, Caroline. "A Different Reality: Feminist Ontology." In *Beyond Domination,* ed. Gould.

———. "The Moral Implications of Regarding Women as People: New Perspectives on Pregnancy and Personhood." In *Abortion and the Status of the Fetus,* ed. William B. Bondeson, H. Tristram Engelhardt, Jr., Stuart Picker, and Daniel Winship. Dordrecht: Reidel, 1983.

———. "Theories of Sex Difference." In *Women and Values: Readings in Recent Feminist Philosophy,* ed. Marilyn Pearsall. Belmont, Calif.: Wadsworth, 1986.

———. "A Theory of Health." In *Concepts of Health,* ed. Caplan, Engelhardt, and McCartney.

Wolf, Susan, ed. *Feminism and Bioethics: Beyond Reproduction.* Oxford University Press, 1995.

Zohar, Noam. "Prospects for 'Genetic Therapy'—Can a Person Benefit from Being Altered?" *Bioethics* 5, no. 4 (October 1991): 275–88.

Index